NINE RUPEES AN HOUR

Aparna Karthikeyan is a storyteller and an independent journalist. She volunteers for the People's Archive of Rural India (PARI) and has written for them, as well as for *The Hindu*, *The Caravan*, *The Wire*, *Scroll.in* and other publications on culture, books and livelihoods. She has authored books for children, and published short fiction. She lives in Mumbai with her husband, daughter and dogs.

Praise for *Nine Rupees an Hour*

'*Nine Rupees an Hour* may not succeed in reversing the pitiless course of history, and "make whole what has been smashed". However, as a counter-narrative of our times, it can add to our collective memory and shape public conscience in the times to come. And that possibility is a testimony to its value and triumph.' – N. Kalyan Raman, *Open*

'[D]iligently researched and faithfully written ... not a polemical tract though. It contains illuminating and moving narratives about a wide array of extraordinary everyday people who lead spirited lives, even as they linger on in their vanishing livelihoods. The author has brought to bear her excellent story-telling ability to ask a searching question: what kind of society allows its most creative craftspeople to wither away in the name of "creative destruction"?' – Raghunathan Nageswaran, *TheWire.in*

'Karthikeyan resists easy choices. She opens a rare and realistic window into a world on the edge, keeping its occupants and their unequal struggles in focus. Her gaze is not invasive; neither is it gentle. It is unsparing but humane, ever mindful of the dignity that lingers among these resilient men and women.' – Uddalak Mukherjee, *The Telegraph*

'The stories tell us yet how people living in rural areas are highly distressed by a constant economic struggle, social discrimination and political exclusion. Packed with statistics, facts and expert views, it is a must-read for anyone seeking a profound understanding of the countryside and traditional livelihoods.' – A. Shrikumar, *The Hindu*

'Their life stories are rendered by the writer with sincerity (she has certainly spent time with her subjects to get "into" their lives), compassion and a journalistic precision for information ... her rendition of these extraordinary lives (hidden from plain sight in a society that is quite unidirectional) is poignant without being frothy or sentimental.' – A. Srinivas, *The Hindu BusinessLine*

'This is an important book. It provides an insight into agrarian distress, skewed policies, farmers' changing lifestyles and disappearing livelihoods ... *Nine Rupees an Hour* is a book with a big heart. It also raises a lot of troublesome questions.' – Sushila Ravindranath, *Deccan Chronicle*

context

NINE RUPEES AN HOUR

Disappearing Livelihoods of Tamil Nadu

APARNA KARTHIKEYAN

cntxt

First published by Context, an imprint of Westland Publications Private Limited, in 2019

Published by Context, an imprint of Westland Books, a division of Nasadiya Technologies Private Limited, in 2022

No. 269/2B, First Floor, 'Irai Arul', Vimalraj Street, Nethaji Nagar, Allappakkam Main Road, Maduravoyal, Chennai 600095, Tamil Nadu, India

Credit for representational sketch on p. xx: TP

ISBN: 9789395073233

10 9 8 7 6 5 4 3 2 1

Typeset by R. Ajith Kumar
Printed at Parksons Graphics Pvt. Ltd, Mumbai

For
all those who told me their stories
and
the People's Archive of Rural India,
from where this journey began.

Contents

Introduction

When a livelihood dies
a way of life vanishes;
and the language too
is diminished.
—Cho Dharman

Let me tell you a story. Make that ten. Stories of everyday people who do extraordinary things to earn a living—like Soundaram, probably the only woman to own over half a dozen of the fiercest and finest stud bulls; Kali, perhaps the only male dancer who is accomplished in both Bharatanatyam and folk dance; and Tamilarasi, only the second girl to perform in an all-male, all-night folk theatre. Then there is Rayappan, who climbs hundreds of palm trees every week; Selvaraj, the nadaswaram maker, who makes wood sing, Krishnamoorthy, who has created ten thousand sari designs by hand, and Zeenath, who weaves exquisite silk mats on a floor loom. There is Kamachi, who has spent most of her life dancing on stilts, with a dummy horse strapped around her waist; Chandrasekaran, the sickle maker, who gets iron to yield to him; and Podhumani, who coaxes the parched earth to bear a crop, rushes back home to cook another meal for her sons and her husband, and is back again on the field, to put food on your plate and mine.

Though 68.8 per cent of India's population lives outside its cities,[1] the rural has been steadily forced out of the nation building process and our imagination. The rich get richer with land, water and resources snatched away from the rural poor. This savage inequality means that a minimum wage worker in rural India has to work 941 years to earn what a top paid executive at a leading Indian garment company earns in a year.'[2] Privileging and pandering exclusively to the urban elites will not just diminish and destroy the rural economy. What future does a country have if farmers who subsidise the country's milk and meals continue to be financial martyrs; artisans who stitch the rural economy together are systematically marginalised; and artists who perform about a glorious past are sent home to an uncertain future?

But why would we care when we do not know the people who put food on our table and culture in our lives? When their stories and struggles are brushed aside in the race to build dysfunctional smart cities and missions to the moon? When we blithely furnish our homes with beautiful Pathamadai mats, whose makers earn just nine rupees an hour? These highly skilled women make an average of just a hundred rupees a day. Farmers fare better, but only just. The backbreaking work they plough into an acre of paddy nets them about two hundred a day. Palm tree climbers? Roughly two hundred and fifty, but only during a limited, unpredictable season.

The rural economy is delicately and tightly intertwined. A good year—when the rainclouds behave and the earth obediently produces a bumper crop—benefits everybody. Why must rainfall have any bearing on the livelihood of, say, a nadaswaram maker? The logic is bafflingly simple: when there are good rains, the agrarian classes organise bigger weddings and more of them, and invite musicians. This drives up the demand for nadaswarams, favouring local makers. A bad year, is a bad year for all.

I began this journey—as a storyteller and witness—discovering my home state, its culture and people, in July 2013. It started with a fan mail to journalist P. Sainath, who was then setting up a mammoth archive to document the lives of 833 million people in rural India. He invited me to be a part of the now four-year-old People's Archive of Rural India. Without a formal degree in journalism and armed with only curiosity and a camera, I travelled across my home state of Tamil Nadu, to Madurai, Sivagangai, Kancheepuram, Tiruppur, Ramanathapuram, Tirunelveli and Thanjavur districts, to document traditional livelihoods.

These men and women, shared their dreams and defeats, triumphs and tears with me. They spoke as they worked under the scorching sun or rested briefly in the shadows of tall palms. They told me stories of pride and despair, of love and laughter, in rooms lit only by oil lamps. And hope.

They yearned for their children to receive good education and a well-paying job. 'Let this end with me,' they said about the occupation their ancestors had survived on for centuries. They did not have much of a choice, not when they were growing up. Their children do.

What is a livelihood? Sainath defines it as work that supports a person's life, and is sustained by natural (and sometimes related social and cultural) resources. This takes care of the practitioner's essential needs, across a lifespan, even if their earnings seem meagre or irregular to a city dweller. When the resources disappear or are destroyed, or access to them is barred, that livelihood is wrecked.

It is different from a job, where skillsets are transferable. 'A clerk in one company may be dependent on the job they are holding, but can fit into other jobs of a similar description. Now, suppose you are by tradition and skill an inland river fisherman, if I privatise that water, then you're out. You've lost that livelihood and can't simply just find another river. You were supporting yourself and your family through that resource. Millions of livelihoods have been devastated in this way in India,' says Sainath

For a state that prides itself on its culture and valorises it in the popular imagination, Tamil Nadu is an ironic example of how traditional livelihoods fare in the country. Touted to have great developmental parameters and ranked high among India's 'best performing states', the Tamil Nadu model comes in for praise in *An Uncertain Glory: India and its Contradictions*. The authors, renowned economists Amartya Sen and Jean Dreze, point out that during the 1970s and 1980s, Tamil Nadu, 'much to the consternation of many economists, initiated bold social programmes such as universal midday meals in primary schools and started putting in place an extensive social infrastructure—schools, health centres, roads, public transport, water supply, electricity connections, and much more.' The result is 'today, Tamil Nadu has some of the best public services among all Indian states, and many of them are accessible to all on a non-discriminatory basis.'[3]

Why, then, are livelihoods in the state under threat? Cho Dharman, an award-winning writer from Kovilpatti, has an answer: The corporate model is breaking up the relationship between farmers and their crop, the land and its people. When a livelihood collapses in the countryside, those supported by it often have little option but to migrate to towns and cities in search of work.

'When you move from paddy to prawn culture, over a hundred days of labour is lost,' says Sainath. 'Because one acre of paddy will employ several people at different times in a year. When that land is used for aquaculture, all you need is one watchman with a stick to chase birds.' These internally displaced people may even find menial work in, say, a top corporate. 'Sometimes, the same people whose work in the fields used to put food on the table of the techies, now serve coffee in their canteens.'

Livelihoods 'that relied on a measure of self-sufficiency, personalised vending and household participation have been displaced by nucleated wage labour and the co-option of the traditional weaver, metal-working artisan, carpenter and potter into the carousel of mass production,' says Gopalkrishna Gandhi, former governor of West Bengal and a long-term observer of Tamil Nadu, having served in the state's Indian Administrative Service from 1968 to 1985.

Every livelihood documented in this book requires prodigious skillsets and is physically gruelling. Yet, despite being central and integral to society—keeping alive breeds of native cattle, preserving a wealth of colours and designs in everyday aesthetics, ensuring food security—much of the work is financially unrewarding and the craftsmanship is largely unrecognised.

The poor pay is determined by a market founded on skewed ideas of what is skilled and worthy work. Amit Basole, associate professor of economics at Azim Premji University, explains that there are several definitions of skilled work and, by extension, of unskilled work. 'A crude one equates skill with years of formal education. In this case, anyone who is not formally educated is unskilled. A more sophisticated definition looks at the amount of learning/training involved in a particular kind of work. If it requires relatively less training [say a few days], it is considered unskilled work. There is, of course, a school of thought that says no work is unskilled, no worker is unskilled. But this is a moral position.'

In an essay in *The Caravan*, Basole says about the skilled and the schooled: 'India is triply disadvantaged. As in many other societies, we suffer from the "head versus hand" hierarchy, which ascribes higher status to purely mental work over work that requires physical labour. In India, that hierarchy is also encoded in caste, with mental labour assigned to dominant castes and physical labour assigned to oppressed ones.'[4]

A similar argument defines and distinguishes art from craft. A widely held Western idea of art is to restrict anything utilitarian to the realm of craft, says Sainath. 'A product of craft is something which has constant and wide replication, a specific use, plus a restricted number of patterns. The main differentiation made by many is to look at art as creative, and craft—even when highly skilled—as mechanical and unthinking.' But what about the brilliance of the handloom weaver? 'Subtle little variations, small, yet visually captivating—are these art, or craft, or both? Who is to say our craftspersons are not also artists?' Except 'there isn't an impenetrable Great Wall between the two. Standardisation and homogenisation,' he points out, 'are what capitalism brings, not our artisans.'

What further complicates matters in India is that livelihoods are closely linked to caste. Writer, feminist and activist Bama framed her argument with Ambedkar's words: Caste is not a division of labour, it is a division of labourers. That the State has done nothing to recognise skilled livelihoods, deters people outside the community from taking up an occupation usually confined to a narrow caste group. This perpetuates the caste structure, placing the burden on a particular community to continue the legacy, while also gradually obliterating the livelihood itself.

The most visible victims of these are sanitation workers. The National Commission for Safai Karamcharis notes that 194 people have died cleaning sewers—an occupation that was declared illegal in 1950—in Tamil Nadu between 1993 and 2018. They were all Dalits.[5]

Education is often 'the only real path available to break away from other kinds of societal structures and hierarchies. Dalit parents must (and do) send their children to school, because education empowers, it's not just about earning money,' says Anurag Behar, CEO of Azim Premji Foundation. 'India has made dramatic progress in the last twenty-five years in getting the young into schools.' At the degree level, Tamil Nadu has a peculiar advantage: according to the All India Council for Technical Education, 533 colleges in the state offered a bachelor's degree in engineering in 2018–19. Unfortunately, as many of the families I interviewed told me, a 'degree education' does not always lead to a good job, or 'placements'.

'India faces a shortage of quality jobs—that is, productive work with commensurate remuneration. Jobs should be aligned with grounded aspirations and aptitude,' says Sabina Dewan, president and executive director of Just Jobs Network. 'Take the example of a security guard: a twenty-one-year-old kid, stuck in a mind-numbing job from eight in the morning to eight in the evening, with little to do but stand in front of a gate for a relatively low wage—how long do you think he will stay in the job?'

Actual change can only come, 'if people outside the community begin to recognise and respect the dignity of labourers and their humanness,' says Bama. For now, it is a 'utopian dream, for work to be fully independent of caste in our country. Almost all goods are produced by everyday people. The ones who benefit are usually the privileged and dominant groups, who reap cash rewards for the hard labour that somebody else puts in.' Policy changes, few and far between that they are, cannot affect a change without a fundamental shift in attitudes, without the 'annihilation of caste'.

When livelihoods are demolished, it is not just the economy that disintegrates. Culture does too. Across India, livelihoods shape culture. Food, sport, clothes, worship, leisure are all influenced by local and long-standing occupations. And in turn, they anchor and sustain livelihoods. When this link is broken, 'the same culture, which may have sprung from the livelihoods of many villagers, could become a revenue stream for the elites in the cities,' warns Sainath. Heritage weaves and heirloom paddy varieties might, one day, only survive in upmarket boutiques and food stores. This uneven switch will also impact the environment and natural resources.

'One does not have to be a Ruritanian romantic to lament the demise of the cottage as a production venue in which there was a mutuality of capital, labour and technology,' says Gopalkrishna Gandhi. 'We have to unjudgementally recognise the fact that the overtaking of the "traditional" by "new" successor livelihood modes is universal and has been known to every generation.' But having done that, we need to see if this process robs current times of something aesthetically valuable, whether the loss of skill and know-how is irretrievable and whether the technologies that replace it are 'adverse to livelihood stability, heritability and quiddity.' Simply put: whether in this process of replacement, 'both producers and users have suffered.'

Then again, 'who values native knowledge?' asks Dharman. He recalls going to the field with his grandfather as a young boy. 'We've always had eighteen palm trees in our fields. Weaver birds build their nests on these. My grandfather used to walk around the trees and count the nests. I didn't understand what he was trying to do. People who came that side would ask him, "What do the rains say?"' His grandfather would pronounce his prediction based on the direction the nests faced, and he would turn out to be right. This native knowledge is not celebrated, says Dharman, because people who make policies do not know the land.

Why does the job of preserving tradition fall on those who have already spent centuries labouring to keep it alive? Why ask practitioners to absorb shocks of a magnitude that could bring corporates to their knees? A palm tree climber in a tiny village has to cope with cyclones, slippery barks, low prices during a glut, and traders who cap prices. He becomes a one-man army, fighting for survival and his family's future while nurturing the state tree of Tamil Nadu all along. All this, with no formal financial aid, or any other kind of state assistance.

Given how quickly Tamil Nadu is urbanising, protecting our culture is 'tricky, as it often flies in the face of new aspirations,' says A.R. Venkatachalapathy, a Tamil writer and professor at Madras Institute of Developmental Studies. 'How can you interest youngsters who aspire to eat pizzas and burgers, in nongu and padhaneer?' Taste is aspirational too. How these fit into our cultural memory and history is as important as how they fit into the economy. White sugar and white rice illustrate this best. They pushed palm jaggery and millets—produce that are kinder to the soil and rural economy—out of fashion. 'Organic products' may be a fad in the cities, but without local demand, those industries will never truly flourish. 'I find it hard to believe that a nation, which can send a satellite to Mars, cannot find a simple, elegant mechanism to climb a palm tree. The technological institutes don't come up with solutions. If you ask them, they say they don't have an incentive to do so; who will fund such projects, they ask.'

In this fast shifting cultural landscape, what have the last few decades meant for traditional livelihoods and the people who depend on them? What form of intervention will help keep these art and craft forms alive? To keep cultivators and cattle breeders solvent? Can the state sponsor or support a revival? Do caste and gender affect outcomes? Have awards mattered? Has the awarding of a geographical indication made a difference? Forced to sell their agricultural land, compelled to migrate to overcrowded cities, having little choice but to join the lower rungs of the labour market, heavily disadvantaged by a lack of formal education, isn't this too, a violence?

It is these transformations, aspirations and disruptions that I have documented: by chronicling ten important occupations—and the people who practise them—from Tamil Nadu. In 2015–16, on a fellowship from the National Foundation for India, I produced a series on the vanishing livelihoods of rural Tamil Nadu, building on earlier work I had done for PARI. The pieces appeared in PARI, *The Hindu*, *Open*, *Fountain Ink* and *Frontline* as articles, photo essays and video documentaries. This book is born from that series and includes additional reporting and interviews; four profiles are exclusive to *Nine Rupees an Hour* and were completed in 2017–18.

Each standalone essay in the book foregrounds the voice of the artist, craftsperson, cultivator and cattle breeder, and seven in-depth interviews with experts seek to provide context and commentary. Together, I hope they will present a nuanced picture of ten of the state's traditional livelihoods.

These stories can never be completed. Each day, each season, brings new challenges, opportunities and dreams. They deserve to be told, need to be told, not just because they get such little space in mainstream media but because, even when narrated, they are often reduced to a shallow feature. As skin-deep as the make-up on dancers' faces before a performance. But when the make-up fades away, and the dummy horse, stilts and sequined blouse are packed up, the true story trickles out. Kamachi told me hers the third time we met, in her house in Thanjavur, seated across the formica-topped dining table.

She was, I learnt, a grandmother, a mother, a wife, a farmer, a cook *and* a performer. She heaped my plate with rice and sambhar, and railed at the lack of patronage and a system that offers handouts in place of opportunities. She asked me how she could compete with younger, prettier, fairer dancers one-third her age. She showed me her photo albums, and we smiled at old sepia pictures, when she too was a young girl. 'Now I'm sixty-seven,' she said. She did not look it, certainly not when she wore her costume and danced to the beat of the Maratha drum. She looked, instead, like a queen: the queen of poikkal kuthirai.

This book is about the men and women who struggle every single day to keep alive the culture that we wear as a badge of honour and brandish about in the name of regionalism or patriotism. Their stories are important not only because their livelihoods are ancient, complex and beautiful but also because they are vital to a way of life—without which we would be a lot poorer.

Representational Sketch of Regions Covered*

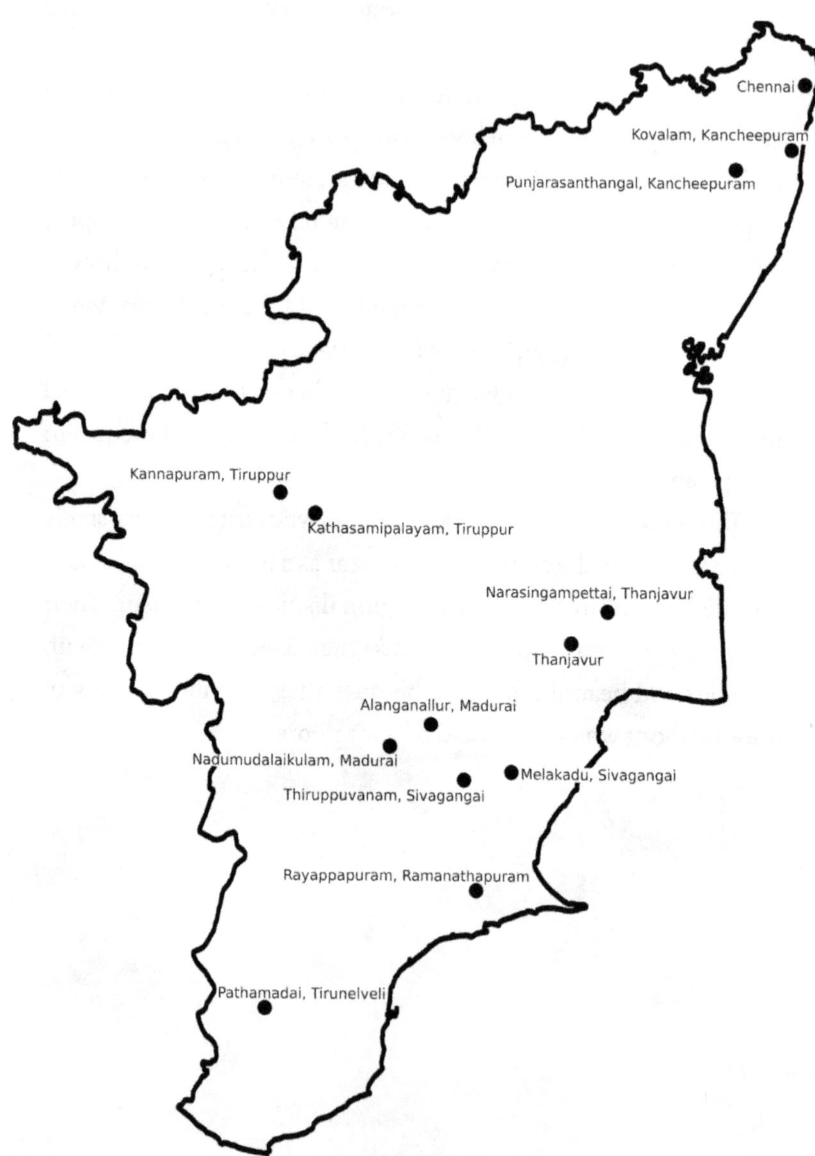

*Not drawn to scale

Part I

A Sickle ...

Let Them Eat Rice

The lotus pond was muddy and brown. It was the first one to the left on the long, winding road to Nadumudalaikulam, a hamlet deep in Madurai district. It was only February of 2018, but the pond had already turned into a sludgy pool. The leaves were withering, the flowers pale and wilting. All around, abandoned straw-yellow paddy fields were drying up. In a week or two, these soft sepia tones would deepen. The lotus pond would disappear. And the dusty earth would crack open, crying for rain.

'It has never been this bad,' said full-time farmer J. Podhumani, as she scythed the tall stalks of maize to feed her three cows. But that year, Madurai, and all of Tamil Nadu, hadn't recovered from the terrible drought of 2016–17, the worst in over a century. As a result, in the cluster of hamlets in Mudalaikulam village, Chellampatti block—which includes Nadumudalaikulam—paddy was grown only in 150 out of the usual 3,000 acres.

When I first visited Nadumudalaikulam in January 2015, it was lush. December rains had greened the hills and filled the ponds. Egrets perched on trees like white flowers. In every field, women stood in rows, ankles deep in slush, and pressed short green shoots into the wet earth. It was punishing work, but the women moved swiftly and gracefully through the squelching soil, not once stopping to stretch their backs.

The very next year, rains failed spectacularly. The Tamil Nadu government declared a drought across the state on 10 January 2017. Headlines in newspapers and tickers on TV channels announced that it was the 'worst drought in 140 years'.[1] The state received only 168.3 mm of rainfall during the northeast monsoon of 2016 as against an average of 440.4 mm—a deficit of 62 per cent. Out of 16,682 revenue villages in the state, 13,305 were identified as drought affected. The state requested a sum of ₹39,565 crore from the National Disaster Response Fund as drought relief.[2]

The Centre approved only ₹1,447.99 crore, less than 4 per cent of the amount requested.[3] Farmers from across the Cauvery delta districts of Thanjavur, Thiruvarur and Nagapattinam—the state's most fertile region, now cracked and brown—gathered in Delhi to protest and seek compensation. They stripped, drank their own urine and sat waiting under a crushing summer sun. Politicians, journalists and photographers came, but their demands—for a farm loan waiver, drought relief and the setting up of a Cauvery River management board—remained unfulfilled.[4] 'Since October 2016, more than 600 farmers have committed suicide in the state,' P. Ayyakannu, who led the Delhi protests, told me in January 2018. Although the National Crime Records Bureau recorded 381 suicides in the farming sector in the state in 2016 alone,[5] it responded to an RTI query on the number of farmer suicides in the state for 2016–2018 with: the 'data ... is not available with the bureau.'[6]

But the troubles with farming run deeper and longer than the recent drought. P. Sainath, who has extensively covered the agrarian distress in India for over two decades, wrote in *The New York Times* in April 2018: 'Policy-driven agrarian distress is very real. India's last national census—conducted every decade—in 2011 recorded nearly 15 million fewer farmers than there were in 1991; that's a dropout rate of about 2,040 every 24 hours. Many of those fell from being farmers to being landless agricultural labourers, into the ranks of the agrarian underclass.' He also noted: 'Between 1995 and 2015, the National Crime Records Bureau logged over 300,000 farmer suicides.'[7]

'It's nearly impossible to be a full-time farmer and make enough money,' Podhumani's husband Jeyabal told me. He pointed to a group of men under a banyan tree. 'None of them can live off agriculture alone. One drives tractors, the other ferries construction materials on lorries, the third runs a bakery. And I work as a swimming instructor in Madurai city, 25 km from here.'

'With little rain and hardly any water in the rivers, paddy farmers are only reaping debts. Cash crops and flowers are no better,' said Ayyakannu.

Why then are farmers like Podhumani and Jeyabal, both in their late thirties, attached to raising paddy? 'It's prestigious,' they said. 'And when there's water, it's profitable. It's also relatively less labour intensive than vegetables or flowers. Except during transplanting, harvesting and weeding, a couple can handle three acres of paddy on their own. You need three times the number of people for a third of ladies finger.'

Oryza sativa, rice, has always been grown extensively in India, its history of domestication going back several millennia. India is the second largest producer of rice, after China, and in Tamil Nadu, rice is grown in 42 per cent of the cropped area.[8] But when rains don't arrive on time, paddy fails spectacularly. In 2016–17, rice production was less than half of what it was the previous year: down from 73.75 lakh metric tonnes to 35.54 lakh metric tonnes.[9]

When Jeyabal was a young boy, there were one or two good rains every month and plenty during the monsoon. 'Now, there are a few good rains during the monsoon. And after, none for months on end.'

Since their lands are not directly irrigated by rivers or canals, Podhumani and Jeyabal depend on the rains to fill the local ooorani and kanmai, ponds and lakes, to raise three crops of rice. The first pokam, or crop cycle, is sown in October and harvested in February, the second lasts from February to May, and the third from July to October. Rice is a thirsty crop and guzzles 5,000 litres of water to produce a kilo; the hardier millets need only a fraction of this, about 250–300 litres per kilo.[10] In 2017, when the northeast monsoon failed again and the water bodies went dry, all the couple got from their first pokam was dried up clumps of paddy, and they were already ₹5,000 down. They could not do anything about the 3 acres of land they had leased, but applied for government insurance for the 1.5 acres they owned. They received nothing. 'They tell you to come back the next day with one set of papers, the day after with another, and so on. I can't do all that. I need to go to work. Podhumani has to graze the cattle. Who has the time for this?'

During a good season, the couple harvest thirty-five sacks of paddy an acre, out of which they retain four sacks for themselves, including one for re-sowing. For a farmer, food and fortunes are ruled by the elements, but crop varieties are mostly decided by the local shop. In Jeyabal's case, it is nine kilometres from their village in Chekkanurani town. Though he has tried different varieties of paddy, it is not comparable to the range that was available to his grandfather in the 1960s—a staggering 70,000.[11] But back then, few people grew rice in his village and until he was in class five, Jeyabal's family ate nellu saapadu, or white rice, only on special occasions like Deepavali and Pongal. The staple food was the healthier millets. Ironically, as paddy cultivation was scaled up through hybrids, by 1991, 'over 75 per cent of India's rice production was coming from less than 10 varieties.'[12]

The family sells their paddy to the trader at only ₹15–₹21 per kilo (a 66 kg sack fetches them ₹1,000–₹1,400). But if they have to buy rice from the market, it would cost them ₹50 per kilo. The couple counted fifteen stages of expenditure—from sowing to the commission they pay the trader—and arrived at ₹25,750 per acre as their input costs. 'At the very minimum, a sack has to fetch ₹1,500,' said Podhumani. 'Fertiliser costs are leaping,' she added, using gulping sounds, 'gappu, gappu,' to denote their quick upward leaps.

'If the next generation needs to farm, the rates have to be sustainable. What happens now? If there's a lot of production, the rates sink. If it is low like this year, the price is higher at about ₹1,700 a sack,' said Jeyabal. 'And whether the production is good or bad, our work is going to be the same. We can't increase or decrease the labour, can we?' asked Podhumani. Together, they labour eight to ten hours daily for three months. Their wage, which they have never calculated, comes to roughly ₹200 per person, per day.[13] 'Why should my sons want to do this work?' asked Jeyabal.

So who makes money from paddy cultivation? The traders. 'They buy the paddy from us. They dehusk it and sell the rice. They determine the buying price of paddy. They also determine the selling price of rice. Both are in their control. It is not possible for the average paddy farmer to become—or replace—a trader,' said Jeyabal. 'Who has the time?'

When the unrelenting drought got worse, Jeyabal decided to abandon paddy and switch to millets and cowpea, alongside dairy farming. A lot of thought and traditional wisdom went into these choices. Jeyabal explained how the soil in rain-fed lands, called karisalbhoomi, like in Ramanathapuram district, retains a hint of moisture for weeks. Whereas Nadumudalaikulam's earth, a mix of semmantharai and karumantharai, red and black soil, holds water for only a few days. 'Ours is ideal for millets.' It costs about ₹7,500 to raise an acre of cowpea or maize. The risks are lower too, unlike for paddy, where even one downpour before the harvest can ruin the entire lot. 'Take a few grains of ripe, wet paddy and rub it between your palms. It will break. Who will pay a good price for it?' asked Podhumani.

But the couple did not once complain about their bhoomi, their earth, not even when the drought killed their hopes. They referred to it with affection, never anger.

To tide over the drought, they also pooled in their savings, borrowed some money from Podhumani's sister, and bought two cows for ₹50,000, to add to the one they already had. 'I tried getting loans from the bank,' said Jeyabal. 'I heard they were giving money to buy goats and cows. But I was made to run around for over a week. They told me to get sureties from the company I sell the milk to. I persisted for a month and then gave up. We bought the cows anyway.'

Small farmers in Melakadu hamlet, in Sivagangai district—about an hour's drive to the west from Nadumudalaikulam and part of Chettinad, famous for its cuisine and architecture—are also rapidly abandoning paddy cultivation. Situated in the state's rain shadow region, water has always been a problem here; rainfall is often patchy and has been distressingly meagre in the last few years. All around, palm trees are dying, paddy fields are turning fallow and ponds are drying up. To get water for agriculture, borewells have to go down a thousand feet and wells are routinely deepened.

And yet, the Sivagangai earth gives. In the early morning light, it is the red of ground chillies; in the cooler months, it is as hard as jaggery. One shower and it turns fragrant.

Tamil Nadu gets most of its rain from the northeast monsoon, from October to December. That rain is nothing like the sudden summer showers that come with their own band of thunder and strobe lightning. The spells are short and ferocious—as fierce as the day's heat—and the earth is quenched. During the monsoon, the rain is moody, and the sky, often bruised and brooding. The farmers wait, those who have sown after the first shower, anxiously, and the others, eagerly. When the rain comes—a slow, steady downpour—the goats and cows are brought in and people move inside their tiled houses. And smile.

Inside a newly built house in Melakadu hamlet in Muthur village in Sivagangai, Chandra Subramanian, a single woman farmer, was also awaiting the rain in November 2017. 'That acre of land that's been fallow for so long? I'll till it and plant more sampangi [tuberose] flowers. But first, I'll put in a new irrigation system with butterfly sprinklers. It will water the plant from the top, the flowers will be beautiful and fresh, as if it has just rained.'

Married at sixteen to her aunt's son who lived in Tiruppur district, famous for its garment factories, Chandra came back to her maternal home in Melakadu when her husband took his own life. His suicide had come within forty days of a road accident that killed her father. 'My father was his uncle, he meant everything to my husband. He was shattered when my father died. Depressed, he hung himself.' Chandra did not divulge more. She was twenty-four then, and her kids were four and one. But she did not have the luxury of mourning, and loathed being pitied by the older women. She told them to stop depressing her and carefully weighed her options. She decided against picking up tailoring again—the work she had done with her husband in Tiruppur—and also against studying. A job meant long hours away from the children. Opting for the degree route to a better life required her to first clear the twelfth board exams, again keeping her away from the children.

So she decided to take up farming, which she sees as a flexi-hours job. She appreciates the convenience of working in a nightie in her backyard—their fields are right behind the house. Her mother divided the family's twelve acres among her three children after her husband's death. Now, mother and daughter live together on Chandra's share of four acres and grow flowers.

Like everybody else in the region, they too initially cultivated paddy. When their family migrated to Sivagangai from Salem about twenty-five years ago, land was cheap, water was plenty and the fields were green with swaying paddy. Later, many switched to sugarcane, a thirsty crop, pushed by sugar companies, who subsidised drip irrigation for sugarcane cultivation. When the water table plummeted in 2014, after years of poor rain, many farmers sold their farmlands as real estate and moved to towns and cities. Those who held on—some for lack of opportunity, others because they worship the land they work on—switched to other crops. Chandra tried vegetables for some years and sold them herself at a local shanty. In 2017, seeing a neighbour plant sampangi, Chandra decided to try it out.

That year, thirty-five of the forty houses in Melakadu had at least a small patch of sampangi, Chandra told me one early November morning. The sky was black and moonless. Wearing a shirt on top of her nightie, with a blue, striped scarf, Chandra stood alone, encircled by a beam of light from her headlamp. It was not quite four o'clock, but she was hard at work, delicately breaking the stems and dropping the flowers into a sack tied to her waist. Already, a tenth of her two acres were plucked.

The peak season was over and she had only thirty–forty kilos to pick, down from the sixty–seventy kilos from a few months ago. It did not reduce her workload much though; she still had to walk between every row and inspect every stalk and stem because a fully bloomed sampangi is of little commercial value. It helps that Chandra is nimble. Forget a bulging sack; it was not easy to walk between the rows even with just a camera, in the night. Neither was it easy to engage in a conversation with Chandra, who moved quickly, twisting and turning, as if she were a wooden top in a nightie and a scarf with a miner's lamp on her head.

By half past five, the picking was nearly done. The sky lightened, fog caressed the palm trees and the animals in her farm stretched and yawned. Kannama, the cow, woke up with swollen udders and tugged on her ropes as Azhagi, the almond-eyed biscuit-coloured calf, cried for her mother. Chandra's six-year-old daughter Iniya came out of the house, her bangled hands rubbing against sleepy eyes. Nine-year-old Dhanush followed her and headed straight to the calf. As soon as he untied her, she ran to Kannama and suckled hungrily. The children tied sacks around their waists and, without being asked, picked the remaining flowers, quickly.

Chandra emptied the flowers from all their sacks into a bigger one that had her name inked on it. She lifted the corners—as if they were ears—and hoisted it up on one slender shoulder. Balancing what was probably four-fifth her body weight, she walked gracefully and placed the sack on the veranda. She asked the kids to fetch oil and a bucket. It sounded like a strange combination till she sat on a small stool next to the cow and greased the udder with the oil. The milk hit the bucket loudly at first, turned frothy and soon filled it up. 'Stay for tea,' she ordered. 'I have a gas connection now, it won't take long.'

Podhumani and Jeyabal's three cows give twelve litres of milk, the two hybrids produce five each and the indigenous, two. The daily earning, collected every ten days, comes to ₹300, a third of which goes towards feeding the cows. They have ₹10,000 left over in a month. With this amount and Jeyabal's salary of another ₹10,000, they pay interest on previous loans of ₹3.3 lakh that subsidise the farming. Much of the principal amount still needs to be paid. But it funds small dreams.

One of Podhumani's is to have a roof over her house. 'A pucca, concrete roof. Flat.' The large front room of their house is divided up into cooking and living spaces by a short, whitewashed mud wall. 'Tomorrow, if someone wants to marry my son, won't her family ask if the boy's house has a proper roof?' she said, looking up at the tiled roof.

The couple's married life too began like a dream, the dream of a young girl-farmer.

Podhumani was the youngest of six daughters, with a boy born after her. Her father, who chopped and sold firewood, got lucky when he found a cow in the open. He brought it back home, and from that one animal, which he worshipped as 'Saami madu', God's cow, he bred and raised a hundred. Despite their poverty, the family never sold milk or any of the cows. 'Only bull calves were sold, as my father thought of cows as God's, like the first one he found.' From the money earned by selling ten or twenty bull calves every year, her parents took care of the children and got the girls married.

As children, Podhumani and her siblings were sent to graze the cattle. When they grew to about four feet tall, she raised her hand to indicate the height, they were sent to work as agricultural labourers. 'It's only now that you have machines to harvest paddy. Back then, everything was done by hand. So they used to take us kids early in the morning and bring us back late. Where did we have the time to study?'

Although Podhumani never had a formal education, she learnt about the earth and farming. It was also in the fields that she first saw Jeyabal. She was sixteen, he nineteen. It was love, as they say, at first sight.

'I had flunked my tenth exams, so I went to work,' said Jeyabal. 'That year I was harvesting paddy over here, she was scything over there. A year later, we told our families we were going to marry.' He smiled as he recalled the memory.

Their second son, who was sitting by the door on a palagai, a low wooden stool, also grinned. He nodded when I asked if he knew of this story already. Podhumani clearly wanted him out but instead of asking him to leave, she giggled.

Jeyabal's friends used to tease him about how he could marry a girl taller than him. 'So he sent a bunch of young boys to measure my height,' said Podhumani.

'One metre and seventy-four centimetres,' said Jeyabal proudly, 'that's how tall we both are.'

'We managed the opposition from the family, mainly his. They asked how he could marry a woman without a gold chain. But we did, three years after we met.'

'The day we got married in 2002, a drought began, and for three years after, there was no water,' said Jeyabal. Until then, a happy-go-lucky young man, he was interested in and good at sports, and that is what he pursued and won: kabaddi matches and discus and shotput competitions. He was a champ in jallikattu too. Podhumani fetched a pile of his certificates from a bureau. Jeyabal listed his prizes with longing. 'Gold coin, kuthuvilakku [traditional brass lamp], TV, cycle, I won everything.'

But after marriage, he couldn't keep playing games. It was around 2002–03, that young men from Jeyabal's village ventured out, for the first time, to find work. He too went to Madurai and found work at a construction site. Before heading out everyday, he helped out in the family farm in Nadumudalaikulam, then in his father's name.

He became a swimming instructor in 2008. His salary was ₹4,500. In 2010, when he was handed over the responsibility of his share of the family land, he became a full-time farmer, apart from holding down a day job.

Meanwhile, Podhumani worked in the field of a wealthy landowner in the village, Ochamma Gopal. Her daily wage then was ₹60, half of what it became seventeen years later. 'I didn't go to too many people's fields to work. I had two sons and I was busy caring for them. It's not easy to work with small children to care for.' With everybody in the village out in the fields, the kids had to be taken along too. The women work till the day before they deliver and are back in the fields a month after childbirth.

In late 2017, Jeyabal's family land was transferred to him. 'We figured it would be helpful to have it in my name. Banks ask for land as surety for loans. If we don't have any, the interest rate is higher and they just make us stand around.'

But despite all the hardship, Jeyabal still has faith in his land. 'If there is water, and we have paddy growing in our fields, we'll never be able to sleep.' He is hopeful that the hard labour will be worth it. 'If I grow paddy on three and a half acres, and I get about two lakh rupees after the harvest, it will be great! It will also make raising the cows easy; there will be feed for them. Maybe next year there will be rain.' This predictable income is possible only with paddy and food crops. Cash crops can bring in a bounty harvest, but they come with very high risks.

Podhumani too shares his dream of paddy cultivation and is determined not to give up farming. 'I am very keen to work on our own land, to raise paddy; maybe we'll do it again soon.'

While Jeyabal and Podhumani at least have each other, many farming families are broken.

A few minutes after Chandra and I reached her neighbour Poovayi's house, it began to rain. The courtyard turned slushy, the dogs got wet, the firewood that was cooking their rice sizzled and died, and roosters took cover under a steel cot. As we settled on the cement floor inside the house, the power went out. Colours faded, people became silhouettes, until Poovayi's thirteen-year-old daughter Priyadarshini brought a brass lamp, rubbed five cotton wicks between her palms and lit them one by one. And in that room, where everything was touched by a golden light, two single women who farmed for a living—S. Poovayi and her mother-in-law M. Sivabhagiyam—told me a story.

It wasn't a happy one.

Four male members had died on that piece of land in twenty-five years. Poovayi's father-in-law was the first and then her brother-in-law. Tragedy hit closer when her eldest son, a bright lad, drowned. Poovayi's husband, Subramani, was devastated. He drank pesticide late in the night, but came running to the field at 2 a.m. when Poovayi was plucking tuberose and told her what he had done. They rushed him to the hospital, where he held on for two days. And then he was gone, leaving her with two children, some debt and plenty of uncertainty.

Fifteen years ago, Poovayi came to Melakadu as a young eighteen-year-old bride. She helped her husband and his family cultivate paddy, vegetables and eventually, sugarcane, in the twelve acres the family owned. Back then, there was water at two hundred feet in the borewell. 'There was one good rain almost every month, which kept the soil wet for some days. It increased the water level in the well, we managed,' the women told me. But the last four or five years had been disastrous. 'You're lucky if you find water at a thousand feet.'

The water-intensive sugarcane mercilessly perished, along with their efforts and money, as soon as the soil turned dry. The motor had to run for three hours a day to water an acre of sugarcane, double the time it takes to irrigate sampangi.

Poovayi has mature sampangi flowering in one acre and two-month-old saplings in another. There is little water to cultivate the remaining ten acres. 'We've sunk a lakh for each acre; we start seeing a profit only after the first year, when the yield is good.' Cash crops—particularly flowers like tuberose, which are used in garlands—fetch different prices on different days, unlike food crops. Festive and auspicious days see it climb, sometimes to over ₹300 a kilo. A glut in the market on a 'karinaal', an inauspicious day, when no wedding or function takes place, and the price plunges to single digits.

Now, Poovayi and her mother-in-law work from midnight to five in the morning to pluck the flowers, ten hours of work daily between them. Chandra teased, 'These two are slow; that's why it takes them this long.'

'It's true, I cannot work like her,' said Sivabhagiyam, laughing. 'I'm slow and sleepy. So in the middle of the night, I milk a cow, heat it, make myself a glass of kaapi, wear two shirts and go to the field.'

'Not just that,' said young Priyadarshini, 'Paati even cooks and eats at midnight.' Her grandmother laughed, as she handed out fistfuls of sooyam to everybody. 'Eat, eat,' she ordered.

As we snacked on the deep-fried sweet, the children fetched albums and photos. Shyly, Priyadarshini showed photos of her father, mother and brothers. She held out her favourite—her father, his trousers folded, standing in the sea at Rameshwaram. Poovayi picked it up gently, as if it were fragile, and stared at it. Only Murugesan, the youngest, seemed untouched by the grief. He smiled happily as he grabbed the portraits. 'My father, my brother,' he said, the smile not leaving his face when he spoke of the two who had died some months ago, too young and too unaware of what had hit his family.

Irrespective of the presence of men in the family, women end up doing a lion's share of the work.

Podhumani's day begins before the cock's crow, even before the sun. 'I wake up by half past four or five. First, I put the rice to boil. Then, I milk the cows. My husband cleans the yard, gathers the cow dung and heaps it to one side. Next, I milk the cows, he delivers it at the collection point.' By then, the rice is done and Podhumani makes a kozhambu, or curry, to go with it. 'At about seven, my son needs to be packed off to school.'

Alone at home, she fetches water, about ten pots, from the tap nearby or from another a little distance away. Since the grass is poor and scant, she cooks some millets for the cows, which she mixes with readymade cow feed and water. By then it's ten, a good five hours since she has been up. 'There are some small jobs in between: washing the vessels, clothes and school uniforms,' she said, but didn't complete the list, because, she considers her 'work' to begin only when she sets out to graze the three cows, walking many kilometres. 'It's not easy to find a patch of green during the drought.'

When the sun is high, she ties them in the shade of scrawny trees and fetches water for them from the house. Over the rough and tumble paths, walking briskly, she makes it home and back in forty minutes.

While the cows rest and chew cud, Podhumani gathers their evening and night feed: usually grass plucked from wherever she can find it and maize stalks they raise. Holding the stalk, which is taller than her, she hacks at the thick stem with a sickle. She feeds a bit of it to the cows and saves the rest for later. 'I walk along with the cows and see that they eat properly.' The milk output depends on the cattle's intake; even a slight fall in the output takes days to build up again. She has to dash home for lunch and back, and then finally, around half past five in the evening, she drags the cows back home, hurrying to milk them by six, feed and water them, and prepare dinner for the family.

'If there's agricultural work—this year there's none—that too has to be done between all this. What can we do? The drought means more work with animals and no work with the land. If there is water, life would be so much easier. If only the pond would fill up, we can farm for two years. If only ...'

While Podhumani's day goes by fetching ten pots of water, tending to half-dry plots of maize and cowpea, and milking the three cows, Jeyabal spends the day standing beside a beautiful swimming pool filled to the brim with good quality water.

Podhumani gets very little time to rest and Sundays mean more work. 'Everybody is at home. The kids will want special food. They complain that house is cooking meat and this house is eating fish,' said Podhumani. The family can attend a wedding as long as it is nearby, so they can milk the cows in the morning and be back in time for the evening's milking. 'In the one hour we've spent chatting here, I could have grazed them a bit, they'll milk 100 ml more,' she confessed, but not accusingly, only to explain how little time she gets to stay indoors, in the shade.

She instead spent that one hour cooking me a meal of rice, sambhar and venjanam, or a side of vegetables, a meal she prepares for her boys to take to school everyday. But for herself, she only packs some watery rice, with pickle or a brinjal dish, to take to the fields. She pulled a sackful of cowpea, which she often cooks with. They rustled and rolled in her hand. 'Some days, I peel and eat this when I graze cows. I can't always come back home to eat on time. This helps me get by,' she said and offered me some: they were hard to bite but rewarding in their flavour. 'It's nice,' she said, 'isn't it?'

Old age does not exempt the women from hard labour. As I ate, Jeyabal's seventy-year-old mother was out in the fields, even though she is financially secure—she owns some gold and even lends out money. Her husband was busy playing cards in the afternoon shade of a neem tree, his hair as white as his hoicked-up dhoti, surrounded by other men, whose wives too were out in the fields. Unlike many of them, Jeyabal lends a hand whenever he is home, even though Podhumani loathes asking for help.

Jeyabal has one other advantage that most women and many men from the interior villages are denied: access to other work. Women work longer hours for less pay. And often, there are few opportunities besides farming or working as day-wage labourers. 'If not for her,' said Jeyabal, 'I can't keep up with two jobs. And we cannot run our house.'

Women in India own around 13 per cent of farmland and do over 70 per cent of the agricultural work.[14] With few exceptions, women fare abysmally across the world when it comes to farmland ownership.[15] They work twelve to thirteen hours more per week than men in the developing countries of Africa, Asia and the Pacific; yet, their contributions are often 'invisible' and unpaid.[16] In South and East Asia, the number of women 'agriculture holders'—decision-makers and managers of the holding in essence—is still not high enough, considering they do a large part of the work. Malaysia tops the list with 27.5 per cent of agriculture holders being women and Bangladesh is at the bottom with 4.6 per cent.

Despite the punishing schedule followed by women like Podhumani, Chandra and Poovayi, the census does not count their contribution as work. The data from the last published 2011 census pegs the workforce participation rate for rural women at 30.02 per cent, while men fare better at 53.03 per cent. On the ground, the reality is altogether different. Almost every woman in a village toils at home and in the fields. While the housework is unpaid, the wage for women agricultural workers is about half of what men get. To skew things further, the 'weaker sex' gets the tougher work on the farm. Men prepare the field—a job that traditionally pays well and is now increasingly mechanised—and build varappu, or boundary walls. But 80 per cent of the transplanting and weeding, both of which put enormous strain on the back, legs and hands, is done by women.

Jeyabal too acknowledged this disparity. 'When a couple farm, the woman lands the bigger share of work. Take someone like me. I go to work all day. When I'm around—morning and night—I'm only supervising. She does all the executing—weeding, watering, fertilising, inspecting the fields for pests. Seventy-five per cent of the work is done by the ladies.'

The pay gap—for the same work—is staggering. According to the Labour Bureau, in 2018, male workers in Tamil Nadu were paid a daily wage of ₹404.67 per day for sowing/transplanting and a female worker, ₹254.94. For harvesting, it was ₹444.36 for males and ₹265.83 for females.[17]

Not just women, the economy itself will benefit from bridging this gap, said Jayati Ghosh, professor of economics at Jawaharlal Nehru University, New Delhi. 'It improves household incomes, usually leads to more spending on welfare of children, adds to rural effective demand and therefore has significant positive multiplier effects.' The most effective way of bridging this gap, she explained, is to provide public employment at equal wages, and this would set the market floor. 'We already have evidence of how this can work with the MNREGS [Mahatma Gandhi National Rural Employment Scheme]—where it has worked well and employed more women workers, it has also played a big role in reducing gender wage gaps. However, its spread is still insufficient to eliminate the gap [which, incidentally, is among the highest in the world]. Even worse, a lot of public employment actually exploits gender discrimination in the labour market to hire women as "voluntary workers" [in anganwadis and as Accredited Social Health Acitivists, or ASHAs] at well below minimum wages, thereby intensifying the problem.'

Agricultural labour fetches ₹120, while the MNREGS could pay up to ₹140; but the latter is hard to come by and sometimes, badly timed, competing for labour during planting and harvesting seasons. 'There aren't enough workers then. We have to lure labourers with higher rates, or by throwing in a meal of tea and vadai,' said Jeyabal.

In Melakadu, and all of Sivagangai, the situation isn't any different. It is difficult to find local labour, and landowners labour on their fields, including for the most intensive job of weeding. 'Out of twelve acres, two have flowers. Where is the water, manpower and the money to cultivate the rest?' asked Poovayi. 'When my husband was alive, he took loans to put in drip irrigation and farm inputs. The outstanding has grown to ₹8 lakh. We're still repaying that.' The private loans she takes come at a hefty interest rate of 3 paise–4 paise per rupee, which comes up to ₹3–₹4 per ₹100 a month: a whopping 36 per cent–48 per cent per annum. Not surprisingly, the loans quickly grow out of control.

Yet, the women are clear that they don't want to access banks for loans. 'See, we work so hard, why should we go to the bank and get insulted? They want surety—land documents—and if there is the slightest delay in repayment, they send people home to collect. It's so embarrassing.'

'Also, we're both single women. Men can go, speak to four people and get loans. What can we do?' Chandra complained. 'They ask a person to sign for surety. I have my mother, Poovayi has her mother-in-law. Both women are over sixty. The banks assume they'll die soon and tell us they are not eligible. Otherwise, they ask us to bring children over eighteen years of age. Our children are young. Where do we go? Who do we bring as nominees and sureties?' she raged.

The women's troubles with the bank are endless. Chandra continued, 'You might hear banks say that they support single women and farmers. But ask us, we'll tell you how it really is. Rather than go and beg random people to come and sign for us, we just get loans outside and pay the high interest rates. It is a question of our self-respect, our dignity. When I go to an office or a bank and introduce myself, I'm asked to wait in the corner. Where are the chairs for the people who grow your food?'

When I spoke to Jeyabal later, he pointed out that it wasn't easier for a male farmer either. 'You can quickly get into debt. One failed harvest, and the money sunk in is lost. Besides daily and unforeseen expenses, there's also the rent on the leased land that has to be paid.'

Despite their obvious pride in and love for their land, Podhumani and Jeyabal don't think farming to be a suitable occupation for their children. 'My sons Akash [16] and Harshavardhan [14] will not want to farm the way we do—lease land, struggle for water, raise paddy—all because we both like agriculture,' said Podhumani. In a rare admission, she talked of how they toil endlessly to cultivate the land. 'Besides, what do we have to show for the work we do? Won't my sons ask us, "You worked every day, what have you made?"' But then, she argued, how could they see any sizeable profit when there's so little state support? 'After six years, we're still waiting for an electricity connection for a borewell. They say they will give it when the government is stable. It might even take two more years. When will we ever own more land and farm our own fields?'

'People are abandoning even money-making occupations,' Jeyabal joined in. 'Take sickle making. The sons don't want to get into it, even though the makers decide the final price of the product. Now compare that to farming. Can I set the buying price of paddy based on input costs and my labour?' Moreover, his sons are not trained for farm work. 'They're raised in a village, but they're not hardy. They might not be able to become policemen or join the army. Maybe all they are fit for is a software job.'

Poovayi's daughter Priyadarshini had to pitch in to help after her father died. 'From 18 July, I have been taking flowers to the lorry,' she piped up. 'It was a Tuesday, I circled it there,' she said, pointing to the calendar. Her mother did not share her enthusiasm, but she was clearly grateful. When her husband died, the women had no means of getting the sacks of flowers to the collection point, from where it went by truck to Mattuthavani, Madurai's busy flower market. It has to be done in the wee hours of morning; the walk is too long and the load too heavy. Neighbours and friends helped out for a bit, but salacious talk about the men who lent a hand put an end to that quickly. Poovayi was heartbroken all over again. She swore she would quit farming and go back to her mother's village. That is when Priyadarshini offered to carry the flowers herself. At five every morning, balancing over twice her body weight on a small 80CC bike, she drives nearly five kilometres on the narrow roads. At the collection point, the men receive her warmly. 'They all know her, they come running when they see "Subramani's vehicle". One of them holds the bike, another lifts the sacks on to the lorry. I never wanted to make her work, but there was no choice,' said Poovayi, her eyes downcast, her voice trembling.

The two older women are firm that Priyadarshini should not end up as a farmer like them. They don't want her to work on the land, though they have a sizeable holding. 'Enough, let her go and do something nice,' said the grandmother, sighing. 'Whatever they want to study, however much it costs, I want it for them,' insisted Poovayi. Priyadarshini wants to be an engineer. Murugesan is undecided. 'I work night and day for them. You know, we cannot sit for a moment when we pluck flowers, my half a minute of rest is when I transfer the flowers into the big sack. Then there are the cows and goats and hens. When I'm exhausted, I just crash.'

Even Ochamma, who owns over ten acres and a deep borewell, confessed that she farms because it is a prestige issue. She too is not spared from the fear of failed harvests. 'If we let our fields turn fallow, people would gossip that we're broke. That would be embarrassing. We're not looking at profits. Ask Podhumani how much money I lost last year.'

As Jeyabal walked back to his bike after inspecting Ochamma's fields on her request, a small puff of dust rose and fell with every step. 'Do you want to see the well?' he asked, walking towards it. The well's walls were velvety brown and cool. 'How can we make money from farming?' he asked, as we peered into the deep, black well. 'In my father's time, the men were stronger and more skilled. They even built bunds themselves. But my generation is losing vital knowledge. Now, we only know how to break them to regulate water levels. We pay others to ready our fields.' He predicted it would only get worse in the coming decades. 'I was not educated. My options were limited. But my sons tell me: if you want money, we'll earn it from Madurai. They don't want this life,' he said, waving his hand at the acres and acres of paddy fields.

'Protests Must Never Stop'

P. Ayyakannu was streamed live into people's living rooms from Delhi's Jantar Mantar in 2017, where he participated in an ingenious protest along with other farmers for 141 days. Their demands were profitable pricing, interlinking of rivers, individual insurance, pension and compensation for crop loss during the worst drought in 140 years. A lawyer by profession, he also farms his twenty acres of land in his hometown, Musiri in Tiruchirappali district. He was the state general secretary of the RSS-affiliated Bharatiya Kisan Sangh, but quit the organisation when the Bharatiya Janata Party did not fulfil their promises. He then founded the National South Indian Rivers Interlinking Agriculturists Association and continues to protest for farmers' rights.

You have been protesting since 2000. What is your main demand?

I have been fighting for something straightforward and simple: fair prices for agricultural produce. In 1970, a tonne of sugarcane fetched ninety rupees, which was also a teacher's salary. Now, the same teacher earns fifty-four thousand. But my sugarcane only fetches two thousand five hundred rupees. Do you know why? 95 per cent of the teachers protested every year; they were ready to go to jail. So their salary went up 600 times. Despite some farmers protesting, we only got 28 times more. Farmers cannot participate in the same way that teachers or others from the organised sector can, because the farmer does not have a fixed income. And if he went off to jail for ten days, his crop would wither. The loan he took to cultivate the land would mount. That's the life of a farmer.

Is farming profitable now, even if it doesn't match up to the rise in incomes?

It is almost impossible to farm now. My annual crops of banana and sugarcane died because of lack of water. The paddy crop, which needs water only for three months, also died. Even the coconut trees died. But the government refuses to give me compensation. When I racked up a loss of one lakh after my banana crop failed, I was offered one rupee per plant, a total of thousand rupees.

But the input costs keep rising. A kilo of punaaku [cattle feed] that I got for twenty-five paise in 1970 now costs fifty-five rupees, up 220 times.

The meteoric rise isn't true for agricultural produce though. Then, we could sell three sacks of paddy and buy a sovereign of gold. Now, the rate for the same eight grams of gold is twenty-four thousand rupees. When paddy has gone up by only 22 times, gold has shot up by 200 times. How do we buy it?

Why has the government not fixed this disparity?

It comes down to electoral politics. Two out of every three Indians has something to do with agriculture. But not all are cultivators. Only twenty crore people grow paddy. They want a better and fair price for their produce. But the remaining hundred crore don't want it to rise. Who will the government support?

Among the twenty crore, eighteen have some sort of political affiliation. They will vote only for the party they support; they might not change their loyalty just because they got a higher price. Once, a senior politician openly told me that if they help a corporate, they get 30 per cent in kickbacks, which they can use during the elections. He asked me, 'What's the point helping farmers if they won't even vote for us?' The pattern is similar among other producers—wheat farmers and sugarcane cultivators. The prices are kept down for the sake of the vote bank. The only time a farmer is trotted out as the backbone of the country is during elections. The rest of the time? We're slaves.

Is this why so many farmers are taking their lives?

Farmers are enslaved by their debts and are dying because of it. Bank managers ask us if we eat food or shit, and order us to repay our loans. They say they'll lose their jobs, that their bosses are threatening them. If we tell them there is no water, the wells and lakes have dried up, they tell us to sell our land and house. We try and explain that we get offers of only two lakh for land that should fetch ten lakh. The retort is, sell your house then. If I plead that we cannot possibly sell our house, he asks why I buy a new saree for my wife or a new dhoti for myself if I cannot pay back the loan. It's demeaning.

How did the central government respond to farmer suicides in the state?

The government completely denied it, and blamed all suicides on family matters, fights and alcoholism, anything but the actual reason: unprofitable and unviable farming. Governments routinely disregard our petitions.

One of the reasons for this is also the skewed and unrealistic perception of agriculture. There was a sensational report on a cash crop in the agricultural supplement of a popular Tamil magazine—'If you invest four lakh rupees in the medicinal plant kanvali kizhangu [flame lily], you will get a return of seven lakh.' It is pure humbug. I spent three lakh and cultivated it on three acres after signing an agreement for buy-back of the tubers for twenty-five rupees a kilo. But the price fell, and they never came to buy it. The fields just rotted, and I finally got thirty thousand rupees. Deducting the expense to transport it, I made a 'profit' of ten thousand. This is the trouble with such reports and advertisements.

There are ads which assure you that roses will bloom into money—panama malarum roja. In half an acre, make four lakh a year. But the chaps who actually cropped the flowers? They are burdened with huge debts.

If a high court judge reads such a report, he will think I can make eighty lakh rupees by cultivating roses on ten acres. He thinks that compared to his salary, we're very well off. He tells us off for coming to the court. He doesn't know how badly I've fared actually cultivating it!

How many of your sangam's core demands—for profitable prices, insurance and pension schemes for farmers—have been met?

Not one. And how will it be? In the national annual budget, shouldn't the amount allotted to the people who are in agriculture and allied industries not be in proportion to the population? And yet, we're only allotted barely 2 per cent of the budget. This is the crux of our problem.

North India constantly faces floods. But Tamil Nadu suffers without water. Even after the Supreme Court orders, Karnataka does not release water. Kerala does not. And Prime Minister Modi ayya does not help us.

It is in their own interest to cripple small cultivators and hand over the agricultural industry to corporates. Their coffers will fill up. But farmers will unite. We need a socially minded and secular government. Otherwise we cannot survive. First, we had the White and Green Revolutions around the 1970s. Then tractors replaced our cattle. My father and grandfather lived and aged gloriously since their farming was organic. Now, at forty years of age, everybody has sugar and BP. Why? Because we smother our crops with fertilizer and pesticides. Every evening, brinjal, ladies finger and greens are bathed in chemicals. When I was young, roosters and hens lived four to five years. Now, broiler chicken are killed in three months. These hormones and chemicals from the food and meat we eat mess with the biological rhythms. Ask questions and politicians hide behind a 'spiritual' screen.

But questions—and protests—must never stop.

Singaravelan: Fighting for the Bulls

No one offered to fetch the bulls. Three were grazing under the slim acacia trees that cast soft shadows. The biggest, Singaravelan—a tribute to his good looks—was nearly six feet tall with a heavy neck, great hump and sharp horns.

Three men, all muscular arms and moustaches, stood around and watched the animals. One of them had brought along his daughter, a little girl in a red frock, who was eager to meet the bulls. There was pride in the men's eyes; livestock keepers and farmers, they recognised the bulls for the fine specimens they were. But there was also a primal fear.

'Let my wife Soundaram come,' sixty-year-old Ramasamy, the oldest in the group, told the girl when she asked him to bring Singaravelan to her. 'Only she can catch him.' Singaravelan flicked mud up with his horns and snorted. 'If I go near him, he'll make a fuss. But she will easily get him.' The girl nodded and settled to wait patiently for his wife Soundaram Ramasamy—the only woman bull-keeper in the Kangayam region, near Coimbatore, and a legend in her own village, Kathasamipalayam.

Shadows shimmered in the noon heat by the time Kaalakaramma, or bull-keeping woman, as Soundaram is known in these parts, arrived. Small and slight, wearing a silk saree and roses in her hair, the fifty-year-old walked briskly up to Rajini, an enormous black bull. Gently rubbing his flank and face, she called him 'kannukutti', young calf, and led him by his rope. Then she went back for Singaravelan. When she wrapped her hands over his great height and hump, and posed for pictures, they appeared—woman and bull—like best friends.

Soundaram is as rare as her bulls, which belong to an indigenous cattle breed called Kangayam, named after the region; it is unusual for a woman to rear over half a dozen stud bulls (the number varying between six to twelve in the years I interviewed her, from 2015 to 2018).

Native to the Kongu region in western Tamil Nadu, Kangayams are strikingly handsome animals. With soaring humps and sweeping horns, they are tall and hardy, can withstand droughts and thrive on dry grass. Over the last two decades, the preference for exotic and crossbred cows that yield more milk over indigenous cows, and for tractors and tubewells over bullocks has savagely reduced their numbers. They continued to be bought by those who race in bullock carts in rekla and breeders who seek out the finest bulls to sire untameable champions for jallikattu—both traditional sports that involve indigenous breeds. Then, in May 2014, the Supreme Court banned the games, and native breeds took another massive beating.

According to the Indian Government, the country has 190 million cattle (excluding buffaloes)—more than the cattle population of the United States and the European Union put together. In 2016–17, India's total milk production was worth ₹61,4387 crore and its total beef production was worth ₹25,332 crore.[1]

While these numbers suggest a healthy and booming cattle economy, they tell only part of the story. The latest available government cattle census from 2012 threw up some worrying data.[2] Since 2007, cattle numbers have fallen by 4 per cent. The population of indigenous cattle—the thirty-seven indigenous Indian breeds recognised by the National Bureau of Animal Genetic Resources, belonging to the sub-species *Bos indicus* and characterised by the humps on their backs—dipped 9 per cent, to around thirty-eight million; and that of indigenous bulls and bullocks a full 19 per cent. The only numbers to rise were of 'exotic' cattle, or animals of European descent, and of exotic-indigenous crossbreeds, which together shot up by 20 per cent.

A census done today would paint an even more alarming picture of the situation of indigenous cattle. (Due in 2017, the twentieth livestock census began in October 2018;[3] the report is yet to be released.) Take the Kangayam breed, one of the five officially recognised indigenous breeds of Tamil Nadu, alongside Pulikulam, Umblachery, Bargur and Alambadi. According to official figures, as late as 1996, there were nearly 500,000 of them,[4] but the 2013 breed survey[5] puts the population at about 193,445.[6] Today, conservationists estimate Kangayams in the state to be down to about 100,000.

Traditionally, most agricultural households kept indigenous cows, which provided manure, birthed calves, produced enough milk for household use and which could also be put to plough, making them a good financial proposition. Stud bulls were raised for breeding, while bullocks (castrated bulls, usually from desi breeds) were used for ploughing, to draw water and for their manure. This economy sustained many native breeds for centuries.

With the advent of mechanisation and the decline in the need for working farm animals, that economic calculus changed. Cows became valued primarily for their milk, and this made exotic and crossbred cows—useless in the fields but good milkers—particularly attractive. Jersey and Holstein Friesian cows of European descent, and crossbreeds of these with indigenous cattle, can produce twelve litres of milk or more per day, while indigenous breeds like Kangayams give only about three. Though native cows are much cheaper to maintain—production costs per litre of milk works out to roughly half of the ₹17 per litre sunk into exotic cows, which require special feed and medicines, and also more hours of care—their low productivity means they do not offer quick returns, at least in the present market greedy for milk. The Centre's data proves this—at the national level, milk from exotic and crossbred cows accounted for 55.61 per cent in 2014–15, and in Tamil Nadu it took an incredible 90.98 per cent of the share.[7]

'There are few sectors where governments have done greater damage than they have in cattle,' said P. Sainath. 'Sturdy local species that took millennia to evolve have been decimated—by government order.

'Indigenous breeds are low maintenance and perfectly evolved to the weather and climate of their region. Exotic species have evolved to cope with the climate of Europe, including some of that continent's colder regions. They actually suffer terribly in, say, the heat of Yavatmal, or elsewhere in India. They are far more prone to disease—some farmers joke that keeping these means having the vet almost always at your home.' Yet in many states, 'local breeds were treated as little better than vermin in the 1960s, 1970s and 1980s. We now see the price of that madness unfold.'

India's white revolution or Operation Flood, which began in 1970, and substantially increased the availability of milk across the country, transforming it from deficient to surplus, relied on crossbreeds. According to the National Dairy Development Board, India had 178 million cattle in 1970 and produced 20 million tonnes of milk. By 2012, the country had 190 million cattle but produced 132 million tonnes of milk—a 560 per cent increase in milk production with only a 7 per cent increase in cattle population. Much of the productive gain is due to the replacement of indigenous cattle with exotic and interbred cattle, and the market incentives that drive that trend remain unchanged.

Sainath gave the example of the Vechur breed in Kerala to demonstrate how native breeds have suffered because of State policy. In 1961, the state imposed the Kerala Livestock Improvement Act, which mandated castration for mature indigenous bulls in order to promote crossbred varieties. This severely depleted numerous indigenous breeds, including the Vechur—the world's smallest breed, about 90 cm tall.

Vechurs were saved by Sosamma Iype, who led a concerted breeding effort in the late 1980s and 1990s to revive their population. Iype retired as a professor of animal genetics and breeding and is now the director of the Vechur Conservation Trust.

With the shift to more intensive farming, the poor are the first to lose their animals, said Iype. 'If the cattle, which are a part of the village ecology, are lost, it means the ecological balance is lost. Food security is lost. The whole economy is affected. ... The most high-producing cow is not the most profitable one,' explained Iype. 'It depends on the input-output ratio. '

Iype pointed out that many of India's indigenous breeds are on the verge of disappearing, like the Alambadi in Tamil Nadu. Yet, there continues to be an official bias against them. 'The irony is Indian breeds like Ongole, Sahiwal, Red Sindhi, Kankrej and Gir taken to other countries are performing very well as pure breeds,' said Iype. 'It is due to the strict adoption of good breeding programmes. Brazil is exploiting Indian breeds on a large scale'—though primarily for beef, not milk.

The Indian problem is reflected globally. 'There are thousands of cattle breeds in the world,' said Iype. 'But a handful, like Holsteins, Jerseys, Guernseys, Ayrshires and Brown Swiss are the top ones, with Holstein being the most popular. This breed has spread to 128 countries already.' Naturally, these breeds 'are replacing the adapted indigenous cattle'.

This comes with consequences in terms of genetic variety. 'In the case of world-dominating breeds,' said Iype, 'one thing to note is the use of very low number of bulls.' Particularly with the rising use of artificial insemination, where frozen semen from a single bull can be used to impregnate thousands of cows. As a result, the calves have a 'high percentage of the same genes. This is not a healthy situation.'

A depleted genetic pool increases the risk of inbreeding down the line, which can lead to mutation and weakened resilience against diseases. Iype predicted that as global temperatures rise, water levels drop and new diseases emerge, 'a handful of breeds with a lot of homogeneity may not save us.' But, she lamented, India has not successfully created even a single new breed in its research institutions.

Karthikeya Sivasenapathy, head of the Senaapathy Cattle Research Foundation in Kuttappalayam village, Tiruppur district, spoke of the huge financial pressures on farmers when they switch from zero-maintenance indigenous varieties to high-maintenance exotic ones. The Kangayam breed, like many other indigenous cattle, require relatively little water, making them suitable for dry areas like Kangayam region. They also range freely, feeding on what is normally considered poor pasture. The move towards exotic cattle means more and more land must be cleared and dedicated to raising fodder suitable for them, at a cost to biodiversity and water resources.

With indigenous cows, if the costs saved on grazing land are factored in, Karthikeya argued, their 'milk is priceless.' The pursuit of 'a short-term gain in milk,' said Karthikeya, 'has decimated many indigenous varieties.' This revenue cushions farmers from the long-term tragedy that is the loss of a species. This is true across large parts of India—the Khariar breed in Orissa, for instance, became almost extinct when the state government promoted exotic and crossbreed animals in the late 1970s and 1980s. Established cattle economies are also further upset by politically motivated bans on cattle slaughter.

With this unfortunate State bias against indigenous cattle, it is individuals like Soundaram and private organisations who have taken on the responsibility of conserving them. In Tamil Nadu, for instance, according to the 2015–16 policy note of the Animal Husbandry, Dairies and Fisheries department,[8] 178 of the 250 bulls in state-owned breeding centres are either Jersey or Jersey-cross. Only eight were breeds indigenous to the state: four Kangayams, two Pulikulams, one Bargur and one Umbalachery. (The policy notes of the following years do not include a break-up of the number of breeding bulls.)

By mid-2018, Soundaram's farm surpassed this: it had twelve Kangayam bulls and six calves. Two were typical black and white ones called mylai, four were sevalai, the red ones, and six kaari, black. She also had seven cows.

Twenty years ago, Soundaram and her husband Ramasamy presciently began to raise Kangayams. They started with cows and when one birthed an exceptionally good-looking male calf, they decided to keep him. With Karuppan, or the black one, their stud farm was born.

The couple carefully selects each of the bulls for his good looks and fine features. To procure the animal, they rent a tempo, scour the countryside and cattle fairs, and pay between ₹25,000 to ₹40,000 for a calf. The grown-up bulls fetch good prices. Soundaram was offered ₹3 lakh for Singaravelan, their biggest bull, in 2016. But she did not sell him.

'It is not a business,' Soundaram told me emphatically when I enquired about her business model. 'We do this because we like it, because we want to keep the breed alive. If we wanted to make money, we'd raise sheep.'

Soundaram claimed that if not for the income from her sons—one an engineer, the other in finance—working in Chennai, the cattle farm could not be managed. Maintenance of each bull costs ₹200 per day, apart from the rent paid for the grazing land. The couple have leased thirty acres of Korangaadu—fields that house about twenty-five varieties of vegetation and rented out as pasture land, a speciality of the Kongu region. They also had to convert their vegetable farm to raise maize and millets for cattle feed. Times of drought, which are getting more frequent, further increase their expenses. 'If there is rain, then the Korangaadu will be filled with grasses and plants and the bulls can graze freely. But now? We have to give them supplementary food like cotton seed and cattle feed.' The only thing that she does not have to pay for is the immunisation. A young vet from her village comes by and injects all her cattle for free.

The farm, Soundaram explained, is not only a financial burden but also physically demanding. Her days begin and end with the animals. She takes the cattle out to graze at eight in the morning and is back by lunch time. She sets out again in the afternoon, with water and food for the animals, and returns in time to milk the cows.

Soundaram has one other passion: roses. The roses on her head, orange as corals and pinned into her plaited hair like ornaments, were from her garden. On her ears were maatal, a thin gold chain that runs around the earlobe and supports the weight of heavy earrings. Her neck and wrists were circled with a chain and bangles, and there was plenty of the colour in her sari.

Sitting on the steps leading up to the veranda of her new house, Soundaram served me sweet tea and biscuits. Bright and modern, the house was built in 2012. The wooden doors were varnished and ornate and the living room furnished with large, comfortable sofas.

Everybody in her family, including her widowed mother, spend their days worrying about the height and heft of the bulls, anxious to keep them plump and in their prime. As stud bulls, their good looks are vital.

Soundaram, who does much of the fetching and carrying and handling, is thin. The distance between the various pastures and her house ranges from half a kilometre to a few. The fields are small in size and rented for the purpose. Though she takes the water pots on her two-wheeler, which she calls 'Scooties' (for TVS Scooty), she walks at least twice a day to fetch the bulls.

'Only we, the people of the house, have to look after them, especially when a cow comes for servicing. No other man will come for such a risky job. They don't want to walk the bull or give it water. They'd rather live, you know.'

On an average, four or five cows are brought from a 150 km radius to mate with her studs everyday, though there are days when nobody comes. She doesn't have the time to cook—her mother takes care of it—and has to forgo even family functions. 'People just turn up with their cows. They expect us to be home all the time.' The whole exercise can cost the cow's owner up to ₹4000, including transport, food and a payment of ₹500 to Soundaram for the stud, which she claims is cheaper than some others. Though artificial insemination costs as little as ₹200–300, cow owners prefer coming to bull rearers like Soundaram as they get to pick a bull of their choice. Soundaram keeps rare kaari and sevalai bulls too, as breeders and wealthy farmers prefer them.

In recognition of her conservation efforts, Soundaram was given the Breed Saviour Award in 2010 instituted by the National Biodiversity Authority and LIFE Network. 'My relatives were impressed that I went to Madras to get an award, for raising bulls!' The couple is keen to start raising more cows too—not for diary, but to breed their own stud bulls.

Soundaram took me to see her animals. The field where they grazed was a short walk away. The ground was gravely and spongy. Sparrows and mynahs perched on the white acacia trees. And beneath them were her majestic bulls, the only sound came from their soft breathing, rising and falling rhythmically. She petted them gently and one offered his face, tilting it so she could reach it better, aware perhaps of her small stature. People in the Kangayam region used to buy cattle as an investment, in the same way the city folks buy stocks, Soundaram told me. 'But it's hard to get fields to rent. People ask why a woman should rear bulls!'

For five decades, until the late 1950s, Rao Bahadur Nallathambi Sarkarai Mandradiar, Karthikeya's great-grandfather, almost single-handedly bred generation after generation of animals to fix and improve the defining Kangayam characteristics: the majestic hump, the black markings on the head, hump and shoulders, and the wide, curved horns. This work was extraordinary, not least because it was accomplished by just a single man and his herd.[9]

Karthikeya and his father Sivasenapathy established the Senaapathy Kangayam Cattle Research Foundation in 2008. The organisation conducts research, organises cattle shows, works to raise awareness about the importance of indigenous cattle, liaises with government officials to promote helpful policies, and breeds Kangayams. The foundation's most prized bull, Bulli, until he died in 2018, sired over two hundred calves a year, including with cows belonging to independent breeders, for which the foundation does not charge any fee. Karthikeya explained how the economics works for small and individual breeders: 'They make their money selling bulls in their prime, for a nice price. Typically, they buy calves for ₹30,000–₹40,000. When the bull is about 2.5 years of age, it begins servicing cows, and the charges range from ₹500–₹2000.' But this money only covers the expense of keeping the bulls. 'They make a tidy sum when they sell it at about 5 years, for ₹200,000–₹400,000, and then invest about a tenth in a new calf. The rest finances the family's capital expenditure.'

But conservation efforts by individuals, pioneering and noble though they are, cannot solely sustain a cattle ecosystem.

There is still one thing left that bulls are widely valued for, primarily in Tamil Nadu: pride. And that pride is bound to traditional sports: the massively popular jallikattu and the relatively elite rekla. Kangayam bulls participate in rekla, while Pulikulams are preferred for jallikattu; the former are taller by a third and their hump is often too pronounced and easy to grab in the contest. However, Kangayam bulls are used by breeders to improve herds of Pulikulam.

Historically, jallikattu had enormous cultural significance in the state, and finds mention in Sangam period poetry—from the third century BCE to the fourth century CE. In its contemporary form, the sport involves letting bulls loose, one by one, into a crowd of men, who try to grab their humps or horns and hang on as the animals either buck thrice, turn thrice or run fifteen metres. Men who successfully 'ride' the bulls and bull-keepers whose animals defy the bull-catchers' efforts are both given rewards. Keepers take their bulls to multiple jallikattus each season, and the renown of both keeper and animal increase with each 'win'.

Alanganallur, near Madurai, hosts the biggest jallikattu in the state and its very name has become synonymous with the sport. When I visited the town on a quiet afternoon in April 2016, jallikattu enthusiast Saravanan Kumar described with great excitement the atmosphere during Pongal, when the sport is usually conducted. 'Tens of thousands come—tourists, foreigners. It's a great celebration,' he said. At the deserted town square, he showed me the vaadi vaasal, a narrow brick enclosure with high walls that hold in the bulls before they are released. It was painted like a temple wall in red and white stripes and had a large picture of a charging bull painted on one side. Saravanan, a contractor and builder, also pointed to a nearby house that he rents to watch the event.

His bulls, Sevalai and Kari, have run in numerous jallikattus and have won Saravanan a mixie, a fridge, a cot, a CD player and a fan. 'Once, I got a goat kid,' he told me, laughing. But 'the jallikattu prize is only for pride. You get a bicycle; it costs ₹3,000. We spend so much more on the bull.' After each successful jallikattu, he used to take his bulls out on a procession, with his prizes held high, led by a dancing crowd.

P. Rajasekhar, a businessman based in Madurai, who presides over the Jallikattu Padhukappu Peravai, Forum for the Preservation of Jallikattu, walked me through how the economy of jallikattu works: 'The events are free, the prizes are small.' The expenses of rearing a bull are far too great to be compensated by the grinder and mixie and bureau that are given as prizes. 'But, it is a way—perhaps the only way—for coolie labourers or landless women to make money. All they need to do is raise a male calf. If it shows potential—scratches the ground, shakes its head when a stranger approaches, tries to butt them—the animal's value soars.' A rearer could earn ten times more from a promising male calf, he said, than from raising ten goats.

Beyond the monetary and material awards, the real lure is the chance of celebrity and prestige, strong enough for thousands of keepers to maintain indigenous bulls, even at great cost. By all the accounts I heard, it takes at least ₹500 a day to care for and feed each jallikattu bull.

Animal rights activists have been demanding a ban on jallikattu for at least a decade, alleging that the sport exploits the bulls' natural fears as prey and that bull-keepers and event organisers mistreat the animals to rile them up before releasing them into the arena. They have footage and evidence to back their claim. It shows bulls being beaten, prodded with sticks and sickles, having their tails pulled, twisted, bitten and sometimes broken, having irritants rubbed into their eyes and noses, and apparently being forced to drink alcohol. In 2016, breeders and bull-keepers I spoke to flatly refuted this. They declared their love for their bulls, and insisted they would never let them get hurt. They said they were ready to obey any regulations on organising jallikattus.

For Tamil political parties, defending jallikattu and rekla is a political obligation. 'There are community votes at stake,' P. Ramajayam, a political analyst with the Centre for Study of Social Exclusion and Inclusive Policy in Tiruchirappalli, told me. 'Rekla is dominated by the Gounder community in the western districts, and jallikattu by the Thevars in the southern districts.' Between them, in their respective areas, the two communities influence electoral results in about 60 out of the 234 state assembly constituencies, Ramajayam explained.

Bulls brought all of the state to a halt for seven days in January 2017 when Tamil Nadu erupted in what is now known as the jallikattu protests. The Marina Beach in Chennai witnessed something extraordinary—tens of thousands of urban Tamilians came out in support of jallikattu, a rural sport many young urbanites have never seen. The largely peaceful protests had men, women and even children holding placards and shouting slogans, calling out the state and central governments for not keeping their promise to hold the ancient Tamil sport in time for Pongal that year. The scale of the protest had the national media come down to the often ignored Chennai.

The protests were successful, with jallikattu and rekla taking place again after the state government passed an ordinance on 21 January amending the national Prevention of Cruelty to Animals Act 'to promote and follow tradition and culture, and to ensure survival and continuance of native breeds of bulls.'[10]

The ban on jallikattu, while seeking to protect Kangayam and Pulikulam bulls that are primarily used in the sport, jeopardised the future of these animals. When the bulls disappear, then the collapse of the breed is only a matter of time, regardless of how many cows there might be.

The three-year ban was also the tipping point and savaged the already diminished native cattle economy. For hundreds of years, Kangayam cattle have been bought and sold at the Kannapuram cattle shanty. Every April, the fair coincides with the festival of Goddess Mariamman and stretches for about a kilometre on either side of the Trichy–Coimbatore highway. Organisers said that up to a hundred thousand people visit the fair daily and many stay on the grounds with their cattle. They erect small, temporary sheds, with Casuarina poles and plaited palm leaf roofs. In that dappled shade, they conduct business, quoting prices to prospective buyers, counting bundles of cash wrapped in white towels, shaking their heads when the prices do not match.

Traditionally, many cattle fairs happen around annual temple chariot festivals, called ther, such as the Kannapuram ther and Anthiyur ther in Erode district, explained Karthikeya. 'A big wooden chariot is taken in procession around the temples. Devotees, livestock breeders, sellers, traders—they all visit.' I visited Kannapuram in April 2016, two summers after the ban on jallikattu.

Lorries turned in from the highway all day, from which men unloaded the cattle. The floor of the vehicles was covered with hay, to cushion the feet and provide fodder. Each animal was coaxed out, and they leapt elegantly and landed neatly, kicking up a small cloud of dust. The stud bulls looked menacing, while the castrated bullocks and cows largely placid.

Symmetry and good looks, especially in paired bullocks, is a specialty of Kannapuram—traders here pride themselves on this. Small farmers tend to go to Anthiyur, especially those who do not care if one animal in a pair has a rounder neck than the other.

'Everyday, around one lakh people visit Kannapuram ther,' said R. P. Palanikumar, one of the fair's organisers and Karthikeya's uncle. 'People come from Thanjavur, Nagapattinam, Pudukottai, Kumbakonam, besides the neighbouring districts. Almost every household used to buy a bullock for fieldwork.' Until tractors replaced them, that is.

In the morning, people walked around with neem twigs in their mouth, cleaning their teeth. Food stalls sold millet porridge with pickles and fried baby chillies as accompaniments, a local staple.

There were few women among the many white dhotis. The absence of female calves was equally glaring but only because they were being bought unlike bulls, bullocks and bull calves.

By eleven, the sun was white and blinding and the ground hazy with heat. It was hot for April and scorching even in the shade of the scrawny trees. Men fashioned their towels into turbans, hitched up their dhotis and lungis, and folded them over their knees. They searched and sat in slivers of shade—by the side of the water lorry or under a shack. But the cattle stood tall and unflinching, a testament to their hardiness. They drank some water, chewed some cud and sent flies packing with a flick of their tails.

Soundaram and Ramasamy, who visit the fair every year, sold two bulls for ₹1.3 lakh that year. 'Had there been rekla and jallikattu, they would have easily fetched ₹2 lakh. The calves we bought for ₹60,000 are now worth less than half the price.'

Other cattle rearers I met at the fair too complained about how the ban had affected the prices further. Thirty-two-year-old Anbalagan Mani from Coimbatore sat on the hard-baked earth next to his pair of bullocks, huge and handsome with great horns and chiselled faces, poster boys for the Kangayam breed. Passers-by stopped to admire them and said they looked like Nandi, Lord Siva's mount. But Mani was unhappy. 'Had the ban on the games been lifted, these would have fetched me ₹2.5 lakh. Now? I don't ask for even ₹1.3 lakh for the pair!'

K.C. Doraisamy of Thottipalayam, Vellore, who had been coming to Kannapuram for forty-six years, said, 'The Supreme Court ban on jallikattu has affected us badly. For a month before rekla, we give the bulls maapillai saapadu, a groom's feast. Rekla lasts just ten minutes, but animal welfare activists went and banned it.' After the races, the bulls change hands, often bought by people who own small tracts of land in hilly areas. 'The bulls are used to plough the uneven land.

When the animal gets older, they are used to pull rubber tyre carts. There was a whole system in place.'

In the early 1990s, Doraisamy remembered, the fair saw nearly hundred thousand heads of cattle. That dropped by 50 per cent after farming activities were fully mechanised in the region. But during the period of the ban, the situation got even worse. 'There are only around 5,000 animals here today.'

Large numbers of indigenous bulls were also sent to slaughterhouses during the ban, said Vikram Dorairaj, a volunteer at Velliangiri Gaushala, a cattle refuge on the outskirts of Coimbatore, supported by textile businessman Siva Ganesh. Bulls and bullocks, unlike cows, can be sent to slaughterhouses after getting a 'fit for salughter' certificate, when they are over the age of ten and cannot be used on fields anymore. Dorairaj and his team went around to buy bulls from farmers and breeders, including poor labourers, who, with no profit in sight, could no longer afford to keep them.

People were desperate, said Dorairaj, and were willing to give up animals in their prime at very low prices. 'If farmers were selling it for ₹15,000, we paid ₹20,000 and told them they could come anytime and visit their animal in the gaushala. ... For the farmer, this was a good deal, far better than selling it to the butcher for ₹15,000.'

Of the 1,900 animals that the gaushala housed in May 2016, 231 were past jallikattu champions, bought for ₹50,000 each. 'No other gaushala would take them,' said Dorairaj, as 'they are very hard to maintain.' At Velliangiri, there were veterinarians and caretakers who had previously worked in jallikattu arenas.

'We are not looking at breeding the bulls,' explained Dorairaj. 'And we are not against beef. What we recommend is: when you take it for slaughter, take it peacefully.' He explained that existing regulations on slaughter are routinely flouted. 'Pregnant cows are routinely trafficked because calf leather is very expensive. Also, instead of the recommended number of six animals in a truck, thirty are taken. Calf meat is in great demand. Just yesterday, a truck heaving with twenty-two calves, all three or four months old, was caught.' He showed me pictures of the incident on his phone.

Dorairaj was in favour of stronger enforcement of regulations but was resigned to the fact that 'you cannot police every slaughterhouse.' Even with all his sympathy for the animals, he did not see much point in having blanket bans on cattle slaughter or beef consumption. Each animal, he said, costs ₹100 a day to maintain. For jallikattu bulls, the sum was many times that. How, he wondered, could the government replicate this model of care for all animals in the country past their economic use?

Many of India's politicians and policymakers do not seem to have considered this problem. The large majority of Indian states have restrictions on cattle slaughter. Calls for a nationwide ban on cattle slaughter and beef consumption are getting louder.

The Tamil Nadu government banned the raising of bulls exclusively for slaughter in 1958, following which the demand for male calves fell steadily. Cow slaughter is completely banned in the state.

Karthikeya's position was clear: for indigenous breeds to be economically viable, any bans that choke business for bull-keepers must go. Strong male calves must promise a profit and farmers and cattle rearers must be able to sell unproductive animals for slaughter to raise money to invest in young calves. Very few people can afford to keep cattle just for sentimental reasons. He sees Hindutva activists railing against cattle slaughter and animal rights activists opposing bull-taming sports as being largely similar in their failure to understand this. Both lobbies, in arguing for the protection of cattle, are jeopardising the future of indigenous breeds. It is not just jallikattu and rekla in Tamil Nadu, he continued, 'but bullock-cart races in Maharashtra, stone-pulling in Andhra. Kerala, Karnataka, Punjab, Haryana, all the places where there are very good Indian breeds were targeted.'

'This ideological insanity comes from people who know nothing of cows or their role in the rural economy,' said Sainath. He described the effects of what he saw as official interference in the traditional cattle economy. 'The cattle markets are in collapse. Farmers are not buying cattle as they do not know what they will do with them when they are non-productive. Farmers with cattle in badly drought-hit areas just have to stand by and watch their cows die—they can barely feed their families—as they can't send them to the abattoir. The idea, of course, was to hurt the Muslim community. What happened is that everybody has taken a pasting. The Muslims, of course. But also the Maratha and other Hindu farmers are stuck with cows they can't sell, Other Backward Caste groups that deal at the cattle markets where prices have collapsed, and Dalits in the Kolhapur chappal industry have been badly hit by the shortage of hides. Generally, it's been a disaster all around.'

A strong and open beef industry could support indigenous cattle with incentives to keep the animals for more than just their milk, but the political climate is unlikely to allow one. The present dairy market, meanwhile, does little to encourage indigenous breeds.

Karthikeya suggested one possible step forward—increasing the procurement price of indigenous cow milk. All indigenous Indian cattle—and buffaloes—give what is called A2 milk, with a different type of protein from the A1 milk produced by exotic breeds. Proponents of A2 milk claim it has health benefits over A1 milk, but this has not been fully proven. Still, in many countries, A2 milk is marketed as a premium product with higher prices—and global demand for it is growing. In India, however, government-stipulated procurement prices do not distinguish between A1 and

A2 milk. In Tamil Nadu, official dairy schemes pay farmers between ₹24 and ₹28 per litre, irrespective of the kind of milk.

Some livestock keepers in Tamil Nadu, already market A2 milk straight to consumers at ₹100 a litre. In Kannapuram, they told me about 'waiting lists' in towns to get such milk. In Karnataka, the state milk federation ran a pilot project last year to market A2 milk at higher prices. But not everyone is convinced that such efforts can translate into a viable market. Saravanan, for instance, was cynical. 'In Chennai or Bengaluru, they will buy it even if it is differentially priced. If you go to him,' Saravanan pointed to an old man sitting under a tree in a village, 'and tell him, "This is A2 milk, give me ₹70 for it," can you imagine what he will say?'

The Tamil Nadu government is now investing more effort into promoting indigenous breeds. Besides setting up breeding centres for Kangayam and Bargur cattle, the 2018–19 policy note of the state's Animal Husbandry, Dairies and Fisheries department noted, 'Production of indigenous bull calves for cross breeding as well as pure breeding was undertaken by induction of 50 Tharparkar heifers/cows procured from Rajasthan and these are maintained at District Livestock Farm, Chettinad.'

But whatever encouragement such efforts—a reaction, perhaps, to the successful jallikattu protests—might offer, without a market for indigenous cattle, there is little reason for significant numbers of people to continue raising them.

'If there is an economical gain,' Karthikeya assured me, 'people will be ready to care for the animals. Have you heard of any NGOs working to conserve sheep or buffaloes? If there's a market, it takes care of itself.'

When the ban on jallikattu and rekla was lifted, 'the prices of Kangayam bulls went up 100 per cent,' said Karthikeya. Interestingly, the jallikattu protests increased the demand for not just native bulls but also Kangayam cows. Breeders and farmers use the word 'craze' to describe it. Animal welfare organisations have appealed against the jallikattu ordinance, but 'the government of India and the Supreme Court are more sensitive than before,' said Karthikeya. Some of those gains were, however, destroyed by the terrible drought in Tamil Nadu in 2016 – 17. In 2018 and 2019, the Kannapuram fair was a success, but there were also distress sales 'because there is simply no water or food.' However, Karthikeya remains hopeful that after the awareness created by the protests, people will come to buy the native cattle breeds so important to Tamil Nadu.

For Soundaram, Kangayams remain very dear. 'I love the bulls like my sons,' she said, holding the massive Singaravelan, who stood meekly next to her. It is the couple's careful grooming that removes the menace from the animals. 'When they get four teeth, uncastrated bulls turn aggressive,' Ramasamy explained, referring to a local way of determining the age of the cattle. 'We train them to be docile. If not, nobody can handle them!'

Soundaram showed me her photo album with some pride. The images of her at work were shot over the years. There were several with her holding the ropes of bulls, as gently as one would a pet dog's leash. There were pictures of her supervising the mating of cows. In one, she stood with her saree hitched up and tucked into her waist, her hair pulled into a bun, her slender arms stretching to secure a rope around a visiting cow; in another, she was right next to the bull, holding the rein, as it mounted a cow; a slip of a woman beside the big, muscled bull. 'My bulls need me beside them all the time.'

Because it is so unusual—a woman with twelve bulls—people troop in everyday to see Soundaram's farm. 'They come from Pollachi, Coimbatore, Erode, Thiruchengode and Madurai and ask us how we raise them. They also take pictures with the bulls.'

Though not all livestock keepers do, Soundaram and Ramasamy name their bulls. She gave the etymology of the names with a shy laugh: 'Rajini is a showy bull. Just like the film star he's named after, he does a lot of stunts. Singaravelan is very handsome, but he's hot-tempered. He's our angriest bull, and most valorous. Srinivasan is like the God he's named after, the reigning deity in Tirupati hills. He's patient and gentle. Anybody can catch him and stroke him. Natarajan is dignified, his walk is very grand, but he won't trouble anyone. Valaiyanoor is now in the Andamans. He was red in colour, a sevala kaalai.'

Soundaram keeps the lineage of her favourite bulls alive by retaining the best of the bull calves they sire. Singaravelan's two-year-old son, Murattu Kaalai, named after a famous movie starring Rajinikanth in the role of a bull tamer, is now in great demand and services a lot of cows. The bull calves of Natarajan, Srinivasan and Rajini are also in her farm.

Her bulls are also well known for producing twins, she said happily. 'Why, just recently, a cow gave birth to two female calves.' The family had phoned to tell Soundaram about it.

As we stood on Soundaram's fields, watching the bulls graze, I asked her to name her favourite. She said she liked them all. I asked her to name the strongest. 'All our bulls are strong. And they come running to me when I whistle.' She then put two fingers into her mouth and whistled—a piercing, shattering noise. It startled me, and the birds, but the bulls only looked up. She whistled again. They lowered their heads and went back to grazing. She walked up to two of them locked in mock-fight, gently pushed their entwined horns away and then stroked one of them.

One of the bulls was to service their own heifer. Soundaram's oldest son, Kanagaraj, helped his father hold the cow. Soundaram fetched a young bull. He went up to the cow and sniffed her rump. In one swift movement, he mounted her, forelegs clasping the cow, the union quick but powerful.

As Soundaram fetched the bulls from the fields, they walked behind her obediently, like school children, snapping branches off trees, chewing on the leaves. Buses, cars and lorries stopped to let them pass—a slender woman and her hefty bulls, who together owned the landscape.

‘Groundwater Is a Dangerous Gamble’

S. Janakarajan is an economist and a professor at the Madras Institute of Development Studies (MIDS). He is the president of the South Asia Consortium for Interdisciplinary Water Resources Studies (SaciWATERS). He has carried out many research projects in several river basins with particular reference to surface and groundwater management, problems of water market, water rights and water laws. He is an expert on agrarian development, environment and climate change. He has authored several books and is published widely, in national and international journals.

The farmer suicides we saw in Tamil Nadu since October 2016 are said to be because of a double burden—debt and drought. Could one of them—water—at least have been managed better?

India is the largest user of groundwater in the world and the current and future scenarios are absolutely scary. Around 70 per cent of India’s gross cropped area (GCA), 80 per cent of the country’s drinking water needs and roughly 90 per cent of our industrial water requirements are met through groundwater. The key stakeholders—policymakers, bureaucrats, academics, media, leave alone the general public—don’t really understand that we’re heading towards doomsday. At the same time, the long-term trend in rainfall, in a hundred years, does not show any decline. Why then has there been a secular lowering of groundwater tables and an increasing mismatch between extraction and recharge?

Take Tamil Nadu, where the average rainfall is 970 mm, and all along the coast, it is over 1000 mm—it is not a rainfall scarce state. But due to global warming-induced climate change, the rainfall spread has changed. We get heavy showers on a few days with very little change in the total annual rainfall. The important question is if there is a way to adapt. Even if we receive an entire season's rainfall in five days, we have to find ways to save that water. We need to maintain the many thousands of small water bodies that exist in the state. They are not merely water bodies, they are important hydrological units—a recharge structure. These small water bodies farm ponds, temple tanks, spring channels, irrigation tanks and so on. All these are in poor condition and desperately in need of maintenance. It's important that we adapt to changing rainfall conditions. But nothing of that sort seems to be on the cards. We simply sit and mourn the situation. Shouldn't there be better imagination and commitment from policymakers, bureaucrats and water users?

The conditions are not great in the remaining 30 per cent area that is cropped with surface water. This water is heavily polluted and further affected by river sand mining, encroachments and diversions. We have the Ministry of Environment, Ministry of Forests, Ministry of Water Resources that spend thousands of crores to maintain our waterbodies, rivers, groundwater stock and so on. But our burden on all these is increasing. About four thousand crore rupees was sanctioned in the last few years to clean the Ganga. Has the river been cleaned now?

How dire is the water situation across the country and state? And what are the fallouts of its mismanagement?

Groundwater use has become a dangerous issue for the farmer's well-being; it's a gamble. Without any information, he invests in a borewell. If he's lucky, he strikes groundwater in one stroke. If not, for a single borewell, he may have to dig four trial borewells to check for water availability. Even if he finds water, he does not know the number of acres he can irrigate or when the supply will end. So, if he has invested five lakh in the borewell, and if it only works for two years, he ends up paying interest on the loan, and tries to sort this out by digging another well. Finally, farmers get into a debt trap. This is what leads to farmer suicides. Go to Vidharba, Karnataka, Orissa, Andhra and Tamil Nadu—wherever farmer suicides are reported, if you go deep into the reasons, you'll find that in 70 to 80 per cent of the cases, it's because of the lack of returns from investments made on groundwater.

What are the repercussions of failed wells? One is obviously suicides. Farmers also abandon agriculture and migrate. Two, the entire economy will collapse. Because we're talking about sixty-five crore people who are dependent on agriculture. And agriculture contributes to 17 per cent of the country's GDP [Gross Domestic Product]. Without this, the economy will collapse for lack of foodgrains, water, employment, and because of huge levels of migration, urban pressure, rural poverty converted into urban poverty and, most importantly, food insecurity. There will be total chaos. This sounds like fiction, but it could happen. To prevent all this, the need of the hour is to take continuous and sustainable steps to recharge groundwater.

Can the groundwater that is sucked up be replenished if there is a good monsoon?

For this, we need to understand the dynamics of groundwater—hydrogeology. There are different stages of groundwater development. The first stage is when the extraction is less than the recharge. This is a happy situation. The second is when the extraction and recharge are equal. This is still okay, and you can sustain it. The third is when we take more than what is recharged. This is also okay if it is a temporary phenomenon. But if it continues, the rate of decline in the groundwater table will increase. That's more worrying. This year it might decline by two metres and the following year by three, and then four. This is called secular lowering of water table and will lead to an ecological problem. It's even worse when groundwater is extracted in an unsustainable fashion, and the area is declared as an 'overexploited' red area by the Central Ground Water Board. But if groundwater is taken out over and above this, it's called mining of groundwater, and there is absolutely no possibility of recharge. It's gone.

In many places in Tamil Nadu and across the country, we are mining. Punjab has five rivers and their groundwater situation is one of the gravest in the country. Sometimes, they get tanker water from Rajasthan. Throughout the country, we have either secular lowering, overexploitation or mining of groundwater. Even in places that the Ground Water Board calls 'comfortable', the quality might be bad. The water may contain arsenic, flouride, iron and so on. This cannot be used for drinking or agriculture.

It's in this context that we need to view India's 50 per cent population depending upon agriculture. Furthermore, about 70 per cent of agriculture's water requirement is met from groundwater. This is why farmers cannot handle successive drought years.

What is the solution for sustainable agriculture, especially with the looming threat of climate change?

There are two parts to it. One is sustaining the soil and environment. The other is sustaining groundwater. To sustain soil, you need to get rid of chemical inputs. During the Green Revolution in the mid-1960s, productivity increased, but beginning from the 1990s, it started declining. Soil quality decreased and our food now is mixed with chemicals, due to the heavy application of NPK [nitrogen, phosphorous and potassium]. As for water, from 1965 to 1990, wells were reasonably thriving. But from the 1990s, it became a villain. Compounded by free electricity, wells became a potential threat to farmers' well-being. Alternatives touted now are sprinklers and drip irrigation. But for both, capital and maintenance costs are very high and not viable for small farmers, who make up 80 per cent of the farming population in India.

Let's talk about Tamil Nadu, which can be divided into three parts. One is hilly. The second is the hinterland, which is dry. The third are coastal areas facing problems because of seawater rise, climate change, seawater intrusion, erosion and accretion. Mangroves are vanishing, shrimp farms are emerging, which results in salinity of soil. And sea level rise is expected or already happening. If there is a one metre rise, Nagapattinam will go under the sea. In the hinterland, it is dry, and groundwater is declining. In the hills, deforestation is rampant and that has the impact of global warming–induced climate change. Yet, what are we discussing everyday? Sensex, NIFTY, growth rate. These growth rate figures don't mean anything. You know why? These are gross growth rates.

Any manufacturing activity produces negative impact on our natural capital—water, land, forest, carbon space, surface water, groundwater. If I were to calculate the growth rate, I would calculate the cost of damage done to groundwater, river, agriculture, soil and environment, and deduct these environmental costs from the earnings. Finally, one might end up with a negative rate, because, ecological and environmental damages have cumulative impacts. Once we reach the level of mining groundwater, it is a permanent ecological loss. What are its costs? Ecosystem valuation is so important that nobody knows how to do it! Mining, thermal power, nuclear power, many chemical and fertiliser industries are all killer industries as they don't take adequate precautionary measures to prevent pollution. They just contribute to killing our ecology and environment. They simply contribute to erosion of our natural capital. But we're proud of our growth rate! Such growth rates are neither maintainable nor sustainable.

Fifty Feet Above ...

... sarattu, sarattu, sarattu. A short, muscular man shimmies down a palm tree in a minute, placing his right foot here, his left there and lands gracefully on the ground. Fifty-four-year-old Anthony Rayappan scales the equivalent of Mount Everest in a week during the season. It is what keeps him and his family from going hungry.

Rayappan lives in Rayappapuram hamlet in Ramanathapuram district, a region famous for its palms—the state tree of Tamil Nadu—and infamous for its droughts. His father and grandfather were palm tree climbers; when in class five, Rayappan quit school to do the same work. When he was young, he climbed without a care, about the height of the tree or the width of the bark; he just went up and down swiftly: sarattu, sarattu, sarattu. But the adventure of climbing turned into a responsibility, a job, a livelihood, after marriage, when his own family grew.

Deep inside the palm grove where he works, the new fronds are the only green in the brown landscape. The earth, the bark, the dried fronds and even the karupatti, or palm jaggery, made from the tree sap, range from a pale sepia to a rich chocolate brown. The work huts strewn around too are a shade of brown, built from parts of the tree—thatched roofs fashioned from palm fronds, the insides furnished by cots made of thick, dried palm stems and every joint held together with palm fibre.

As we spoke inside his work hut, a country chicken pecked on grains at Rayappan's feet. 'My son's fussy,' he said, 'he won't touch broiler chicken. Neither will my daughters. So we raise our own.'

Palms are ancient, hardy trees requiring little water and care, and flourish in this dry, dusty landscape. All along the road to Sayalgudi, a town near Rayappapuram, women, and sometimes men, wheel home plastic pots of water on purpose-built, hand-drawn wagons. There are long queues for water lorries, at hand pumps and dug wells. In the few places that borewells reach the groundwater, paddy and peanuts are grown, and stocky, straw-filled scarecrows work round the clock to keep peacocks away. But they come anyway, dragging their tails like glittering ball gowns, and peck every last morsel from the fields.

Palm tree climbing, as an occupation, has changed little since 1848, when Sarah Tucker marvelled at the dexterity of the climbers in *South Indian Missionary Sketches*: '... some of our English boys who pride themselves on the ease with which they can climb an oak or an elm would be puzzled to know how to reach the top of palmyra.'[1]

The branchless tree is indeed a puzzle but not for the palm tree climber. It is tall—between forty and sixty feet in these parts—and scaly and stout at the bottom; the top is slim and crowned by a shaggy mop of leaves that rustle and rub in the breeze. The prize, for the climber, is the sap that oozes from the paalai, or inflorescence.

As soon as a new paalai emerges, Rayappan pounds and crushes its tip until it produces sap, which is collected in terracotta pots coated with slaked lime to avoid fermentation. This process is known as panaiseevaradhu, or slicing the palm. Once the sap, or padhaneer, is ready for collection, Rayappan straps a palm fibre harness around his ankle, slings a tin can over his shoulder and climbs. One moment his body is flat, pressed fully against the tree, with only a leather chest guard between his skin and the sharp bark; the next moment he slides his feet up and crouches. Swiftly alternating between these two motions, he reaches the top, manoeuvers between the fronds with grace, reaches out for the pots, empties out the padhaneer into his can and makes his way down. And then he goes up the next tree. And the next one. Until he covers about thirty trees in the morning round. He'll repeat this again in the evening. And the next day, every day, for six or seven months during the season: from February–March until about September.

Before the padhaneer sours, he empties his cans into an aluminium pot near his work hut. From here, his wife Anthony Rosary takes over; she boils the padhaneer—a thin, sweetish, translucent liquid—until it becomes karupatti, brown and hard and sweet as jaggery. This traditional sweetener is the family's only source of income, since toddy, or kallu—the sap that ferments into an intoxicating liquid in unlimed pots—has been banned in the state since 1987.

Early every year, Rayappan leases a hundred to two hundred palm trees, paying a fixed rate to the owner of the trees, who offers no guarantee of a good harvest. In 2018, it was ₹24,000 for two hundred trees. For this, he borrows from the jaggery trader who reserves the right to buy all of Rayappan's karupatti later in the year. The moneylender-trader not only determines the rate but also decides when to sell it in the market to earn himself a profit, usually a fat one.

Rayappan spends half a year climbing and tapping padhaneer, while his wife makes karupatti, to pay back the loan and interest. Usually, the whole family—including schoolgoing children, goats and chicken—migrate into the palm grove for over six months and live there with no water, electricity or pucca housing. In 2018, however, with very poor yields, they stayed in Rayappapuram every night and travelled to the grove in the day. They also borrow to tide over the lean, non-productive months. In a good year, the family might have a little left over to feed themselves for a month or two. But that is rarely the case. Most months, the income is slender and in the off season, it is reed thin. And often, in the red. The only assured income—the word is used loosely here—is from the sale of karupatti. There are several factors that impact this, primarily the capricious rain, which reduces sap production. In years of drought, they make only three kilos of karupatti per day, instead of two kottons—each kotton is ten kilos—during the peak season. Though the price of jaggery goes up when supply is low and the demand high—in 2018 it was twice the previous season's rate—it still won't pay off even the interest, let alone the principal.

From this unpredictable production of karupatti, Rayappan has to feed his family, take care of sundry expenses and, of course, pay back the loan and mounting interest. The work hut is sparse; there is the sturdy, tall, palm stem cot that he has made, and his bicycle. A drawstring bag hangs from the roof. Inside is his phone, which at work he tucks behind his head, in the folds of his towel. When it rings, he presses the speaker button and talks at fifty feet above the ground, as he empties the pots of padhaneer.

During the off season, there is simply nothing to do. When I met Rayappan first in November 2017—back in the village, after the palm season—he was looking for work on a dhoney, or fishing boat. Rayappapuram is small, the houses tidy and sturdy. We sat outside the church in the village square near his house. It had been a bad year. Rayappan got to go out to sea just once and was paid ₹350 for it. If there is no work on the dhoney, there is just no work.

'Where is the water for agriculture? So that's gone too. What's left then? We sit around in tea shops, pretend it's the legislative assembly and talk, that's our only work.' But even to just sit around, read papers and drink tea, he needs money. As we spoke, the church clock announced it to be two in the afternoon and suddenly, as if awakened by the gong, a thunderstorm painted the sky with white lightning and the earth with muddy brown rivulets of water.

Typically, climbers don't own land. If they have a cow, that brings in a little money. Rayappan's gives six litres of milk a day and some of that is sold. The last time the family cleared their loans was in 2011. There is a minimum of ₹10,000–₹15,000 outstanding at the end of each season, and the family is constantly caught in a cycle of debt and loans. In October 2017, it was ₹14,000, after paying off ₹1,30,000 of the previous loan, spending ₹300 everyday on food, and covering for other expenses. By February 2018, the outstanding amount had climbed to ₹1,75,000, because of 'nalladhu-ketadhu', good and bad: festivals, functions, buying cattle feed during droughts and medical emergencies like his son's appendicitis surgery that cost ₹55,000.

Formal loans are hard to come by. Rayappan said he has heard of bank loans. 'But when people we know went to apply, they were asked to bring someone well off to be a surety. Will the wealthy come if we ask? Will they sign on our behalf?' Besides, traders keep cash ready when climbers fix a wedding in their family, knowing they will come around to borrow. 'Who do you think we go to, if we want to preserve our dignity? Banks who turn us away or traders who come home and give us money?'

Uzhudavan kanakku paathanna uzhakku kooda minjaadhu—If a farmer counts all his costs, he will not be left with even his measuring cup. S. Sathaiah, who has been working for the welfare of palm tree climbers since 1989 and is the director of Rural Workers

Development Society (RWDS) based in Ramanathapuram, referenced this popular Tamil saying to illustrate the plight of palm tree workers. 'If the palm climber's family added up all their labour, would there be any money to call as profit?'

The over-dependence on the trader and the lack of financial inclusion ensures there is none. 'Each family has a loan of a lakh or two lakh rupees. The interest rate is three paise, which comes to three thousand per lakh, per month. The Tamil Nadu government's Primary Palm Jaggery Cooperative Societies gave short-term loans to the climbers and also bought the karupatti, cutting out the middle men. But now it's stopped and the society exists only in print. Why can it not be revived, like agricultural societies that help farmers with loans, fertiliser and seeds?' asked Sathaiah.

Even during the rare good season, it is not all easy. It would mean climbing up to fifty trees thrice a day, resting for barely an hour or two in the hot afternoon, and then back again, looking up at the scorching sky, scraping against the bark, and down again to the brown, baked earth. 'Yes, my body aches, I take a painkiller,' said Rayappan. 'There are calluses on my palms. I cut the hard skin off with a blade. In high summer, when the temperatures soar into the forties, my skin is full of prickly heat. I put oil when I sleep, it's gone by the morning.'

What really bothers Rayappan are his knees, especially when they begin hurting high above the ground. 'This year's alright. But last year was bad, I couldn't sit like this with my knees folded. My legs would get stuck like this, when I was halfway up a tall tree' he said, holding his legs out straight. He would stretch, twist and release the joint mid-climb and only then could he come back down. The herbal medicine he took somewhat helped and he is now '90 per cent better.'

Climbers have no safety gear, no harness or helmet, nothing but the hard earth and thorns to cushion a fall. All they wear are a pair of shorts and a dhoti scrunched up over it. Their heads are covered with a cotton towel fashioned into a turban. Until eight years ago, Rayappan climbed in the nights too without any light, even on new moon days. Once, he felt something sting and mistook it to be a thorn. When he reached the leafy crown of the next tree, he felt breathless and giddy. He was treated for snake bite by a local healer.

Rayappan carries considerable weight on his arms and shoulders; the heaviest is a t-shaped, stand-like piece of wood called murukkuthatti, which the climber places at the bottom of the tree trunk for support during his descent. A small piece of dense wood attached to it also serves as a sickle sharpener. Tin cans, Rayappan usually carries two, and a wooden box with a supply of slaked lime are tied to his waist. The tin cans are used to transport collected sap, while the slaked lime is reapplied on terracota pots. When he is done with the day's sap collection, he hangs the cans with the padhaneer on either end of the murukkuthatti and walks back to the hut with about ten kilos balanced on his shoulders.

The palm's bark is frighteningly spiky. From the base of the tree, the scales stick out like blades. 'I don't feel it,' said Rayappan. 'The skin on my legs and hands have thickened. But if you were to step on it, the spikes would pierce your skin, as if to ask who asked you to climb it.'

The energy expended by palm tree climbers is high and close to marathon runners, given the physical exertion and utilisation of both muscular and skeletal strength, often under conditions of high temperature and humidity, said Dr Poornima Prabhakaran, additional professor and deputy director at the Delhi-based Centre for Environmental Health (Public Health Foundation of India). 'The effects on upper [shoulder and elbow], lower [hip and knee] and the smaller joints of hands and feet, given the agility and grasping power required in this task, cannot be discounted. ... The long-term effects on cardio-respiratory function can also cumulatively affect health outcomes with age.'

The climbers get a raw deal for so risky a job, said Sathaiah. 'Take insurance. The government-run Palmgur Federation gives climbers a license every year and a policy of ₹100 is issued in their name through New India Insurance. In case of death, an autopsy is conducted and then a lakh rupees is released. However, in case of falls, things get tricky. The sum assured, ₹50,000, is not given for fractures but only for loss of a limb.' Fractures and other injuries, which are not liable for compensation, incapacitate the climber and put him out of work for weeks.

Palm tree climbers and their families might have mobile phones and television sets, their children go to school and might even find opportunities to pursue other occupations, but the work itself has not changed much from what Tucker saw 170 years ago. The job is as treacherous, with falls, fractures and death.

> You will readily suppose that this is a dangerous as well as difficult employment; a single false step among the leaves, or one moment's letting go his hold in ascending or descending, precipitates the poor Shanar to the ground, and the half-yearly reports of the missionaries frequently contain the account of one or more of their people who have been found dead or dying at the foot of their trees.[2]

Palm trees are not privileged any more than the climbers who tend to them. According to the state government's Tamil Nadu Palm Products Development Board, more than half the palm trees in the country are in the state: 5.10 crore out of 8.59 crore. But a tree census now would give a very different picture, said Sathaiah.

Despite palm being the state tree, it is chopped indiscriminately to fire brick kilns. And the wood fetches only a pittance. By his estimate, 1.5 crore grown trees have been felled till date. 'We've been planting 10,000 every year near the seashore to contain erosion. So there are lots of young trees. But the adult palm, which can live up to 250 years, is being destroyed!'

Sathaiah spoke eloquently and in chaste Tamil. He comes from a family of palm climbers and like Rayappan, tapped the trees as a young man. For the last ten years he has been crying hoarse—protesting, fasting, fighting—that the trees be protected. But governments don't listen, he said. 'Palms are ancient trees. Thiruvalluvar, the great Tamil poet, wrote the *Thirukural* entirely on palm leaves. The trees—and their produce—are central to the village economy. They house so many birds and insects. They are hardy and do well in these dry areas. Should the government not step in to preserve them?'

Palms originated in Africa, said D. Narasimhan, retired professor of botany, from Madras Christian College. 'We cannot exactly tell when it came to the Indian subcontinent and whether it was through the sea route or land. But its glorious past does not help it today. It's a neglected tree, one that does not get the attention that mango or paddy command. And that's because it cannot benefit the powers that be. Unlike, say paddy, there's no industry around it. Palms are marginalised trees that grow on their own outside the village; they don't need fertiliser or much care. They can withstand droughts, and so many can be packed within a small area.' It can also withstand cyclones. When Cyclone Gaja hit Tamil Nadu in November 2018, one crore coconut trees fell,[3] but palm trees stood tall.[4] The tough and hardy palm can be used to tackle climate change and frequent droughts. And that is not all.

A classical Tamil poem, *Tala Vilasam,* lists 801 uses of the palm. In Sathaiah's office were decorative and utilitarian objects made from palm leaves—boxes, hats, baskets, bottle holders, and visiting cards and wedding invitations made from palm frond. 'Plastic is taking over the world, but palm leaf products can replace it. It's biodegradable and costs only five or six rupees. Plastic maybe cheaper, but this will employ thousands of families too!'

'If you go to Canada, you will see the way maple sugar and syrup are marketed,' said Narasimhan. 'It's not a patch on palm jaggery, but it's promoted vigorously. During the season, they have maple sugar tourism. Let's have palm sugar tourism. That way, the pride of the products and the people will increase. And if we promote the trade globally, the caste stigma—because of which people leave the occupation—will disappear.' Palm tree climbers are also wrongly thought to belong to just one particular community, that of the Nadars, said Sathaiah. 'But there are twelve communities, including Dalits and Muslims, who depend on the palm for sustenance.'

Unlike refined cane sugar, the global villain, karupatti, which has medicinal values, is loved by everybody. In the excellent and exhaustive book on palm trees, *Panaimaram,*[5] R. Panchavarnam writes about karupatti's nutritive benefits. 'The jaggery contains appreciable amounts of vitamins of B group and minerals. Iron is present in a form that can be easily assimilated. Due to the higher content of non-reducing sugars in palm jaggery, it is used as an energy food for convalescence.'

Among the reasons for the decline in rural livelihoods is a larger shift in focus—from sustainable local economies to a gigantic industrial one. Individuals struggle to cope and compete with big corporates who sell similar products for a fraction of the price, because they cultivate it in thousands of acres. Sugar scores over palm jaggery for the same reason, as the latter is neither cheap nor widely available. 'The government provides incentives to sugarcane factories and also forces this water-thirsty crop on farmers burdened by debts and droughts,' said Sathaiah.

'Tamil Nadu has forgotten biodiversity-based livelihoods,' said Narasimhan, 'But other countries are doing this very well. Laos and Cambodia are doing excellent work with their palm trees.'

In Tamil Nadu, the stigma of toddy affects the state support extended to palm workers. 'Climbers are harassed and false cases are foisted on them, even if they're bringing down padhaneer to only make karupatti.' Sathaiah wants the ban on toddy to go.

The history of the ban[6] on brewing palm toddy is long and complex. Among Indian states, it was Tamil Nadu that first introduced prohibition in independent India in 1948 on Mahatma Gandhi's birthday. This stayed in place until 1971, when the sale of arrack, toddy and Indian-made foreign liquor (IMFL) was permitted. Two years later, toddy shops were closed once again, and the granting of licenses for tapping and drawing, and permits for possessing and transporting toddy, was resumed only in 1981. But this was, once again, revoked in 1987. Since then, toddy and arrack remain prohibited in the state, whereas, IMFL is sold through state-owned TASMAC (Tamil Nadu State Marketing Corporation Limited) outlets.

An article published on 31 January 1987 highlights the irony of this ban that shuttered 16,000-odd retail arrack and toddy shops.[7] The official reason was to stymie 'the liquor addiction among the poor and the heightened social tensions this was generating.' But the ban only covered 'the poor man's drink, and not the more expensive IMFL.' It was clear 'that there is a deliberate attempt to aid the strong and influential IMFL lobby.'

Sathaiah wondered why 'toddy, which has 4.5 per cent alcoholic content, is banned, while whiskey and brandy, which have more than 40 per cent, are not.' The TASMAC website registers its turnover for IMFL spirits and beer for 2016–17 at ₹31,243 crore.[8] Women vigorously protest against TASMAC outlets, said Sathaiah, given the financial and health burden on their families when their menfolk get addicted. And yet, it is only toddy that is banned. 'Is it because,' he asked sharply, 'the free availability of toddy would impact the sale of IMFL?'

Because of this misconception that the men brew toddy and also because tapping is viewed as a primitive, hereditary occupation, the younger generation is reluctant to take up this work. Police harassment is not unknown. 'After the toddy ban, all climbers were viewed with suspicion,' Sathaiah said. 'The sugar content is high only in Kadaladi block in this district, giving about 140 grams of karupatti per litre of padhaneer. In Mandapam block, it's about half that.' When the percentage of sugar is poor, climbers need to collect more padhaneer for the same amount of jaggery. While in Kadaladi there are 550 families tapping palm, Sathaiah predicted the numbers to have fallen dramatically in the other ten blocks of Ramanathapuram. 'The men have moved on to construction work, fishing and wood cutting. Before the ban on toddy, there were ten lakh families who were dependent on the palm in the state. Today, that is down to about half.' At RWDS, they have over ten thousand registered members from Ramanathapuram.

Supporters of the toddy ban—including governments—cite adulterants, especially the sedative chloral hydrate, added to toddy as the reason for the ban. There have also been several instances when people died after consuming spuriously brewed liquor.

But Sathaiah is vehement that the ban on toddy tapping must be revoked. Vesha kallu, or poisonous toddy, is usually the work of middlemen, he argued. 'Shouldn't the government work to stop the adulteration?' he asked. 'Our slogan has been: "Kalluku kadai vendam, kallukku thadai vendam."' Don't ban toddy, but don't sell toddy through shops. 'Just like a milkman sells fresh milk, a tapper must sell his toddy directly. The onus will be on him to supply good quality.'

He is not alone in viewing palm tapping as a viable livelihood opportunity. Defending Telangana's plans to increase the number of palm trees,[9] the state's excise commissioner R.V. Chandravadan said to the media, 'Pure toddy has low alcohol content and has medicinal value if consumed fresh. As far as the apprehension that consumption of toddy induces crime is concerned, the complaint is generic and baseless.'[10]

Apart from allowing the tapping of palm neera, or unfermented sap, just like coconut neera, the climbers have a host of other demands to stabilise and strengthen the business: Palm tree climbers should be recognised as farmers and the government should strictly monitor the felling of palm trees, allowing only old or sick ones to be chopped down for firewood.

'Most importantly, there should be technological advancements in the lives of the palm tree climbing families,' argued Sathaiah. 'Why can't the state help develop ladders or lifts that will make the job less risky?' The climbers' work environment hasn't changed at all, he pointed out, whereas in fishing—boats, nets, methods, storing, selling—everything has been modernised. 'Where is the change from their grandparents' time in palm tree climbing? If the work becomes more modern, less risky and the rewards better, it will surely attract young men and women.'

Men should be given hydraulic climbers to scale the trees. 'Why would young men want to do this knowing their skin will become scaly and thick from hugging the coarse trunks? The women need sheds with chimneys so that they can make the karupatti in a smoke-free hut. The process will also become hygienic. The way it's done now, sand and ash fly in. A pre-fabricated structure with a good stove and chimney will cost only two lakh per unit. The government can do it. They have to!'

The state must also extend short-term loans, like for farmers, to palm tree climbers, so that they are not dependent on middlemen and traders for their livelihood. 'If we're not in debt, we can set a price for the product,' said Rayappan. 'We don't have to give everything to the trader at a price set by him, and then ask him for money for food.' The government could also purchase karupatti directly at a fair price, cutting out middlemen.

But beyond such policy changes, an attitudinal shift is required in the way the economy is managed. While corporate honchos who have defaulted on loans and engaged in data fudging get to plan their escape to a comfortable life abroad, people like Rayappan and Rosary are systemically excluded from accessing financial assistance.

Though Rayappan's neighbour in the grove, Rajendran Chellaswamy, was firm that 90 per cent of the climbers have gone on to do other jobs, Rayappan disagreed. 'Once a palm tree climber, always a palm tree climber. It's only the children who are leaving this. We're keen they get educated and take up other jobs.' Only those who drop out of school end up as climbers, they said, holding out their educated children as examples. 'And they learn from their fathers, long before they're eighteen. You can't just pick it up as an adult.'

'I started going to school when I could touch my left ear with my right hand like this,' said Rayappan, taking his arm around his head to touch his earlobe. He laughed as he described this novel 'test' to admit children to school but the smiled vanished when he talked of dropping out.

'Even today, when climbers die, the last thing they tell their son is how much debt they have,' said Sathaiah.

And yet, quitting is not an option for Rayappan. 'How can I? I keep hoping that once in ten years we'll have a good year and we can wipe out our loans. If we get ₹2,000 a day for six months, won't we be well off? Which job will give so much in a day? It's like a lottery. And then we'll forget the pains and troubles. Yes, there are times when we're scratched and we bleed. My wife gets tense when there is no money. But we will forget everything when the going is good.' Except, he does not want this life for his four children.

The couple's oldest daughter is married and has two sons. The fourth and youngest is twelve, and their third child, who wants to become a doctor, is seventeen. But Rosary isn't so sure. 'How can we educate her? We don't have money. She will have to drop out after twelfth.'

Rayappan's only son and his second child, Parloga Raj, had a twin who died soon after birth. The twenty-one-year-old has seen his parents toil for little gain. Though he had his moments of fun in the palm grove—catching rodents, dangling from cloth swings hung from trees, eating nongu, or palm fruit—his childhood was not easy. He walked miles to get a bus, studied by hurricane or oil lamps and lived in the grove for six months every year with his family.

Raj is a fan of computers, and wants to set up a shop to repair them. He is among the few from the village to have graduated and has a bachelor's degree in computer applications. 'He can repair any computer! He does it for free,' said Rayappan, adding in a low voice, 'I've been asking him to charge for his services.' He is proud of his twenty-one-year-old son, who has taught himself C and C++ and to repair hardware by watching YouTube videos. 'All the money I make will go to my parents,' said Raj, determined to change the lives of his family members.

'As if,' his mother Rosary dismissed him, laughing affectionately.

Since her marriage in 1990, Rosary—Rayappan's 'Kanmani', the apple of his eye—has been working in a smoky, hot hut for over six months every year. She could not take a break even after her deliveries, three of which happened in a village home, assisted by a midwife. Even when she is unwell, she has to lie down next to the stove and continue boiling karupatti.

As a young woman, life was as hard, having to walk ten-odd kilometres to the well everyday. 'The path was thorny and sandy,' Rosary recalled. 'The well didn't always have water. So we'd scrape at the earth with our fingers and wait for the water to come up. I carried back a big pot with fifteen litres on my head, another with ten on my hip.'

Her living room where we spoke was cooled by a fan and cross-ventilation. There was a television on one side and a tailoring machine on another. Rosary, tall and slim with high cheek bones and striking eyes, pointed to one of the framed photos on the wall: 'My husband loves MGR.' M.G. Ramachandran, a wildly popular twentieth-century actor, often portrayed characters who fought for the economically poor.

When I visited the grove, Rosary was still back at their home supervising the construction of a state-sponsored toilet.

About five hundred metres from Rosary's empty work hut, Muniyamma sat in hers. Smoke curled up from the chimney and hung around, shimmering black in the heat of the afternoon. Her husband Rajendran Chellasamy, like Rayappan, was just back from tapping padhaneer.

On a good day, Muniyamma is stuck inside the hut for at least nine hours, boiling up three batches of karupatti. Every minute she's inside, bent over or crouched next to the wood fire, she's breathing in fumes, her face is scorched and her eyes smart and tear up.

'None of my sisters were married to palm tree climbers,' she said, sighing and stirring. 'My parents did this work. I was the fourth daughter. My sisters' husbands work on salt pans. But they got me married to him,' she pointed outside, where Rajendran was cutting palm fronds.

Despite her angst, she did not once curse her job. Invited to talk about the process and her routine, she spoke at length about the upkeep of the mud stove. With hands darkened by fire, she patted and rubbed the air—this is how she applies cow dung on the stove to smoothen the sides, and this is how she keeps it from cracking from the heat of the burning firewood. What about you, I asked. She wiped her face with the edge of her synthetic saree and continued to stir the padhaneer.

As the sap boiled inside a four-foot wide aluminium pan, over a waist-high firewood stove set deep in the ground, Muniyamma poked with a palm frond at the fizzy, frothy hat that rose to the top and it obediently settled back into the pan. Earlier, she had picked out ants and bees with a muslin cloth off the surface of the freshly tapped padhaneer. Now and then, she added half a pinch of castor seeds—sometimes it is a drop of coconut oil—to keep the padhaneer from boiling over. She kept an eye on the fire beneath at all times, adjusting the heat by adding to or arranging the wood. The liquid became a syrupy caramel and the hut was scented with a sharp, sweet smell, layered with that of wood fire. As it thickened, her strokes got heavier, as if she was trying to row in a sea of brown custard. She poured some of this koocharu, just a stage away from becoming karupatti, into a plaited palm leaf bowl and offered it to me. The warm sweet liquid soothed my throat, but the memory of her labour is bitter.

Muniyamma let a stream of the hot liquid flow from the palm stem and it fell in a thick string. It was ready. Her husband came in to help her lift the pot of hot molten karupatti, over fifteen kilos, off the stove. She then arranged halved coconut shell moulds on a bed of sand and poured the sap into them with a wooden ladle. 'When they're set, I tap them out. Like this,' she said, neatly pressing a solidified disc out of the shell. 'These weigh between 100 and 150 grams. The kids run off with it and sell it to a shopkeeper for twenty rupees and buy some junk food. Those brats.'

Each year, the climbers' families fill a big pot with about twenty kilos of karupatti for their own use, scraping some off with the handle of a ladle when needed, to make karupatti kaapi—black coffee sweetened with karupatti or a concoction of karupatti, dry ginger and coriander seeds brewed together—a staple of the region. The jaggery is also used for making sweets during Deepavali. A popular one is olai kozhakattai, a dumpling of rice flour and palm jaggery kneaded together and steamed in palm leaves. The long, tube-like sweet is richly flavoured by the jaggery and the fragrance of palm leaves. Another is pidi kozhakattai—rice flour kneaded with water, rolled into discs, then filled with crushed palm jaggery and scraped coconut, sealed and steamed on idli plates.

The women in the family—alchemists who sit all day long next to an open flame on their haunches, or a low stool, stirring the boiling padhaneer until it thickens and becomes karupatti—do not have it any easier than the men.

Muniyamma is up at four every morning. She sweeps and mops the house, washes vessels, cooks food, then walks over to the work huts a few kilometres away, removes the previous day's ash from the stove, cleans the vessel and puts it back on to boil padhaneer, and lights the stove. 'If my husband goes out at three in the morning, I've got the fire going before sunrise. I get one batch done between five and half past seven. If he gets out a little later, I delay it a little. And like today, it's over only by half past nine. Then I go out and collect more padhaneer if he's tapped it. The second batch can go on till one in the afternoon. Next, I have to cut down and fetch firewood, cook rice for the afternoon meal, make a kozhambu and give him his meal.' Rajendran comes back for a wash and lunch. Each of his rounds in the grove takes him between three and four hours and each of Muniyamma's in the hut takes two to three.

While she is embarrassed that they don't have time for hospitality, Rajendran joked that they just put their guests to work. 'There's enough for everybody!'

George Monbiot's words would fit her, Rosary's and other women's labour, which is largely unknown and unrecognised: 'If wealth was the inevitable result of hard work and enterprise, every woman in Africa would be a millionaire.'[11]

Women like Muniyamma and Rosary spend much of their day hidden inside a tiny work hut, away from fresh air. The only light they see is what filters in through the chinks in the palm frond roof or tumbles in from the chimney, a square punched out in the wall. Only husbands and children—whom the woman must care for and fuss over when she can—are in her vicinity. If there are other families living nearby, she might walk across for a chat. But often, she does not have the time for it.

'A non-ventilated environment is a perfect recipe for the women to inhale smoke and pollutants from the biomass or cooking fuels. Exposure to these household sources of air pollution can eventually impact respiratory function and cardio-metabolic health,' said Dr Prabhakaran. Children playing in the vicinity too 'suffer from respiratory troubles, apart from the burning/watering of the eyes.'

'The work huts have to be modernised with asbestos roofing, raised stoves and chimneys,' said Sathaiah and estimated that this would cost two lakh rupees per family, an essential cost considering the enormous risks of the thatched roofs catching fire and children falling into the stove pits.

Muniyamma does not have the luxury of worrying about her health. 'I cannot rest for a minute when this sap is boiling. If I take my eyes off, it will brim over and spill, or get hard and lumpy. The day's effort will be wasted. And a thousand or two thousand rupees too.' She pointed to a coin-sized wound on her leg. 'See this? It happened a few days ago. The hot sap spilt. Could I rush off and tend to that? No! I had to stay here and finish my work. When my daughter was very young and I was pregnant with my son, she put her hand in the boiling sap. It was a nightmare! It took so long to heal.'

Like Rosary, she too could not even take a week off during both her pregnancies. 'I worked hours before the baby was born. Then I went to the hospital and had the child. And the day after, I was back inside the palm grove.' Her mother-in-law helped a bit, with whom she left her child in a cloth cradle and went about her work, feeding the child when it cried, rushing to fetch water from seven kilometres away, heating up the padhaneer, making jaggery, cooking, cleaning, toiling. 'I don't want my daughter to do this! She's educated; she's a teacher. My son has a diploma in engineering.'

Rajendran and Muniyamma tried holding on to eight hundred kilos of karupatti until the price increased in 2018. But for them, it never did. 'The trader made ₹800 on every kilo, but gave us just ₹100 over the usual price. We never make a profit. Ever!' Rajendran has plenty of grouses about financial inclusion and how the system is stacked against the poor. 'Why can't banks take pride in helping the needy,' he asked. 'They think we should suffer and die.' Rajendran said this with sudden anger, a surprising fierceness, stressing on the word 'saganam', to die, and his wife laughed softly, helplessly in the background.

Not far from Muniyamma's and Rosary's huts, little Manithurai was playing as his mother Muthumari Kalyanasundaram boiled padhaneer. Muthumari and her family moved eighteen kilometres away from their village Kannirajapuram, to live and work by the side of a palm grove. There are a dozen families in the area and a small grocery shop has sprung up to cater to them. A well is not far away and the kids have company. But it is a hard life.

Few days ago, nine-year-old Manithurai, chasing after a tyre he was playing with, ran into a pile of ash that still had a heart of fire. Before they could take him to the doctor to treat his burnt leg, his parents had a meeting with their neighbours, all palm tree workers, even as their son writhed in pain. It was important to find a doctor who would not judge them for the job they did. 'We can't just go anywhere. We can't go to the government hospital, the timings don't suit us. But so many private doctors speak badly about our work and dismiss our complaints.' Eventually, they took him to a doctor thirteen kilometres away. 'We don't go to a doctor based on his qualification, we go to the ones who don't humiliate us.'

This humiliation happens in schools too, which is why there are many dropouts from the families of palm tree workers. They are teased for coming late during the tapping season when they have to travel from the grove, and for the jobs their parents do. It is also expensive to arrange for transport for the children from the groves that are usually situated far away from the school.

While his mother worked, Manithurai took a break from his playing to tell me that his younger brother is a doctor. That's because his uncle told him he must become one and serve his community. But he couldn't dream of it; he was set on becoming a collector, and his elder brother, the 'military'—an army man. So the boys made the youngest a doctor. 'Paapa is a teacher,' he points to his little sister. And using the present tense, he brought alive all his dreams outside a work hut in a palm grove, somewhere near Sayalgudi.

Panaiyey

Oh, the solitary palmyra standing on the overgrown path
You are the guiding force of our heart
You are the guiding force for our wounded heart.

To the birds that seek you,
To the sparrows and quails,
You feed them with toddy
You feed them with toddy
Till their bellies are full.

I sing of you in awe.
I sing of you in awe.

We chop the spathe,
Shred the leaves.

We cut through the leaf stalk.
And we make you suffer no end
Yet you are nonplussed
Your body doesn't ache
You endure for ages
Holding on to the land
Oh, the solitary palm standing on itteri*
You are the guiding force of our heart
You are the guiding force for our wounded heart.

Getting drenched in rains,
Getting drenched in incessant rains
You sweat it out in the sun
You sweat it out in the scorching sun
You wilt and turn dark
Yet your heart is not broken
Nor your body is shrunken
You endure through ages
Standing tall in the open
Oh, the solitary palms standing on itteri
You are the guiding force of our heart
You are the guiding force for our wounded heart.

—Perumal Murugan [Translated by Kavitha Muralidharan]
From: *Panchabootha Keerthanaigal*

---

* Itteri, a dialectal term used in the Kongu region, is a footpath lined by overgrown trees and shrubs.

'Farmers Have Subsidised the Government'

D. Thomas Franco Rajendra Dev is general secretary of the State Bank of India Pensioners' Association and former general secretary of All India Bank Officers' Confederation (AIBOC). In the mid-1990s, he started a federation of self-help groups (SHGs) in Kanyakumari called Malar, which now has 2000 SHGs and 35,000 members. He has led several nationwide struggles defending the banking and public sectors, and was a strong critic of India's demonetisation in 2016.

We constantly hear that banks exist to serve women, farmers and that more rural branches are being opened. But on the ground, that doesn't seem to be the case. Could you comment on that?

The concept of banking changed in the country after 1991. In 1969, when banks were nationalised, it was to take banking to the common man. We did not talk about profits then. Between 1969 and 1991, the number of rural branches increased, credit-deposit ratio increased, so did the number of small credits. The 1991 RBI data—available as Basic Statistical Return (BSR) data—tells us that 97 per cent of loans and advances given were less than ₹200,000. The majority were less than ₹25,000. Small borrowers were given preference. We had the IRDP [Integrated Rural Development Programme] and other schemes.

But after 1991, when we availed the loan from IMF [International Monetary Fund] and World Bank, we entered into an agreement to privatise, for which the Narasimhan Committee was constituted. The first recommendation was to get rid of priority sector lending, which comprises of agriculture, small industries, village industries, cottage industries, micro, small and medium enterprises. They [the committee] said: Banking is a business, not charity. You have to see what's profitable. They also recommended that the government shareholding be brought down to 33 per cent so that banks are private and can be market-based.

Then the priority sector criteria was changed. 18 per cent of the total credit was meant for agriculture. They diluted this by including agro services. If you had a manufacturing unit for mineral water, that came under allied agriculture. If you do large-scale mango farming—like Ambani—that too comes under the 18 per cent. Second, they also said if a bank is not able to dispense the 18 per cent, they can deposit the remaining money into NABARD's [National Bank for Agriculture and Rural Development] Rural Infrastructure Development Fund. The assumption is NABARD is only going to use it for rural infrastructure development. But that's not real agriculture. Third, all kinds of SHG loans are classified as agriculture, but most of it will be for consumption. Then you have the agri gold loans—you pledge gold, produce some documents that you have agricultural land and take a loan. But here again, it does not really go to agriculture. A study shows that in Maharashtra, 53 per cent of agriculture loans are dispersed in Mumbai city. You can imagine what kind of farming takes place in the city.

What do you think of the loan waivers, is it a solution for the farming crisis?

Farmers are by and large very honest. They might starve, but they will repay the loans. Only when there is a calamity, crisis, drought or when the market crashes—when the price of potatoes and tomatoes comes to ₹2–₹3 a kilo—they find it difficult. The government has to support them. Writing off farmers' loans is necessary during a calamity or crop failure. I have been interacting with farmers' organisations and individual farmers. What they demand is: 'You tell us how much we should cultivate.'

I recently visited Israel. The farmer there gets all manner of support from the government. If they're going to plant potato, they have data available on what the likely price will be, in the Israeli and international market. The government advices how much potato can be cultivated that year, through a mobile app.

When I spoke to farmers in Nagpur, they said, 'Let the agricultural department or the bank tell us—"If you're going to cultivate more of this crop this year, it will be a risk"—then we can decide accordingly.' They have also been demanding minimum support price (MSP), which was recommended by the M.S. Swaminathan Committee—150 per cent of the input cost as MSP including the labour contributed by the farmer and his family. The government plans to implement it, how much, one has to wait and see.

Then, the farmer also requires technology, requires input. Organic farming is picking up. For that you need additional input. Our farmers are very fragmented. Now, NABARD has a concept—it has not been promoted well—called farmer producers' companies (formally, Producer Organisations, PO). Suppose I am a coconut farmer, I can start a PO and add other coconut producers to the company, so we have collective bargaining power in the market and also with the bank. The bank will have faith in a registered company over an individual. This has already come into existence. In mango farming, it's successful. But we need more. Also, this is not a cooperative, but is registered under the Companies Act. It's somewhat like formalising agriculture. You're able to get inputs and technology at a cheaper rate. When you go to the market, you have better bargaining power. Today, unless something like this happens and agriculture is seen as a profitable venture, it's going to be a big crisis, because no farmer's son wants to be a farmer.

When it comes to women—whatever be her livelihood—financial inclusion seems even harder than it is for the male in her profession. Are there any schemes for them and does it reach them?

There are some schemes, for example, for SC/ST [Scheduled Castes/Scheduled Tribes] women for purchasing farmland. But staff strength in the banks has been reduced so much that they find it difficult to cater to small farmers. Instead, it's convenient to lend to groups or to big farmers. Here, I would suggest that women should get into either FCOs or SHGs, or now there are joint liability groups. Seven people, who do the same activity, get together to form the joint liability group. These apply to all banks—public and private sector—but the latter may not be encouraging it much. The rules are common for all.

Informal loans, while easily and readily available for those who might not qualify for bank credit, are also crippling because of the high interest rates. Those who avail it go through life—and sometimes die—with huge debts. Why has it not changed in all these years, despite the Karve Committee identifying usury as

one of the key problems of the agrarian class and recommending nationalising banks back in the 1950s to solve this?

Until 1991, the orientation of the banks was towards service; now it's profit. Larger loans are easy to maintain. Profits are high. For smaller loans you need more staff to be employed; that is not available. There are schemes like the Mudra loan scheme, for which you don't have to give any security. But we found out in a survey, out of a hundred people who apply for a loan, only four get it. The demand in the country is really high and banks are not able to service it. Each branch is supposed to give twenty-five Mudra loans. They somehow achieve this target. They renew existing loans, or a loan under some other scheme is offered under this.

For real benefits, the banking sector has to be expanded. We have a branch for every eleven thousand people. In Sri Lanka or Brazil, it is 50 per cent of that. The moment you have more rural branches, the fellow [at the bank] cannot sit idle. He has to do something. So he will start looking at the people.

How many rural branches have closed from 1991 to 2017?

At least 10 per cent. There have also been mergers. The government itself diluted the norms. Earlier, there was a criteria that a village with a population of five thousand should have a branch. Now they have said it can be a banking outlet. So instead of opening a branch, there's a business correspondent in a village and that's seen as an outlet. He cannot provide credit, but can only make small payments using a POS [point of sale] machine and open Jan Dhan [financial inclusion initiave to provide banking services to every household] accounts. This directly affects the poor.

Is there a ballpark figure for the amount of credit needed from all banks to service the needs of farmers, small businesses, SHGs, etc.? What is the shortfall?

I don't think that kind of data is available anywhere. I also don't think it requires so much money to be invested. It's policy that needs to be reoriented. The government has to enforce existing schemes—a branch for every five thousand people. That branch—preferably of a nationalised or cooperative bank, which cares more for the common man—can be made profitable in two to three years if it functions properly. You don't have to look for huge capital.

Why is the government not doing enough about usury?

Most of the moneylenders are closely associated with ruling parties. They have the support of the police and they manage. Everybody in the village knows who the moneylender is. See, as per the law, they were supposed to have an exclusive tahsildar in every block to supervise the moneylending activity. But nobody has been designated and nobody is monitoring it, unless some episode happens or somebody comes with a big complaint. The government's keeping its eyes closed as their own followers and friends are involved. They are the support base for the political party, they will be funding the election. So that nexus is the root cause.

Usury can go up to 10 per cent per day. There are moneylenders who come to the local market. A vegetable vendor, a lady, will come with just a basket. The moneylender will be standing there. He will give hundred or five hundred. If it's a hundred rupee loan, he'll give only ninety. This lady will take the money, buy vegetables, sell it and by evening return hundred rupees to the money lender. This is 10 per cent per day, 3650 per cent interest per annum.

Could you comment on demonetisation and if the effort, resources, time and money that went into it could have been used to address some of these issues?

Definitely. Demonetisation is a wasteful exercise. It was a kind of imagination that black money was kept in boxes or under pillows. It was in circulation. You know who those black money holders are. Income tax department has the wherewithal to identify them. He won't hide himself—he will dress up nicely, own the best car, have a beautiful house, dine in the best restaurant, which they can monitor. So instead of catching hold of them, they caught hold of all the poor fellows. Even now, I come across women who come with a few five hundred notes and say, 'Sir, I forgot I hid it under the rice pot, please help us, sir!' There were many recommendations on how to curb black money and the government could have followed them by making every transaction transparent. But they did not.

Take moneylending—unless the government comes up with stringent measures, this problem will continue. People badly need credit. When they need the money, they don't think if they can repay it; they take a loan from whoever is willing to give it to them. I have interacted with fishermen from Kanyakumari. Their boats [for deep-sea fishing] cost between ₹60 lakh and ₹1.5 crore. Now, no bank gives them loans. No insurance company insures their boats. So the only way is to go to a moneylender. A group of people go together and get the money. They run it like a chit fund. One crore chit. You take it on auction for ₹60 lakh, but you repay a crore rupees. People say there is no other alternative. And they are confident that if they get a good catch, in two years, they can repay the money. But one collapse, one accident, everything is gone. In the recent cyclone, twenty-three boats were gone. Some with people in it, in some the people abandoned the boat. They are miserable. They say, 'I feel sad

I did not die. If I had died at least my family would have got ₹20 lakh. Now nobody looks at me, I don't have a job, I don't have a boat, give us some rice at least.' Such strong young boys, it was pathetic.

The 2017 drought was devastating and so many farmers have taken their lives in Tamil Nadu. How are they expected to cope with situations like this, which are out of their control? What could the government have done?

We have not been following a proper policy to help the farmer. We have been controlling the price of agricultural commodities, so that a larger number of people get cheaper grains. This has affected the farmers badly.

There was once a Government of India report in the Parliament: Farmers have subsidised the government more than the government has subsidised farmers.

Now what could have been done, or what should be done, is that farmers should be treated as the wealth of this nation. The erstwhile finance minister Arun Jaitley said that the number of people involved in farming has to reduce like in other countries. They cite the USA as an example—only 2 per cent of the people are involved in farming, why should 50 per cent of the people do it here? But our country is different. Farming alone is going to get you food. Tomorrow, if there is an even bigger crisis and we become dependent—that is what WTO [World Trade Organisation] wants—the solution is to import, as it's cheaper. But the moment you become an importer, the prices will keep changing and there will be another crisis.

Village economy has to be made self-sustaining. The decentralised democracy that Gandhi talked about has not been implemented at all. Now, we are trying to centralise everything, which for a country like ours is very difficult; it cannot be sustained, it will not be successful. We require more education in agriculture, more people to be encouraged to take up agriculture.

We should also provide adequate and appropriate technology. We are talking about importing Israeli technology. We have gotten into so many agreements with Israel. Israel is a water-starved state. When I was there, I asked them, 'You say water should not go into the land, it should go directly to the plant. We practise the flooding method because we want our wells to be recharged, our soil to remain healthy, soil organisms and earthworms to be there.' They said, 'It's right for your country, not ours.' But we're trying to implement their technology—have domes under which you cultivate, hydroponics, pivot method, humidification method. In some water-starved regions, drip irrigation and sprinkler might be okay, but not everywhere. We have to find the appropriate method suited to our country. And we have to get into an alliance with the farmers.

Farmers have lost faith in the government. For Cyclone Ockhi, the government announced a relief of ₹23,000 per hectare. The farmers calculated this as ₹5.40 per banana plant. The cost of planting a good quality banana plant is ₹150. What do I do with ₹5.40? The government is callous about the crisis and in finding a solution.

The next is corruption. Farmers have lost faith because, to get any relief or subsidy, they have to spend so much of their money and lose time and work in the process. So they decide to work a little harder instead.

This is the question we at the All India Bank Officers' Confederation (AIBOC) are raising: For what are you taxing people? You don't provide education free, you don't provide healthcare free, you don't provide employment, you don't even provide security.

In the USA, farmers get negative subsidy. They're told not to cultivate and for that the government will give them money. Here, we are only talking of giving input subsidy, which has become a corrupt system. The system has to be changed—you have to provide adequate price, you do not have to provide subsidy for the farmer. For that, he doesn't have to bribe somebody. The market mechanism has to be prepared ahead of time. If that kind of input is made available to the farmer, he will survive, make a profit and sustain his life.

Bankers must have faith in the farmer. By and large, there is a feeling that farmers will not pay back the loan, and will wait for a waiver. A fellow who has repaid will not get a write-off. My demand has been, when you write off during a calamity, write off for everybody, even for the farmer who has repaid. Then the farmer will also have faith, and the bank will also have faith. People will find it worth repaying. But the government's not thinking along these lines. Even farmers' organisations are demanding write-offs without going into the details. There are statistics that show that hardly 15 per cent of the credit is from organised banks, and 85 per cent of the credit is from moneylenders. If you don't write off, what happens to that farmer? The poor chaps who borrow privately are left to their own devices.

Welding Work and Worship

The sickle has a beautiful nose: strong, fine and curved. 'It's hard to shape,' said P. Chandrasekaran, a sickle maker. But that is what makes the Thiruppachetti aruval, named after the village, unique.

We were in Chandrasekaran's pattarai, or workshop, opposite a busy weekly market in Thiruppuvanam village of Sivagangai district. 'Thiruppachetti is over there,' he pointed with his hammer, 'about ten kilometres away. My father, grandfather, all of them lived and made sickles there.'

A curious mix of pucca and kachcha constructions, Chandrasekaran's pattarai has a section at the back that is bricked, cemented and whitewashed; in the front, it is boarded up with asbestos sheets and braided coconut fronds, where twelve sickles of various heights are displayed for sale. On one wall are eight calendars from different years and, on the floor, blue palagais, or low wooden stools, on which the workmen sit. Above the heat and noise that rise from the factory floor, colourful streamers and crepe papers twist and turn in some long-forgotten celebration, perhaps for Ayudha Poojai, the ninth day of Navaratri when tools are worshipped.

When he turned twenty-three, Chandrasekaran moved to Thiruppuvanam, which falls on the route to Rameshwaram, a popular pilgrimage town. 'I came here twenty-five years ago with the clothes on my back. It's busier here, with more customers dropping in. It's quieter in Thiruppachetti, only those who go searching for sickles find the place.' Thiruppuvanam has a population of nearly 25,000. 'People from nearby villages migrate here, like I did, as business is good. Passers-by too stop and buy sickles.'

As he spoke, he hammered a piece of iron that was crimson with heat and kept at it till it turned smoky black. Then, using tongs, he stuck it in the furnace again for it to eat up the colours from the fire, incandescent orange and infernal red. The cycle of heating and hammering went on: five, ten, fifteen times. Finally, after forty-five minutes, Chandrasekaran lifted up the sickle and turned it this way and that. A Thiruppachetti sickle, a child of iron and fire, was born.

The region that is now called Tamil Nadu has a long and ancient iron tradition.

Steel might have been manufactured in this iron ore region well before the thirteenth century BCE, said K. Rajan, professor of history at Pondicherry University and director of excavation at Kodumanal—an archaeological site in Erode district. The region he refers to is Salem, about 250 km north of Thiruppuvanam.[1] 'The occurrence of gemstone, iron, steel, copper-smelting, conch shell and textile industries suggest that this site survived as one of the important trade-cum-industrial centres from fifth century BCE to first century BCE.'[2]

Sangam literature, dating from third century BCE to third century CE, has beautiful and biting references to iron implements, said Dr K. Sundar Kaali, who teaches Tamil language and literature at the Gandhigram Rural Institute in Dindigul. In one famous story,

Avvaiyar, a legendary Sangam era poet, visits the court of King Tondaiman of Kanchi. He is set to wage a war against the poet's friend, King Adhiyamaan of the Dharmapuri region. Tondaiman takes her to see his armoury, stocked with shiny new weapons. A clever and witty poet, Avvaiyar praises the pristine condition of his swords and spears, comparing them to her friend's overused, shabby weapons, which lie in ruins at the smithy. Tondaiman gets the message—Adhiyamaan's weapons are used more often, giving his soldiers more experience in battle—and a war is averted.

A legend from the twelfth century *Periyapuranam* tells a fascinating story of a sickle. Kaali read out the elegant Tamil text, explaining as he went along. 'There lived a wealthy man called Thayanar in Ganamangalam, located in the beautiful, lush Chola kingdom. Everyday, Thayanar took an offering of rice, red spinach and raw mangoes for Lord Siva. The god decided to test his faith. Thayanar's wealth was wiped away; yet, he continued to take offerings to the god. His poverty deepened, but so did his faith. He offered every morsel he could afford to the god, while he himself lived on water. One day, when he went with his offering, the starving devotee fainted and dropped the food. Distressed that he had nothing to give his god, he slit his neck with his sickle. Lord Siva caught his hand, bit into the fallen mango and shouted "*Viddel, viddel*"—stop, stop—and blessed him with the boon to go to heaven after his death. Since then, Thayanar, whose sickle wound disappeared when the god caught his hand, was known as Arivalthayar.'

Thirty-five years of beating the aruval has made Chandrasekaran an indomitable artist of iron.

Without taking his eyes off his work—which would be dangerous—Chandrasekaran spoke about making sickles in his father's factory when he was twelve. 'My day began with agricultural work. My family also cultivated paddy, about fifty sacks of it a year. I had to remove the weeds, water the fields, come home, have a bath and, by half past nine, leave for school.' When he came home for lunch, he was expected to work on a couple of sickles, hammering and lengthening them. He did another hour and a half of work at the pattarai after school as well. When he was fifteen, he went alone to water the fields at night. 'We were raised strictly. Even if I wanted to go for a movie, I had to get permission.' He has done everything—from watering to harvesting to threshing the paddy. 'But farming was never very profitable. Since my father's death four years ago, it has been very hard to look after the land. He worked until the day before he died. We still have our lands, but there are only coconut trees on them. Where is the water to cultivate anything else now?'

Sickle making, an ancient occupation, is still profitable. Every year, in Thiruppuvanam and Thiruppachetti, which have ten pattarais each, highly skilled craftsmen make around 72,000 sickles entirely by hand—about ten a day at each workshop. The sickles are sold between ₹250 and ₹900 apiece and there is good demand. Small sickles are the 'fast-moving' item. Around a foot long, they cost the lowest and are used as an everyday agricultural tool to harvest paddy, reap grass, cut down leaves for goats, prune palms, slice coconuts and hack banana plants. Small, curved, custom-made ones are used to pare fish, bigger ones to skin and dice meat, and large sickles that cost ₹550 are used to chop firewood. 'A big, heavy one is used to fell trees. But, if you use it for five to six hours, your hands will chaff!'

Given their versatility, sickles, in one form or the other, get sold. Well-polished, showy sickles are bought as display pieces. 'It looks handsome and,' Chandrasekaran added, 'it's expensive, costing ₹3,000.' He also makes aruvamanais, or curved blades mounted on a slab of wood—the user sits on the floor and holds the wooden part down with the thigh—a preferred chopping device in Tamil Nadu's kitchens. Brides in the region carry an aruvamanai and a small sickle as part of their trousseau when they get married. 'Unlike cheap versions, ours last for generations!' The wood is replaced with a sheet of metal in the newer versions.

When Chadrasekaran was fifteen—and working double shifts, both in the fields and in the pattarai—his father paid him a daily wage of ₹70. 'It was big money. Other boys got ₹15 or ₹20. But then, sickles themselves were sold only for ₹40–₹60.' Now, sickle prices and wages have increased ten times. 'It was such a novelty then, to see a ten rupee note. Now, we spend freely. A trip to Madurai sets you back by a few thousands!'

The second time I met Chandrasekaran in 2017, two years after my first visit, he invited me home. Built in 2012 and named after his second son Sashi Kumar, it was only a five-minute walk from his pattarai, but a world away from its furnace and ferocious noises. When we reached there at ten in the morning, his wife Vijayalakshmi opened the door and apologised for the clothes and pillows strewn around her older son Santosh Kumar, who was fast asleep on the floor. 'He's here for a function; he works in Chennai,' she said, as she gently woke him and sent him inside. After putting away the clothes, she headed back to the kitchen, where the afternoon meal—meen kozhambu, or fish curry—was bubbling on the stove, but not before she checked if I was the researcher from Germany who had visited them in 2015. When I clarified I wasn't her, she laughed and said, 'That woman was thin.' I tucked my limbs, sucked in my tummy and hoped for the best.

Sitting on the cool living room floor, Chandrasekaran described how the work floor in his pattarai is erected. The first layer is a log of wood buried in the ground. It is longer and wider than the panai—a sheet of iron, which is inserted three inches into the wood to keep it firmly in place. 'The panai is usually a hundred kilos.' A hundred, I asked incredulously. A hundred, he confirmed. 'Because it takes a real beating. Adi vilugum.' It is on this heavy anvil that the sickle is hammered and shaped.'

During the workday, the coal furnace—with a motorised bellow—is lit. A suthil, hammer, and sambatti, an instrument that tempers and shapes metal, are used to make the sickle. 'The sambatti is very heavy. The one we use is about ten rathels.' One rathel is 500 grams. The person who wields it—usually the assistant—stretches, lengthens and shapes the sickle. The senior craftsman holds the red hot iron with tongs and points and directs with a 1.5 kilo suthil on where to strike, occasionally hitting the hot metal too.

Every month, Chandrasekaran buys two hundred kilos of scrap iron at ₹30 a kilo. 'When we buy scrap metal, we choose the pieces carefully. It has to be light but strong, so that the finished sickles don't bend with use.' Mostly, he uses steel leaf springs from buses and lorries. 'When I see the leaf spring, I know how many sickles I will get from it. The metal is excellent and the size works well for sickle making.' The urukku, or steel, from vehicles, ticks all these boxes. Unlike the bulky iron sickles made in his grandfather's time, the ones he makes have a longer life. They are also easier to work on. 'If the piece of metal is heavy, it takes longer to beat it into shape.'

Heating and beating is even trickier than it appears. If heated just past the point when the metal is ripe for hammering, 'it will become watery and run away'. All this sounded more dramatic in his Tamil, a strong regional dialect, which rose and fell with certain syllables and stretched into a melody at the end of each sentence. He also spoke fast, and when I asked him to repeat, he always obliged, with the same patience that helps him carefully shape sickles.

Making sickles is not just hard labour, it is very risky too. 'This is why, even if you're willing to pay money, you don't easily find assistants.' Chandrasekaran employs two young men from the village to help out in the pattarai. 'Who wants to do something so risky?' The fire is a constant source of danger. 'You've got to hold the hot metal very carefully. If not, it can slip from the tongs and hit you.'

'His uncle got an eye injury,' said Vijayalakshmi. 'A piece of sharp metal hit his pupil.' She gasped at the memory, I gasped at the story, but Chandrasekaran remained nonchalant. 'It happens,' is all he said. 'I got a cut on my hand when the sickle landed on it. Here,' he showed me his scarred finger. 'I have so many wounds on my hands and legs. Why, if you take your eyes off for a moment, it will fell you!'

The toll the labour has taken on Chandrasekaran's body is permanent. When one of his assistants is on leave, he has to beat the sickles himself. 'Valikum,' he said. It will hurt. The palms are the first to blister. 'Once the palms become hard, it doesn't matter. Now, after thirty-five years, I feel nothing,' he said, showing me his calloused hands. The room went silent. The body ache leads to another problem, especially among the assistants. 'The hammering is so difficult that the boys go and down a quarter afterwards to forget the pain.' A quarter bottle is the smallest quantity one can buy in Tamil Nadu from state-owned TASMAC shops.

Though it is a hard life, the income has improved in the last few years. At the turn of the millennium, ten thousand rupees was a lot of money. Now, a lakh is not so hard, unlike for a farmer with a small holding. But the sickle making industry is not in any hurry to grow. The craftsmen in both the villages are happy with the small profits—about ₹2,000 on a good day. Like many small self-run businesses, the owners do not take a fixed salary for themselves. 'How can I? If there's a profit, I keep it. If not, I pay from my pocket.'

Is there a way to make this bigger and better? 'Well, mechanisation is possible.' Chandrasekaran has heard of a mechanised factory in Bodhi, near Theni, in the western part of the state. But, he said, one needs a big plot of land and at least ₹500,000 to buy a machine to replace the labour-intensive job of wielding the sambatti. 'The final shaping of the nose has to still be done by hand. I don't think anybody here has ambitions to export sickles.' They are all happy, he insists, with their small investment of ₹10,000 and the corresponding small profits.

Every morning, Chandrasekaran takes a look at the inventory and decides the sizes and quantities of sickles to be made. 'If the sickles accumulate, we stop manufacturing for a day or two.' He does not believe in keeping a big inventory. But a small stock has its uses. 'Sometimes, an outstation buyer will ask for fifty sickles. The odd day, ten or twenty will get sold quickly.' It takes ₹2,150 everyday to keep the shop running. 'Tea expenses are another ₹100. Whether we sell any sickles or not, the daily salary bill for the two assistants comes to ₹1,500. Then there is coal to keep the furnace burning, which costs ₹200. Material is another ₹300, rent ₹100, electricity about ₹50.'

Business is unpredictable but never bad. People come from nearby villages and towns to buy sickles. He also sells to wholesale clients, including a shop in Thirumangalam, where he has been supplying seven hundred sickles yearly for the last two decades. Women too come to either buy or sharpen a sickle. When a customer brings back a blunt sickle, with only the claim that it was purchased from him a few years ago, he always sharpens them, making the tip as fine and thin as it should be, without trying to sell a new one instead. 'After a year or two, the cutting end grows heavy,' he said, referring to the blunting of the blade. The life of a sickle depends on the work, the material it chops or breaks, and the usage. 'A wood-cutting sickle, used everyday, might last three months, four at best. If usage is infrequent, it will retain its sharpness for years.'

Vijayalakshmi joined the conversation now and then, but she was clear that sickle making is not for women, although, Chandrasekaran's mother had worked in the pattarai. 'She's wielded the sambatti. Back then, you didn't always find workers. So my mother and father worked in the pattarai. She only stopped when I grew up and started working,' he said.

'People used to keep sickles at home for self-defense,' Vijayalakshmi piped in. We had an excited two-minute discussion about how gangsters in Tamil films slide out long sickles, called veecharuval, tucked into their backs inside their shirts, only the tell-tale handle peeping out. But Chandrasekaran quickly added that veecharuvals are not made anymore and Vijayalakshami said: 'Yes, they've banned all of that,' with a finality difficult to breach.

Thiruppuvanam and Thiruppachetti get a lot of attention from the press for two reasons. Both, interestingly, are unrelated to the sickle's primary use in agriculture. First, when gigantic sickles are made for temples. 'I've made three,' said Chandrasekaran. 'Each one is eighteen feet long, over a hundred kilos heavy and costs ₹25,000. To make them, I source twenty-foot metal plates used in ship-building.' The giant sickles are not to be used as a tool, but are offerings made to temples. Reporters and TV crews come to take photos and videos and conduct interviews. The other time the media turns up is when the now-banned veecharuval is used in a gang war.

Chandrasekaran's father has made sickles for several movies, including the one named after Thiruppachetti, called *Thirupaachi* starring the popular actor Vijay. 'In the movie, *Periya Veetu*

Pannakkaran, the legendary actor M.N. Nambiar mentions our sickle; it appeared in the famous actor Shivaji Ganesan's film *Mudhal Mariyadhai*; so many have gone for films! I don't always know the names of the movies, but whenever they are purchasing it for a shoot, customers tell me so.'

Sickles and cinema have an interesting and problematic relationship. The 'Madurai formula', as the movies from this region are called, feature men pulling out veecharuvals to dramatic music and hacking off a limb, or a neck. Kaali said that this portrayal is wholly untrue. 'I've lived in Madurai for fifty-five years, and never have I seen a man pull out a veecharuval and kill another! There are people who use them, but it's not a widespread, visible phenomenon. I've only seen it in films.' But this is a recent portrayal. 'The older movies had sword fights. That changed mid to late 1980s, when cinema created regional identities and this became emblematic.' He was referring to films of the late M.G. Ramachandran, in which the weapons were all 'imaginary, they didn't exist in real life.' But the Madurai films, in their attempts at realism, brought in the veecharuval as a weapon. 'Except, that too is cinematic imagination. Madras, Madurai and Coimbatore don't have the kind of big gangster culture depicted in films.' If you were to go by the movies, you only need to walk into a market in Madurai to find groups of gangsters, all with white shirts and folded dhotis, itching to draw the veecharuval tucked into their vest and slay someone.

Apart from the talk about veecharuval that screeched to a halt, the conversation in Chandrasekaran's house had to stop every time the dog barked, loudly. 'It's ours, it doesn't like anybody walking on the road,' said Chandrasekaran, laughing. He called the dog a 'dober naai', a mix of Tamil and English terms for the Doberman breed. It is not yet fully grown but is suitably ferocious, as if it were trying to prove its worth and money.

And hard-earned money it is. 'We don't have a single sickle in this house,' said Chandrasekaran. 'We just keep all the stock in the shop. If it's here, a few hundred rupees stay locked in.' So every time they need to chop something, they go to the shop—a five-minute walk. 'Appadithan irrukum.' That's how it is.

Although many of the makers, including Chandrasekaran, are from the Viswakarma community, who traditionally worked with metal, sickle making is not limited by community nor is it only hereditary work. The only requirement is: 'You should have watched it all your life, you should start young. You can't just jump in one day and start making it. Take my assistants, Suresh and Arumugam. Both their fathers worked for me. When they died, the boys came.' People from other castes and religions too have pattarais. 'Arumugam is a Dalit, and his family members previously worked as agricultural labourers. But where is any coolie work to be had on the fields? There is no water, that's gone, so they come to do other work.'

Viswakarmas, otherwise known as Kammalars or Acharis, fall under backward castes, said P. Ramajayam, assistant professor at the Centre for Study of Social Exclusion and Inclusive Policy, Bharathidasan University, Tiruchirappalli. The community gets its name from the god they worship—Viswa Karman, the divine architect. 'They are highly skilled professionals, with many sub-groups—goldsmith, bronze smith, blacksmith, carpenter and stone mason. Their work is technically sophisticated, they are scholars in measurements, and very professional and skilled in their work. But society does not celebrate their skills adequately.'

In the feudal times, the Viswakarma community enjoyed royal patronage, as their skills were in demand for constructing monuments, temples, chariots and for carving gods and goddesses in stone, rock, metal and wood. They also had the skills to make weapons. 'When they were designated as a backward class in 1971, they lost political leverage, as there are many dominant groups in that category,' said Ramajayam. 'The community tends to be male-centric,' since their work involves making iron tools around furnaces, 'and the men wear sacred threads to claim upper social status at par with Brahmins. But they never controlled their knowledge system and let it spread across the social spectrum.'

The sickle makers of Thiruppuvanam and Thiruppachetti have a sangam, with members paying ₹30 a month. They meet monthly to discuss things like when the new moon day falls—when they usually shut shop. 'But we don't decide rates,' said Chandrasekaran. 'How can we impose that? The sizes of the sickles we make vary and, if someone we know comes and asks, we're bound to give a small discount. We really cannot fix prices in the sangam.'

V. Rajendran, the secretary of the sangam, comes from a family of sickle makers but now runs a hotel. The two men are related—Rajendran is Vijayalakshmi's brother—and so are many who run the association. The seventy members are all from the Viswakarma community, of which only ten are sickle makers; the all-men association also includes carpenters, blacksmiths, goldsmiths, sculptors, copper and bronze smiths. The numbers are only falling, said Rajendran. 'Business is hard. Carpenters and goldsmiths are especially affected, as big chain stores have come in. We have requested for loans at the district level, but they are difficult to come by. Banks ask for security. Most people don't have their own house or land. What will they give?' And so they leave the trade. 'The children from our community have gotten an education, taken up desk jobs. Muslims, Dalits and other communities are now working in the pattarais.'

Chandrasekaran is both pragmatic and a little sad that his sons want nothing to do with sickle making. Like the children of his fellow sickle makers, they have no desire to learn and practise the craft that is synonymous with their villages' names and was passed down for generations from father to son. 'They don't come near the pattarai,' he said. It is also a matter of 'gouravam', or fierce pride and ego, not in the great skill craftsmen like Chandrasekaran have, but in wanting to move away from what is considered to be hard, manual labour.

'So many migrants are here in Tamil Nadu, even in Thiruppuvuanam, from Bihar, Orissa, Rajasthan, working as construction and agricultural labourers,' said Chandrasekaran, hinting at the changing Tamil society, aspirational and moving away from traditional livelihoods. 'What do the boys want? A desk job, an air-conditioned office and a spritz of perfume around their neck,' said Vijayalakshmi. It is what the young everywhere want—equal opportunity, unconstrained by caste boundaries. 'Only those without education end up doing this work. Even my father told me, "Let this work end with me, you go study." But I had no interest. After tenth standard, I came to this work. I want a different life for these boys. Let this hardship end with me!'

Twenty-three-year-old Santosh Kumar, the older son, agreed. To him, sickle making is a sooty job; he does not want to labour next to a furnace all day like his father and grandfather. 'We felt shy to do this and wanted to go out and do some regular work. Most people in my generation want jobs that will not dirty our collars.'

He instead works with new-age tools, with Adobe, Photoshop, Flash, Premier, and Illustrator, as well as 3D software. He has a BSc in animation and is part of a popular Chennai-based YouTube channel that makes political satires. 'After my schooling, I did a diploma in engineering. I didn't like it. I then opted for animation.' Santosh earns ₹20,000 a month, about the same amount each of his father's assistants make in a village where the cost of living pales in comparison to what Santosh would have to spend in Chennai. But his decisions are not just driven by economics. If they were to be, he and his brother would take over their father's business. For Santosh and Sashi, it is a matter of gaining cultural acceptance.

Santosh was wearing what he calls 'city' clothes—shorts and a sleeveless t-shirt—which drew a snide comment from his uncle. The young man replied coolly that if he wore full-sleeved shirts or trousers, people in Chennai would not look up to him. He dreams of working in the film industry and, one day, travelling to America. 'Soon, I have an official trip coming up, to Singapore and Malaysia.' It will be his first trip overseas, and he is excited. 'I'm building my portfolio. Once that is strong, I'll look for other jobs. It's a hot area, and there'll be a lot of demand.' But he comes home even during a three-day break and always visits during the annual temple festival in March. It gives him the chance to tease his parents now and then about the unused air conditioner in the living room. 'He hates sweat and dirt and tells us to put the air conditioner on when he's around; when we don't, he asks if we have it for decoration,' his mother said, grinning. Santosh has also got offers to act in films. 'But he doesn't want to go for all that. My younger one said he'll go; he's asked his brother to call him if there's another chance.' I was curious to meet Sashi, a civil engineering student, but he was out with the car to help out a classmate who had had an accident.

After his son shared his dreams and ambitions, it was Chandrasekaran's turn. 'In five years, I think I'll quit,' he said. 'I want to save for our future, put some money in the bank, and then stop.' His highly skilled but exacting job will remain largely unknown and underrated. But it paid for every brick in their two houses, the bikes the boys drive, their car and Vijayalakshmi's jewellery. Every rupee was earned by the forty-eight-year-old Chandrasekaran, beating and selling sickles.

'Growth Through Justice'

P. Sainath is the founder-editor of the People's Archive of Rural India (PARI), which reports on and records what is easily the most complex part of the planet. He was rural affairs editor of *The Hindu* for a decade until 2014. He has received various awards including the Ramon Magsaysay Award in 2007, World Media Summit Global Award for Excellence in 2014 and Amnesty International's Global Award for Human Rights Journalism in 2000. He has taught at journalism schools and universities in India and abroad. His book *Everybody Loves a Good Drought* was declared a Penguin Classic in January 2013.

How do we keep the skills associated with traditional livelihoods alive, even while dismantling the caste hierarchies that kept them going for so long?

It is a very difficult question. There is no simple answer to it.

Destroying the caste hierarchies, to my mind, takes precedence over everything else. That said, caste in many ways represented the feudal relations of production. That's how they formed caste around occupations. That makes it uniquely different and negatively different from many other relations of production, like capitalist relations of production. For instance, a leather worker in Milan, Italy—for many Europhiles the centre of the fashion universe—

would be recognised as a master leather worker, earning more than the CEOs of some smaller companies there. He would have a client list of some of the great names across the world. But his son or daughter would not be compelled to be a leather worker. They could be a rocket scientist or pizza baker or whatever. But should the child choose to take it up, they have a tremendous advantage and a great deal of respect that they earn from being part of a family that is so highly esteemed in that field. The son of a mochi in an Indian village leads, as his father and sisters and brothers do, a wretched and miserable life stripped of any dignity, condemned to untouchability. And if he wants to try and be something different, there are powerful forces in the village that will teach him why that cannot be. Even today, in many villages, that's the case and it often leads to that person migrating out of the village, the countryside; but what does the person meet in the city? Class contempt. (Not that caste is absent—that is there, too). And not having other skills needed to bring them a life of dignity and fulfilment.

So what we need to do is not just destroy the caste hierarchy but simultaneously create respect for the work and labour that people do, for what they produce. I have always maintained that untouchability is not just a social evil. It's more than that. It's an extremely cruel, vicious but sophisticated form of exploitation by which we keep a large labour force permanently demoralised, humiliated and dependent. So we need to destroy the feudal relations of production completely; we need to accept that if a son or daughter of a potter, weaver or leather worker do not want to be in that field, it's a perfectly legitimate need of theirs and they cannot under any circumstance be compelled. You need to break down the caste hierarchy and when you bring respect and economic returns for that skill, who knows—many other children in the village might want to do it. Look at the way we've destroyed weaving. Several weavers, who for countless years made the famous Kanjeevaram saree, are driving autorickshaws in Kanchi and Chennai, and this is called reskilling. These individuals hold within them cumulatively thousands of years of skill, knowledge and experience. We simply do not respect labour, we don't give dignity to those who do this beautiful work. So, it's a very tough ask.

First thing, break the hierarchy. Second, bring dignity to labour. Third, make these occupations respected, remunerative, even admired. Our multiple societies are full of people with extraordinary skills. You might find that the new generation of potters and weavers and leather workers are not from the traditional castes that were previously condemned to do them as drudgery rather than as creative art. But destroying feudalism not just means economic returns but a very heavy degree of social reform, that person's got to be able to break out of those boundaries and shackles.

However, there are also professions and occupations that you want to see dead. I don't want to see anybody take up or inherit manual scavenging. It is the greatest assault on human dignity that you can think of in a structured way. And it is perpetrated because we are somehow very comfortable with the idea of using the children of our poor to do the dirty work for us. So there are professions that have to be completely destroyed. And there are professions, occupations and livelihoods that have to be preserved. But not as they were in their old context but recreated in a new one.

There was a National Sample Survey that told us that 40 per cent of farmers would quit farming immediately if they had other options. I actually think if the same question was asked with an age bar, under thirty-five, the 40 per cent would go up to 80 per cent. They want to leave because they've seen their parents, grandparents, aunts and uncles go through hell and they don't want to do the same. I don't blame them at all for that. But if farming was restored to a place of dignity, was remunerative, and its social status was reconstructed, it would be a very different thing. In the 1960s and 1970s, in Andhra Pradesh, I can tell you, parents, choosing between an engineer, a doctor and a farmer with ten to twelve acres of paddy, would choose the son of a farmer. Today, nobody wants to give his daughter or son to the child of another farmer. It is because the farmer's universe has collapsed. Thirty years ago, people used to say with pride, 'We are farmers.' Now that it isn't there because of the hell we have inflicted on farming. That was policy driven. The response will also have to be policies, a different set of policies.

At a time when aspirations are at odds with availability of jobs, how can livelihoods absorb and employ the workforce?

Millions of people have been driven out of agriculture and agriculture-related livelihoods, in the name of development, in the name of capitalist society's claim that those removed from agriculture would be shifted to industry. Indeed, Chandrababu Naidu's great debacle in 2004 was based on his attempted implementation of a McKinsey report called Vision 2020, which explicitly recommended that we should remove 40 per cent of the people presently in agriculture. So you remove them and where do they go? A marginal farmer dislocated in Mandya, Karnataka is unlikely to get absorbed in the Infosys workforce even though it is an hour's drive away. So, we have systematically destroyed existing occupations and livelihoods without creating any alternatives. This has happened to farmers, weavers, to the agrarian society at large, in some stupid illusion that industry will absorb them. No such industry exists. What manufacturing jobs have you created in the last twenty-five years of the neoliberal economic policies ruling this country? The one sector that you've created jobs in was the IT sector. And in 2017, the top seven IT firms, which had a pre-tax profit of ₹23,000 crore, laid off 56,000 workers in the mid-senior level. Many of them might have been earning ₹1.5 to ₹2 lakh each. Then the firms would take in fresh graduates at ₹20,000 or ₹30,000 monthly and render unemployed those who faithfully served those companies for ten–fifteen years, and who are going to be in serious trouble because every one of them will have three EMIs—for the house, car and education. How will they now pay ₹90,000 a month? They are finished.

Second, there are going to be fewer and fewer jobs in the kind of development we have undertaken. On the one hand, a lot of jobs are automated, robotised. And on the other, Artificial Intelligence is going to wipe out, on a scale we cannot imagine today, even many middle class occupations. Not just those of workers. In banks, ATMs have replaced so many jobs. But earlier, they destroyed you in one area, because they needed you in another. Now, they're going to have people they don't need anywhere. Huge sections will be completely dispossessed. They'll replace them with automation, AI and machines. You haven't a hope in hell in addressing this question within the current policy framework. You cannot address it when you're grooming and nurturing inequality. Inequality is the womb of violence, the cradle of fundamentalism, the playground of unelected power, and the graveyard of secularism and democracy. You're creating such great, gigantic inequalities. Now, what Mr Mukesh Ambani earned in twelve months, according to *Forbes*—he added $16.9 billion to his wealth—it would take a worker on NREGS, the country's flagship programme, 187,000 years to add that amount on average national rates. Or it would take 18.7 million workers a year to do it. Where are you going to absorb people? Unless everybody wants to be the servants of 121 individuals in this country who are the billionaires accounting for 22 per cent of your GDP.

So there's no chance for any of the aspirations to be met when all that ordinary people do is destroyed or discredited. For instance, we say the workforce participation rate of women is falling. Actually, they are doing more work than they ever did. But you don't categorise what they do as work because it is mostly unpaid work. If you start accepting what they do as work, which it is, their participation rate might probably be higher than that of men. Forget about solving any such problem in an era of neoliberal capitalism when the policy framework is explicitly designed to destroy those millions of livelihoods.

Technology is often touted as a solution to all labour-related troubles. What do you make of this call for machines to replace people?

A great part of this is based on an illusionary understanding of how capitalism developed. The standard thing you were taught about the industrial revolution is: at a time when millions of peasants were being displaced across Europe, when lakhs of peasantry were thrown off the land in England, aha, the Industrial Revolution came along, factories opened, absorbed them ... there was about forty to fifty years of misery, which allowed guys like Charles Dickens to earn a living, and then everything was fine, wages rose, and the Industrial Revolution of capitalism was so clearly superior to everything else. So they will look at the displacement of Indian peasantry, fifteen million fewer farmers in 2011, than in 1991 and say, this is inevitable, this is what happened in England and Europe and the US.

But it's actually not what happened. When peasantry were thrown off in England, it's not as if they all rushed to the factories and wages rose and everything was fine in the industrial working class. Simple economics, simple question—if millions of people descend on the city for work, will wages go up or down? Now your umpteen Tamil Nadu engineering graduates, is their presence likely to make wages go up or down? Companies are willing to throw out those who worked for them for ten–fifteen years to make a cheap saving with these guys. Because there are only so many options for the victims.

In Industrial Revolution England, they had enslaved about a hundred-odd nations, which were colonies, and people had the option of migrating. That's how the US, Canada, New Zealand and Australia were populated by white Europeans. In the case of Australia, you keep hearing this disparaging remark that many of those who migrated were criminals; actually many were peasants dispossessed of their land, fighting for their land, criminalised by the State, and then thrown out. Like here we created criminal tribes. The British did that here. So many of those people were Scots and Irish. A large number of Irish went to the US. People were driven by economic imperatives. Their livelihoods were broken at home. They had the option of going to the white colony, the temperate colonies, the tropical colonies. Even in India, when the twentieth century dawned, there were nearly a million Europeans. That's the way industry would have liked to have kept it. The way the capitalists wanted to keep it. Nineteenth-century London was one of the filthiest places to live on earth, if you didn't live in mansions. Garbage and sewage was on every street, other than the protected, beautiful part of London. That was what a Dickens could see. How horrifying life was for 99 per cent of the people. As these people began to migrate, it pushed wages up. Now the capitalists had to think—if we don't put the wages at this level, they're going to leave. The number of people migrating from the UK between 1815—end of Waterloo—and 1914—start of World War I—accounted for half the annual growth rate of population each year. In that period, fifty-five million people left Europe. And you'll find in Wisconsin in the US, a lot of people of Finnish descent. In Dakota, many descended from Swedes. There are provinces in northern Sweden where a third of the population went. That sends up wages.

What options do developing countries have today? Go out and colonise and make slaves? A lot of this stuff is based on this crazy assumption that this is how it is: agriculture will collapse, industry will rise. Agriculture is indeed in a terrible state, and it's being taken over by corporations, leaving even fewer options and livelihoods. So you have no way of solving this within the existing philosophies and ruling ideologies.

Outside of museums and archives, where will we find the great and good skills of yesteryears?

In India, you can still find it on the streets, always. There are two reasons why museums have never taken off in India. Now there are, I think, children in Mumbai, Chennai, Kolkatta and Delhi, who have visited the Louvre, the Rijksmuseum and other great ones in Europe. But many will be hard pressed to name the major museum in their city. And probably have never set foot in it.

Firstly, it has to do with the class orientation of thinking that everything that is great and beautiful is in the Western museums. Secondly, many of the Western museums are full of relatively young material of a few hundred years. India and other third world countries go back three or four thousand years. But we have never promoted museums in India. Look at the funding for museums. Some of the great ones are in utter disrepair, cracking up. So are libraries and archives. It's a social, political and national attitude to museums. But there's another reason why they've never taken off. The Western museums showcase the best and the most beautiful paintings. I just love the Van Gogh Museum in Amsterdam. They also have exhibitions of other painters, impressionists, etc. The painting styles exist because there are museums. And they have ceased to exist elsewhere.

In India, the beautiful miniatures, the brass work, the carvings/engravings that you see in the museum, you'll probably find someone producing something similar on the pavement outside the museum. In Mahabalipuram, all around those pagodas and rathas, there are people still practising sculpturing forms they claim have directly descended from residents of the ancient town. The fact is, there are descendants of many Indian traditions that have kept them alive. The attitude for a lot of people will be, why do I need to go and see those miniature Rajasthani paintings in the museum when I can buy them off the streets of Jaipur. Many traditions and schools of Western museums are dead but for the museum—and preserved there in mothballs. In India, these are living traditions: the brass work, woodwork, tapestry, embroidery ... all of that continues. It is alive in our society. But they are being destroyed. And therefore one day, you're going to need museums (of a very different kind, I hope from the ones we have now).

Why are time and skills never factored into any calculation of profit and loss, for most traditional livelihoods? Skills that involve the mind/head always factor that in; but rarely those that involve the hand.

Welcome to capitalism.

Also, it's not just time and skills, it's labour itself that they will not respect, because they've got to make their money out of the product of that labour—by exploiting that labour, by keeping the wages down. It's with farming, artisans, everybody. Untouchability itself is such a weapon to perpetuate a permanently demoralised gene pool of labour, whom we can exploit at will and command. Or, let's take farming and how we classified 'skilled' and 'unskilled' when this country became independent.

By the way, no matter what the theory on paper, one shorthand definition you can take of 'unskilled' in Indian society—anything that a woman does is unskilled. In agriculture, everything that the woman does is unskilled. Problem is, women do more work. If you're going to start paying fair, civilised, living wages, your costs are going to go up incredibly. Take, for instance, paddy transplantation. Anyone talking about unskilled and skilled, I want them to do paddy transplantation for five days in the season. Let's look at their rate of failure and success and see how much skill it requires. Paddy transplantation requires incredible amounts of skill. But it's 'unskilled' because it's done by women. Dairy, livestock, all these are called unskilled because they're dominated by women. You and I recognise a weaver as a skilled person. But even that's going. Even though he's a male, it's going. We rate training him as an autorickshaw driver as a higher skill than two thousand years of weaving.

It's to do with labour as a whole; their work isn't respected, and increasingly, we'll use weapons to break that down further. You broke that down by destroying their collective bargaining power and smashing all their unions, which did them a great deal of good. You did all that and now you suffer. What's factored in the calculation, in the capitalistic framework, is profit. And profit depends on how much you can push your costs down. You're going to do everything you can to see that those costs go down.

There's a great erosion of biodiversity, be it in indigenous breeds or seeds. What can the State do and what has it not done?

What can the State do? In this sector, I just wish the State hadn't done anything, if you look at the record of all that it has done.

Again here, for the brainwashed, middle-class mind: what's West is best. So your Kangayam, Gir and Vechur are useless cattle, but Jerseys and Holsteins and Swiss Browns are good. This comes from an urban mind and development mindset that sees cattle purely as milk machines and have no other role. Farmers still have many other roles for cattle, including poor people owning what you think of as emaciated cattle, called scrub or so-called 'nondescript' cattle.

Landowners pay farmers to pen these cattle in their fields after the harvests because their dung organically fertilises the soil. Many Indian breeds were simply swept into this thing called nondescript. Only the most recognised Indian breeds were classified for us by someone else.

It's like foods in India. The British came here. There were incredibly rich cereals, millets that they didn't understand and didn't know. So what they did with your lentils was to feed them to their birds, cattle and livestock. That's how you got the names for your lentils—chickpea, cowpea, pigeon pea. They saw them as inferior foods. They recognised rice and wheat. People in many parts of India consumed millets a lot more than they do today. In Anathapur, till this day, many of the older generation eat ragi mudha. We destroyed many of our cereals, our food varieties, and today, generations are longing for rice and wheat. Only ten or twelve years ago, the government woke up and created a Millets Revival Mission. In fact, food crop itself was declining because we were increasing cash crop production. The British classified our local cereals, apart from wheat and rice—and it's a classification we accepted and used for sixty years in our government documents—as coarse cereals. These are incredibly nutritious and sustainable cereals. This was the downgrading of Indian foods and species. We have absorbed that. And it's very difficult to get (re)habituated to ragi. It needs a revival in the region where it evolved.

If you read my book, *Everybody Loves a Good Drought*, you'll find, we not only despised our local species of cattle but also actively followed and implemented policies that rendered them extinct. Like Khariar and Vechur cattle. The Kerala Livestock Act of 1968 made it illegal for people to breed some of the local species. Where is the question of biodiversity? Then with BT seeds, we have destroyed god knows how many varieties of local cotton. When BT failed—as it was sure to—where are those seeds? They're gone.

If you look at the last two or three livestock censuses, cattle populations have been declining as a whole. Small animal population, owned by poor people—pigs, goats—have seen a precipitous decline in many cases. And desi breeds of cattle account for a huge drop. There was supposed to have been a 2017 livestock census. I believe they started on it at least a year later than scheduled. It's going to show a terrible trend. When I last checked they had still not finished training the surveyors in the use of tabs to digitally record their census data.

Why are the 70 per cent of Indians living outside the great metros so poorly represented in the media? Why are their stories not recorded?

Not only the poor living outside the great metros, even the poor living within are not represented in the media. National dailies publishing from Delhi devote, on average, 0.67 per cent of their front page to rural India, where 69 per cent of the population lives. Why do they do this? Because corporations have reduced journalism to a revenue stream in the last thirty years. For me, paid news, fake stuff, is not an aberration. It's entirely true to the characteristic and logic of profit-seeking corporate media. 'I will do what makes money for me; I will cover you if that makes money for me.' So people don't cover you if you don't add to their revenue.

With all the publicity in the world that experiments by far-off little NGOs and others get, how much has your media spoken about or looked at, let alone celebrated, perhaps the greatest gender-justice-cum-poverty-alleviation programme in the world, which is Kudumbashree with 4.5 million members? Every second household in Kerala—which has a population of nine million—is represented in Kudumbashree, which means this is the poorer population. Also remember, there is a membership limit of one woman per household. Here are people who are doing collective and group farming. At a time when farming is collapsing all over the country, they make profits. They're landless people who have taken lands on lease to make those farms work. But they're not covered because a) they're poor; b) they're poor women; c) they don't make revenue for me.

It's a very different media from what emerged in the freedom struggle—the Indian Press was the child of the freedom struggle. It was idealism driven. Its owners, its editors, were in and out of prison much of their lives. The existing media has converted itself into prisons for employees and re-education camps for their audiences. The richest man in your country is the biggest media owner. It is a continent-sized conflict of interest. It is a herd of elephants in the bedroom. But you don't want to see it. You want to believe that the media is this independent institution. There are lots of independent journalists in those institutions; increasingly, they're being weeded out and thrown out. Journalism jobs are on the decline. Whereas PR jobs are growing at the rate of 3:1 [to journalism] in much of the world, because everywhere corporatisation of the media is taking place, which means the media will be like any other industry. Only worse, because it was not meant to be in that mould. So, you're not going to see a lot of poor people covered.

The fundamental feature of the media of our time is the growing disconnect between mass media and mass reality. Occasionally, there will be times like the Gujarat earthquake or the Kerala floods that forces them to cover things. Once in five years—we still happen to be an electoral democracy—they have to cover poor people. That's what makes the average 0.67 per cent. You remove the election year, it falls to 0.24 per cent.

The media is the most exclusionist institution of Indian democracy, caste-wise, class-wise, gender-wise. And the kind of corporations that own them are rent-seeking, profit-seeking. There's a huge need for diversity in the media, for democratisation of the media. The only genuine efforts that can happen are if there are major non-corporate, non-status media houses which can cover the poor and enable them to find their place in it. When that happens, it also has a forced impact on the corporate media. That they have to suddenly broaden a few things in order to meet the challenge. That's how some of it gets into the corporate media as well.

Besides this, there are thousands of individual well-meaning journalists, in corporate media, whose struggle is always: How do you sell your labour without selling your soul? You have to break the extremely concentrated monopoly ownership in media, if you want your media to be any different. As you know, there are non-corporate, non-status efforts. That's why my friends and I built the People's Archive of Rural India, the only website dedicated wholly to the Indian countryside.

Why does any crisis in farming have a ripple effect in the entire rural economy? What is the solution for this?

You are an agrarian society and agrarian is much bigger than farming. Agrarian draws its name from agriculture, no doubt, but everything in rural India is not agriculture. So not everybody in an agrarian society is directly in cultivation. The carpenters, weavers, potters, smiths—they are all part of an agrarian society. When farming collapses, all those related livelihoods, occupations, all of which fall within agrarian society, take a hit. When farming collapses, the carpenters starve to death. We've recorded cases of that in *The Hindu*. Every village has a couple of carpenter families, of a particular caste, the mistris of the village. Now that person very often draws 30 per cent of his income in cash, the rest in kind. People give so many bags of rice, so many kilos of produce. Now if nobody in the village creates a new bullock cart for ten years, nobody asks for a new plough, nobody asks for repairs of old tools, let alone new tools—the carpenter is finished. Weavers, their first market is the agricultural labourers and marginal farmers who wear the soft white cloth. Now, they're wearing t-shirts from China.

In the larger agrarian society, farmers are a smaller percentage than what people believe them to be. In the 2011 census, the main cultivator—the person who cultivates or works on a piece of land for at least 180 days, if that was the criterion—was less than 8 per cent of the population at that time. But there are millions of others who are connected to farming, part-time; there are others for whom, even if they haven't touched a plough, their output is dependent on what's happening in agriculture. So if you have policies that are destructive to farming, agriculture and rural India—all three of which we have—you're going to have this problem.

Is there an advantage to organising workers of various livelihoods? When and how should it happen?

Of course. Obviously. If the weavers had a strong national association, their bargaining power would have been far greater. Except, the whole nature of our development is aimed at destroying collective bargaining. The bulk of farmers are non-unionised, even though various organisations exist for farmers. And those farm unions that have strength are generally strong in some regions, not so much in others. Weavers are a pan-Indian group. But they're too poor and there are not enough organised efforts to get them together and fight. Farmers are a classic example. When they get collectively organised, they change the terms of trade. They challenge governments and bring them down. Farm distress was an issue in both 2004 and 2014 elections. It went against the governments of the day. But unions have been destroyed in every sector. Including journalism. With that, the independence of the journalist is gone; when you're in an eleven-month contract, and in the eighth month, with three EMIs on your head, the brand manager starts telling you what to do in politics and reporting.

What do you think will be the biggest problem the country faces in the coming years—under employment or open unemployment? Which, in your opinion, is more dangerous?

The single biggest problem the country faces already and which can only get worse in the coming years is gross and utterly ruinous inequality. As I've said in my new introduction to *Everbody Loves a Good Drought*, even in the year 2000, according to Credit Suisse's Global Wealth Databook, the top 1 per cent of the Indian population held 36.8 per cent of the total household wealth. By 2016, their share had risen to 58.4 per cent, far ahead of their counterparts in the US, whose share of wealth in their nation was 42.1 per cent. That also means that the top 1 per cent of Indians held a greater share of wealth that year within our nation than the top 1 per cent of Americans ever did within theirs. The same year, the Databook shows, the bottom 10 per cent of Indians saw their share fall from 0.1 to -0.7 per cent, the minus sign suggesting that the assets of many millions were far lower than their liabilities and they were sinking further into debts.

The next two deciles, just above the -0.7 group, recorded shares of 0.2 and 0.5 per cent, respectively. Club those three together and it means the bottom 30 per cent of the Indian population owned next to nothing.

No society can sustain indefinitely those levels of inequality. The breakdown is already showing in rural distress, in farm suicides, in a thousand ways.

When or how do you think traditional livelihoods can be made appealing/aspirational for the younger lot?

What's actually happening now is that groups of elite society are appropriating those traditional skills. You can see that in weaving and art— where we've already succeeded in taking weavers, the skilled traditional ones, and continuing their bondage in a different form, so that you come out with elite labels which don't tell you who the weaver is (significant in an era where designer clothes have exotic names on them).

When I was a kid, we used to buy cloth for ₹3 or ₹5 a metre, and stitch our school uniforms. Good cotton cloth. On that depended many livelihoods, from the farmer to the tailor. Then we were all brainwashed. The sexy thing in the 1960s was readymade. Kids were dying to be seen in readymade clothes. Here, you had the privilege of tailored clothing, which only the richer millionaires in the West can afford in their countries, and we wanted readymade. Then came synthetics. The most horrendous clothing imaginable for this country. As the weavers are destroyed, a few elite houses come up, which monopolise the weaving sector. And what you could have got from your weaver, if you were willing to pay a decent ₹300, you now pay ₹1,700 or more because you buy it with a label, and only a very small fraction of that goes back to the weaver.

I think it's not enough to make just the livelihood appealing; you have to make the idea of justice appealing. I believe it's there in every young child and among young people, and we spend a lifetime socialising them into losing that value. Growth cannot be only in terms of output and figures. Economists who place people at the centre of their thinking tell you that you have to get your growth through justice. Not with justice, not justice as an afterthought, but growth itself has to come *through* justice.

Part II

... and a Song

Thaka Thari Kita Thaka

It was a boil so big it nearly pushed his eye shut.

It popped up on Kali Veerapathiran's face, near his left eye, three days before a big bharatanatyam performance, making him fret. His mother Ellamalli applied a paste of turmeric and healing leaves of anthimanthaarai. 'How this hurts!' Kali groaned, after sending me a photo—a molehill that looked like a mountain in the close-up. 'How will I keep my eyes open? I look awful. How will I do the bhavam? I'm so nervous.'

It is not unusual for twenty-six-year-old Kali to be anxious before a dance recital. He is a perfectionist and wants everything just so. He worries about the costume colours, about his weight, and about remembering the steps of the complex and long varnam, even after practising it for hours everyday, for many weeks, with the most demanding and caring teacher. He jogs to build up his stamina, goes on a diet, and then he worries about the boils on his face.

But once the velvet curtain goes up, Kali forgets his fears. He just dances.

Kali is not an infrequent performer—he is part of many dance dramas, solo shows and big productions in a year. They are not always bharatanatyam recitals, for Kali is also proficient in three ancient folk styles of Tamil Nadu: karagattam, thappattam and oyilattam. This makes him probably the only folk dancer in the state to have learnt and mastered bharatanatyam.

When Kali was awarded the prestigious Spirit of Youth Award in 2016 from the Chennai-based Music Academy—Carnatic music's 'spiritual home' and the 'fount of knowledge, structure and classicism'[1]—there was much rejoicing. There were also whispers: 'Is he the first Dalit to have won it?' He probably is. Kali was hailed as a promising young dancer, 'talented' and 'hard-working'.

Kali had smashed invisible caste, class and gender barriers that encouraged only girls from upper-caste and upper-class families to take up bharatanatyam, and mostly as a hobby rather than a serious livelihood option. Nobody would have predicted this young boy born to construction labourers from a fishing village, away from the sabhas of Chennai, to have gotten so far.

This is his story.

Thari thana jonnu thimi
Thaka thari kita thaka
Thathinginathom, thathinginathom, thathinginathom

Eight-year-old Kali heard these solkattus for the first time on television, in the film *Thillana Mohanambal* made a quarter century before he was born. Little Kali was enchanted by actor Padmini and her dazzling costume; he was floored by the drumbeats of the mridangam. He watched with unblinking eyes as Padmini hid her face behind red-stained fingers and peeped at the hero Sivaji Ganesan in the song *Maraindhirundu Paarkum Marumamenna*. Kali copied her, as she enacted the navarasas with her eyes and lips, face and fingers. Like her, he wanted to wear salangai, rich costume and fine jewellery. Like her, he wanted to dance bharatanatyam. There was just one problem—nobody taught the dance form in his village.

An ancient and classical art form that originated in South India, bharatanatyam was previously practised by the Devadasi community. Today, it is danced mostly by the upper castes and the moneyed; many of its renowned practitioners live and perform in Chennai city.

However, in Kovalam—only 30 km away from Chennai, where Kali was born and raised— money was scarce and almost never spent on dance lessons. The families, many of whom lived off the sea, would not appreciate their boys taking it up as a profession.

Kali's family are Adi Dravidars, a Dalit community. For years, his parents had carried headloads of bricks and sand all day in the hot sun to build other people's houses. They had met on one such construction site, got married and had six children. Kali, the youngest, never really knew his father Veerapathiran, who had died when he was a baby. Unable to bring up so many children, his mother sent him to her mother. And there, at his grandmother's house, his aunt Rani looked after him like a son.

With big waves and bigger boulders, Kali's childhood was spent happily by the beach. There were women who loudly hawked fish and men who went in catamarans to catch them. There were plenty of tourists and festivals and after school, like all the other boys, Kali played outdoors and watched TV. Unlike the other boys, he also wanted to dance bharatanatyam.

Chennai's classical dance and music scene is fiercely competitive and quietly exclusionary. The classical arts do not reach all the communities in Tamil Nadu today, said Karunakara Menon, senior civil servant and former director-in-charge, Kalakshetra. 'It's still largely upper caste and Brahminical in all the South Indian states, except Kerala. How many non-Brahmins practise classical music or dance? It will be a very miniscule number in the cities. But once you leave the cities, the participation will be more limited.'

Many of the budding artists in the city are also privately tutored and personally groomed. 'Even the simplest things matter: which family you're born in, whether you have a support system,' said Nrithya Pillai, Chennai-based bharatanatyam dancer and teacher and Kali's contemporary. Nrithya comes from the Vazhuvoor Nattuvanar lineage, a Isai Vellalar community,[2] from which bharatanatyam originated.[3] 'If you're rich, things will work for you. By which I also mean belonging to a particular society and having certain connections. You need not necessarily be from a certain community or caste, but it helps if you don't belong to certain castes. It's good for you if you're not a Dalit or an Isai Vellalar, also if you are not dark-skinned.'

Nrithya was questioned on social media for an article she wrote and the 'critic' wondered if she wanted reservation in music and dance. You make it if you are talented, was the underlying argument. 'But,' Nrithya told me, 'this whole thing about merit is bullshit.' She had to fight for her right to perform bharatanatyam when she was nineteen, although she had showed keen interest and talent since she was three. She did not have an arangetram, the debut performance that is every bharatanatyam dancer's privilege and the platform through which a guru presents a student to the world.

People have caste detectors. 'They will scan you and decide whether you deserve their attention or not. If you don't look a certain way: if you're not fair, slim and do not conform to their idea of a conventional good-looking dancer, then they will tell you: "What you're doing is not art."'

Kali and his siblings were supported by his mother's small income from her coolie work. His three sisters too worked in an export company. While his oldest brother did odd jobs, his second brother died of 'brain fever' when he was sixteen. By the time Kali was fifteen, he too had to take on part-time jobs—he handed out tickets at the local cinema, cleaned dining tables at a resort and operated rides in an amusement park. 'I was in charge of the giant wheel. Sometimes, I went and sat in one of the baskets and just kept going up and down, up and down.'

Four years after the December 2004 tsunami struck his village, sixteen-year-old Kali put together a dance for the inauguration of the tsunami relief centre. In the audience were Sara Chanda and Pius Kalathil, who ran Gremaltes Hospital in Chennai, and they were impressed with Kali's show. They offered to send him to dance school and pay the fees.

When Kali set out to visit Kalakshetra on the advice of Chanda and Kalathil, he did not know it was one of the premier dance schools in the country. He mistook it for a forest; it was so full of trees. There, he met Leela Samson, a celebrated classical dancer who was then Kalakshetra's director. She spoke to him kindly and asked him to dance in front of another teacher. Kali hurriedly tied a saree over his trousers and danced to a film song. They told him he had the making of a classical dancer.

As Kali remained undecided on what to do after high school, he heard that the nearby Dakshinachitra, a heritage centre, offered free classes on folk dance—a term that loosely clubs several centuries-old dance forms that originated in Tamil Nadu's villages, and is still practised and performed there, especially during festivals.

In a month, Kali mastered three ancient dances—karagattam—performed by men and women with a heavy pot balanced on the head; oyilattam—a graceful dance, performed mostly by men; and thappattam—in which dancers play their own handheld drums, the thappu. His teacher Kannan Kumar was delighted. But just as Kali began learning a new form, devarattam, he was invited to join Kalakshetra as a student.

The first time Kali performed bharatanatyam—the film-inspired, self-taught version of it—for a school function when he was eight years old, the audience loved it. When he got off the stage, women circled his head with aarti to ward off the evil eye and bought him cool drinks. From then on, for every function at school and at the church, he was asked to dance.

While an eight-year-old dancing to entertain is one thing, an eighteen-year-old wanting to make a career out of it is quite another. Kali continued to have parallel dreams. Sometimes he wanted to act in films, sometimes he wanted to be a teacher, and sometimes he wanted to become a bio-technologist.

His father too had been a therukkuttu performer. From his mother's stories, Kali learnt that his father had an exceptional voice and used to portray Karna from the *Mahabharata*. 'If he acted on this street, you could hear him on the next! His voice had such a throw!' said Kali. 'For three years after their wedding in 1972, appa acted. Then his kuttu teacher died. Other forms of entertainment came in. My father stopped performing. Amma says he was a handsome man, with a big moustache.' Kali twirled the luxurious, invisible one on his face.

Ellamalli had also been an ardent fan of the arts and had enjoyed watching kuttu performances in the village when she was newly married. She encouraged Kali to do whatever he wished to pursue. 'My friends were keen on me joining them in an engineering college,' said Kali. 'But my mother didn't have money for college fees. If I went to Kalakshetra, I reasoned, she wouldn't have to worry about the fees as Sara Chanda would sponsor it.'

Kali did not fully understand what it would mean to be a bharatanatyam dancer. 'In Kovalam, dance is seen as a rich man's art, and not something that needs a formal, college training.' There was nobody to advise him. His maama ridiculed him that it was a waste of time and his friends teased him about becoming feminine.

The first time I met Kali in April 2013, he was a third-year student at Kalakshetra and helped me find my way around the dance school's tree-filled hundred acres. The expressive eyes on his striking face revealed him to be a dancer, even before introductions. I was there to write about the dance school for a newspaper. It was warm for eight in the morning, but the path was covered with fallen leaves, filtered sunshine and pools of velvety shadow. The only sound but for our slippers scraping the dry earth was bird song.

'The silence is calming,' I said.

'The silence was so scary when I joined here. In Kovalam, where I grew up, it was always noisy. I was too terrified to even sleep when I first came here.'

This unsettling silence was the least of Kali's troubles when he set foot on campus. He had never before learnt bharatanatyam formally; all he knew was what he had picked up from the television, and of course, a solid grounding in the folk dances. If the precision of bharatanatyam, its solkattus, were nothing like the folk dances he had trained in, the Sanskrit of Carnatic music was as foreign to him as English. Having only known film songs till then, he could not keep a tune and was not familiar with even the name of any ragam. Kali withdrew, unable to communicate with his classmates, many of them from Kerala and a few from outside the country.

Small-town Tamil Nadu doesn't send as many dancers or musicians to Kalakshetra as Kerala; an irony, given the art form originated in the state. Several reasons are cited for these skewed numbers, including Tamil Nadu's penchant for professional degrees and the arts being seen only as 'extracurricular'. Children might be taught bharatanatyam, they are not encouraged to take it up as a career. It only gets more dire in folk dances.

Menon laid out the differences in, and the reasons behind, the perception of and access to the arts in Tamil Nadu and Kerala: 'In the latter, thanks to a fertile arts environment, they [artists from less-privileged backgrounds] can dance at temple festivals, teach in schools and make a living. Classical art in Kerala today has a very democratic access structure. People from backgrounds traditionally unconnected to the classical arts have started becoming passionately involved in them. This was possible because of a strong and sustained positive intervention by the state government and the creation of independent social institutions such as youth festivals through both private and government efforts.'

For a boy from a Tamil medium school, with little or no exposure to bharatanatyam or Carnatic music, life in Kalakshetra was daunting. The food was strictly vegetarian, lacking in the meat he was used to. Though Kali never faced caste-based discrimination inside the dance school, there were times when he felt left out, being the lone Tamilian on campus.

The rigorous curriculum was also physically exhausting. When his legs hurt, Kali went home to Kovalam and his mother pressed them for him. He cried sometimes, wanting to quit. His mother simply said, 'Okay, then go herd buffaloes.' Kali was shocked. 'Then keep dancing.' She gave him a choice, only one.

At the end of his fourth year in Kalakshetra, Kali rang me one day. 'Akka, you are cordially invited for my exam kutcheri. Please grace the occasion with family and friends.' After a two-tick pause, he asked softly, 'Is that correct English, akka?' It was nearly as fluent and effortless as his Tamil.

'I became a different person in Kalakshetra.'

Even as he struggled with the anxieties brought on by a new environment, Kali began to converse with his classmates through gestures. 'I used dance movements to ask if someone if they have eaten. Then, I asked my friends to teach me sentences in English and used it to invite them home for lunch.' His mother's chicken and fish curries became a big hit among his classmates.

'I was so fat when I joined. I used to dance like this.' He stuck out his bottom to illustrate. 'And my legs would be wonky.' Slowly, he lost weight, found friends and got used to the vegetarian fare of idli, dosa and oothappam in the canteen. 'I didn't always eat like this when I was growing up.'

In the evenings, Kali played football or practised kuttu, a vigorous dance form. His confidence grew, and so did his classical training. He could identify ragas in a trice. At performances in the sacrosanct Rukmini Arangam—named after the legendary dancer and founder of Kalakshetra, Rukmini Devi Arundale—he guessed the ragas and checked with his friends if he was right. He usually was. He had topped his class in his first year, after all.

His dance too had come a long way.

On the day of his exam kutcheri in 2014, Kali's batch of eight danced a margam—a set of dances performed in a sequence. Kali's mother, his brother Rajini who now runs an idli shop in Kovalam, his three sisters and their families, and his friends came all the way to cheer him on.

When I went up and congratulated Rajini, on Kali's splendid performance, he said matter-of-factly, 'We don't understand all this dancing. It's nice that you found it good.' But they were proud of him—they hugged him, and together they posed for pictures to mark the occasion.

Soon after, Kali joined the postgraduate diploma course in Kalakshetra and continued to do well—he topped his class in vocals in the first and second year, passed the degree with a first class, and was declared the best outgoing student of 2016.

'Rukmini Devi laid the foundation for a very democratic access to arts, cutting across economic strata and communities not normally associated with it,' said Menon. 'Where else but Kalakshetra,' he asked, 'do you find a boy from a fishing village, a labourer's son and a Mexican dancing to the same Sankarabaranam varnam side-by-side?'

The history of appropriation of this art form—'where there was once sadir with its "fallen" Devadasis, there was now bharatanatyam, bursting with Sanskritic purity'[4]—and its 'institutionalization' and 'standardization' in Kalakshetra, is long and complex. But for Kali—and for others like him—it opened its gates and embraced a folk dancer from a marginalised background who wanted to learn bharatanatyam.

Kali's aptitude for abhinayam comes from his folk dance training, said Priya Murle, who judged the Spirit of Youth competition and is an acclaimed bharatanatyam performer, choreographer and teacher. 'If you're a little rich girl, you will not have life experiences. For you to say something, you need to have gone through something. Kali's struggle shows in every fibre.'

Many of Kali's teachers and contemporaries recognise his brilliance. 'In all my years of teaching,' said Nirmala Nagarajan, a Kalakshetra teacher and Kali's mentor, 'I have come across very few dancers for whom nrittya and abhinayam are equally strong.'

No other folk dancer has mastered bharatanatyam, said Kali's folk teacher Kannan, and according to him, the converse is true as well. 'There are lots of bharatanatyam dancers who want to learn folk. But their learning is limited to the steps they want to perform on stage. If you balance a pot on your head and shake your hips, will it make you a karagattam expert?' Except, he lamented, that is exactly what happens. 'And you know what? They all get by because they can talk very well!'

While one would assume a dancer trained in other genres to be welcomed into a different style, it is usually not the case with classical forms. Folk dances are not received well in 'formal' settings either, where the art form is looked down upon. Like the time Kannan faced opposition from a Chennai school when he went to teach thappattam. 'I don't wish to name the school, but they asked how something that's played in funerals could be taught to their students. After much debate, that class took place.' When he tried to perform in a sabha, he was asked how something that is danced on the street could be performed there.

Kannan's experience is not an aberration but the norm. As the director for education and culture at Madras Crafts Foundation, when author, educationist and cultural activist Devika arranged for a folk dance recital in Krishna Gana Sabha in the mid-1980s, one of the first to do so, a fight broke out. When she tried to take folk art forms to schools, she faced resistance. 'I brought artists to the city and organised for demos in school assemblies. I worked with two hundred schools. But initially, the schools did not treat the folk artists well; while they were made to sit under a tree, classical dancers were welcomed with a red carpet. After the demo, however, folk performers became heroes.'

Even when setting foot in an intimidating new world with strict lines drawn between what is 'proper' and what is not, Kali did not leave behind his folk training. In his first year in Kalakshetra, he taught Russian and South African students to perform oyilattam on stage.

Kali looks at being trained in folk dance as a huge advantage. 'You need a lot of stamina and energy to perform folk dances. And that really helps when I dance classical.' The folk forms he is trained in were traditionally performed mostly by men, yet they are 'very graceful'. The general perception is that folk art forms corrupt a classical dancer's training. But Kali finds little truth in it.

'In bharatanatyam, there are rules. You hold your hands in a straight line for the natyarambham. I cannot say, I will hold my hands unevenly, instead. There is a specific expression for a certain bhavam.' Whereas, folk dances are less restricting. 'It is joy, happiness, abandon. Nobody will tell you that your hand has to go up this side and touch the ground on that side.' But Kali believes in letting the dances he knows inform each other. He finds shades of bharatanatyam even in salsa, which he learnt out of interest. 'The other students in the salsa class suffered. But I was able to cope because some of the moves require you to position your knees and feet similar to how we do in bharatanatyam.'

In an electrifying performance that Kali put together with his artist friends in 2019 for Svanubhava—a cultural movement which aims to 'cultivate a sensitivity to the arts amongst the future generations of India'—near Coimbatore, the troupe showcased the similarities between classical and folk dance forms: bharatanatyam and oyilattam; kuchupudi and karagattam; odissi and devarattam; kathak and thappattam. The highlight, though, was a question from the audience: Of all the dances that were presented, which was the 'mother dance'? While Kali's co-performer said it was Bharatha Muni's Natya Shastra, suggesting that classical forms were the first to emerge, Kali instead spoke of what must have been the motivation for humankind to have danced: for relaxation, for recreation, after a hard day's work on the field. That first dance—which he desisted from naming or even categorising—gave birth to all forms, said Kali. He effectively upheld the folk forms, but without resorting to putting down another dance form, one which he equally respects and loves.

With two diplomas from a premier dance institution and six years of training in a classical art form—one with considerable social and cultural capital—Kali still found the going tough. He was not earning much and he was no longer sheltered by the dance school. He could not move back to Kovalam, as rehearsals and programmes took place in the city. There were days when he went without a meal. Kali was determined to support his mother financially—who had to quit working as her health deteriorated—and this added to the pressure of looking for a steady income.

An exciting offer to teach in a Texas-based dance school for a year did come his way. But he eventually declined this as he was just beginning to make a name for himself in Chennai and wanted to train further with his bharatanatyam teacher in the city. Another opportunity presented itself, something that better matched his needs at that time—a teaching job in Kalakshetra under the Scheduled Caste quota. One week before the interview, he hurt his leg badly in a two-wheeler accident. He could barely stand on the day of the interview, let alone dance. He did not get the job.

By mid-2019, Kali was making between ₹10,000 and ₹15,000 a month from performances and from choreographing shows for schools and corporates. This was supplemented by a monthly stipend of ₹5,000 from T.M. Krishna's Sumanasa Foundation, which he has been receiving since late 2016.

Whatever money he makes, his first priority is his mother, for whom he sets aside ₹3,000, and sometimes an additional ₹2,000 for her medicines. The rent for his room in Chennai—a small space where he sleeps on a floor mat—eats up another ₹6,000 a month. The room also contains his important possessions: all his awards and mementos. He cooks in the tiny kitchen sometimes, but mostly eats out, in Chennai's iconic thattu kadais, literally, plate shops, which sell affordable food at street corners, and keeps his food expenses under ₹2,000 a month. To get around the city, Kali depends on his scooter that he won as a prize on Zee TV's popular reality dance show, Dance Jodi Dance, in 2018. He paid ₹30,000 as gift tax—on something that costs ₹70,000 in the market—money that he had saved up, little by little.

'The problem for Kalakshetra kids is that they are excluded from all government jobs as they don't have a degree,' said Menon. The dance school awards a diploma at both undergraduate and postgraduate levels. Besides, 'in classical arts, the parameters of success are so completely fashioned by your access, your family position, and in turn by your caste, class or both.'

Kali found the dance community to be welcoming and encouraging, 'and were pleased that someone with a disadvantaged background had made it so far.' Though, nobody mentioned or discussed his caste in front of him. 'People have been good to me because of my family circumstances.' Economic hardship is more easily acknowledged and addressed than caste oppression.

'Dance is now some kind of sacred sacrifice that you don't ask a remuneration for. There are too many teachers in Chennai. Only America and workshops and teaching will bring in money,' said Nrithya. The other option is 'if you have access to a hundred kids from a gated community, with a nice community hall and charged ₹1,200 per kid. But can Kali or I do the same thing?' she asked.

Kannan finds the idea of teaching an art form abroad with the sole aim of making money to be repugnant. 'Is that art or business? You tell me. We're fighting hard to keep folk dances alive. In classical, it is becoming corporatised, a business.' Folk dances were never traditionally a full-time livelihood, said Kannan, making a case for not turning the performing arts into the sole means of sustenance. 'Folk artists used to have other occupations. When there were festivals, they went and danced. And, there were no formal lessons. Whoever was interested came and asked a senior performer to teach them. The student then went for performances with the teacher's troupe. The money, whatever was given, was divided among everybody. When I was young, I have seen nadaswaram players who ran barber shops—the instrument used to hang in their shop walls—and tavil players who ran laundry stores. We were farmers too and we raised cattle. When there were performances, we danced. Can there be festivals all the time? Can the government give us chances to perform all the time? Art might not sustain a family's expenses. If they're not living off this, they will not see it as a business. They will look at the dignity of the performance.'

When Kannan moved to Chennai in the 1990s from Zamin Kodangipatti village in Thoothukudi district, he worked as a security guard at night. 'Every night, I was a watchman. In the day, I went to schools to teach folk dance. They gave me ₹50. Sometimes, they gave me nothing!' Now, at seventy-two, he is probably the only full-time folk dance teacher in the state. He teaches in five schools, one each day of the week, and from this, he earns a fixed monthly salary of ₹25,000, enough for him and his family in Chennai. 'But this has come only after years and years of experience.'

Priya is of the same view, that it is not possible anymore to make a living as a full-time bharatanatyam performer. 'Everybody but the dancer on the stage makes money. To mount a solo performance costs at least ₹50,000. I don't pay for a chance to dance. So many do. A slot is ₹7,000–8,000 and one on weekend costs ₹11,000. But sometimes there are only ten or twenty people in the audience. If you're a star, you'll get more. But only teaching pays the bills.'

Performing on stage also involves paying for the space and the orchestra. But how does Kali manage it with his earning? 'I got lucky with this, actually. My very first solo performance was the Spirit of Youth competition. My guru Nirmala Nagarajan refused payment for teaching me a new set. I offered to collect money and give it to her, but she simply said no. The members of the orchestra also waived payment or took very little. They knew my situation, they never demanded anything.' This was an exception, he added. The rule is, you need deep pockets or connections. 'If you know famous dancers, then you can use that influence to get a performance slot. But so far, I've never paid for a sabha. All my programmes have been as part of competitions.' Dance is what took Kali outside his village, on a train and then a flight for the first time, then for many times after, to places like Malaysia and Singapore. Kali has also signed up for a master's degree in bharatanatyam from Madras University, hoping it would bolster his resume.

But luck is a rare ingredient. Kali's junior, M. Tamilselvan, faced stiff opposition from his family when he quit his job as a draughtsman to join Kalakshetra. His decision meant that the family was once again solely dependent on his aging father's income from his job as a security guard. Having had no acquaintance with dance or music, they resented him, a potential breadwinner choosing dance over a career. 'But my friends are sponsoring my fees. Even if I earn one rupee from dance, it will give me more happiness than what I earn being a draughtsman,' Tamilselvan told me in 2013. Kali's classmate K. Venugopal was more pragmatic. In Malayalam, laced with Tamil words for my benefit, he said, 'You can be a full-time performer only if you're from a rich family. Jeevika kaasu venum illaya, akka.' Doesn't one need money to live, sister?

If teaching options are not open to them, dancers have to depend on the money they make from staging performances. In Tamil Nadu, this is intrinsically linked to the sabha culture. Sabhas are not easy spaces to enter, said Kali. 'You need to be wealthy or famous. You should have family support, connections.' Pointing to his dark skin, he asked, 'If a foreigner and I go and ask for a chance, who will get it?' The question hung in the air, the answer evident. 'It will be very difficult for me if I said "I'm a Kalakshetra alumni. I will only dance in sabhas." Because, then, I will have to pay to perform.'

'I can tell you the politics of this dance in one line,' said Nrithya. 'When it was in my community, we took money and danced. Now, we pay money and dance.' Nrithya's grandfather, Swamimalai Rajarathnam Pillai, one of the keepers of bharatanatyam, used to feel threatened at dance conferences as the grammar of the art changed. 'I remember him saying that celebrated dancers recited shlokas and spoke in fluent English interspersed with dance jargon in Sanskrit. We were always told when we were younger, "Padichittu velaikku poidumma."' Get educated and get a job. Her grandmother used to tell her often: 'Indha paazhum kinathilla unna naan thallavey maaten,' an anguished cry promising never to push Nrithya into the disused well of dancing.

What used to be a dance form practised by the Devadasis is now mostly dominated by Brahmins. 'Many of the sabhas are run by them too,' said Kannan. '90 per cent of the audience is also from this community, just as it is for Carnatic music. They are the ones in the audience who keep talam during the performance. Do you and I do it? Now compare that with tavil, nadaswaram and folk songs—doesn't everybody appreciate it? Aren't there huge crowds?'

Classical music and dance don't have a wider reach because they are held within few communities, added Kannan. 'The classical forms have lots of problems. Reviews in newspapers are fixed or bought. When a well-to-do senior dancer-teacher is on the stage, nobody else appears on camera—not the younger, more talented dancer-students, not the nattuvanar, not the mridangam artist. Isn't this just publicity? How is this propagating the art?' He pooh-poohed the exclusionist spaces: 'Those who perform in sabhas cannot perform on the street; but those who dance on the street can also compete on the sabha stage.' He threw the challenge open to all artists: 'Why don't you take the arts to the streets? Do a good performance in a nice stage outside. If thousand people come to a sabha, ten thousand people will come to the street. Yes, you'll get a mixed crowd—art lovers, educated people, intellectuals, writers, everyday people and drunkards. At least ten people will be inspired to take up dancing. And they won't be put off by your caste or background, whatever it is!'

Kali lives out this philosophy as an artist. In his recent performance in Vaniyambadi, a village north of Chennai, he was paid ₹8,000 for the programme, apart from his food and transport expenses. 'Thousands of people were in the audience. The crowd was "vera level".' The crowd was another level.

Kali's Tamil, like his dance, doesn't belong to just one world, and traverses many dialects. 'I pick them up from all the people I interact with. And I switch between them, depending on whom I'm speaking to.' He sometimes speaks like many of his Kalakshetra friends, using Malayalam words; sometimes, he slips into the Brahminical dialect; at other times, it is the Chennai slang studded with words like 'machan', or bro, and 'gethu', or swag. Sometimes, he also mixes up the many Tamils. His friends in Kovalam scold him if he says '*Anga irrukarache*', the Brahminical Tamil for 'When I was there,' instead of '*Anga irundhappa*', in the dialect of the masses.

Over the years, Kali has taken bharatanatyam to several villages including Kovalam and its neighbouring villages, Mambakkam where his aunt lives, and Mahabalipuram, down the East Coast Road from Chennai.

Sabha culture is habit forming, said Kali. Seeing dancers getting applauded by an elite audience in a sabha, other dancers too desire it. 'Months after joining a dance class, kids want their arangetram. When you're dancing, it hardly matters where it is—a sabha stage or a village festival! I cannot see the audience anyway, as the lights are so bright. When I'm doing a devotional piece, I dance just for God and myself.' What can make or mar a performance is the choice of the repertoire being performed. 'I cannot put up the same set for a sabha audience and my people.' He infused 'my people' with affection. 'The sabha-goers are usually familiar with padams, which are more graceful and slow-moving. They'll appreciate its ragam and bhavam. A crowd in a village festival will grow restless. Only if I dance for a film song like *Azhagu Malar Aada*, will they appreciate it.' The popular song is from a super-hit film from the

1980s, *Vaidhehi Kaathirundhaal*, set to music by the renowned music composer Ilaiyaraaja and has shades of the classical raga Chandrakauns.[5] 'When I perform for this song, they appreciate not just the music, but the bharatanatyam as well.' Kali thinks of what he does as 'smart work'. 'In the beginning, I used to take my classical repetoire everywhere. It bombed.' He tried out alarippu, the rhythm-based invocatory piece that dancers first learn, at local functions. The audience was baffled. 'They didn't enjoy it, even though I put in so much effort. I understood then that you need not only hard work but also smart work. And that is knowing and adapting to the audience and performing accordingly.'

After he lost the Kalakshetra opportunity, Kali decided to start his own dance class in Kovalam and to take both classical and folk styles to children like him, who might have an interest, but not an avenue to learn the dance formally. Outside of a small circle, most kids are reluctant to learn both classical and folk dances. 'They think the former is slow and the latter is boring,' said Kali. 'So they go for Western dances. Maybe they should be taught in school. If they know these dances, they can pick up any other dance form.'

'That a student of mine wants to establish a school and teach both art forms is a source of great pride to me,' said Kannan. In a way, Kali is also following in Kannan's footsteps. 'Devarattam used to be performed only by our community, Rajakambalam Naicker, during festivals and other celebrations in villages of southern Tamil Nadu,' said Kannan. Seeing many appreciate the dance, his brother and he were keen to make it accessible to outsiders. 'We told the elders—who opposed the idea vehemently—that for the art to flourish, it needs to reach everyone. Now, it is danced everywhere.

This only works in favour of the community. For any art that's held within a closed community, it is they who have to make it available to outsiders. Others can't!' In the thirty years that he has observed the performance arts, Kannan does not think folk dances are dying anymore. But neither does he see them as flourishing.

For Kali's dance classes, a family friend and well-wisher in Kovalam, J. Sundar, offered to lend him Bruno Palace, a marriage hall he owned not far from Kali's childhood home, free of charge. On the day Kali took me to see Bruno Palace, he was also working out the many details of running the place. 'What should we choose for their uniform,' he asked his mother, showing her samples of colours and finally deciding on vadamalli, pinkish-purple, for the kurta and a leaf-green for the pyjama. Kali hoped to also make a living off this, charging ₹500 a student for two classes a week.

Few months after Kali started his dance class, his appearances on the second season of Dance Jodi Dance that began airing in late 2017 earned him fans and fame. People in Kovalam greeted him on the street, took pictures with him and congratulated his mother because he was a finalist, but not many were willing to pay to send their children to his dance school. He didn't win the dance show either. But these setbacks neither made him bitter nor unhappy.

In the last year, he made money from performances and did not have to depend on teaching. He is happy that his classmates from economically underprivileged backgrounds, just like him, now have well-paying jobs teaching bharatanatyam. But Kali wants something different for himself. 'If you teach, forty people will know you. If you perform, four thousand people will see you. When I go on a TV show, the audiences are so encouraging, they chant my name, and I feel such a thrill!' He told me this from the green room of a hotel in Karaikudi town, as he was getting ready for a Zee TV show. He WhatsApped me a photo of him, in a mustard yellow shirt and white dhoti, one hand on his hip, the other holding up his veshti in gethu, his chin raised, eyes smiling, confident.

Two years ago, Kali's ambition had stopped at starting a dance school. Now, he has set his goals a little higher, a little further—he wants to do what others haven't quite been able to do—making a living by performing two very different kinds of dances, slaying stereotypes along the way. 'I have a fire in my belly, a burning desire to learn and grow as a dancer. I want to be the best.'

'Is This Work Reserved for Their Caste?'

Bama is a celebrated Dalit woman writer. Fighting impossible odds, she completed her education, and the English translation of her first novel, *Karukku,* went on to win the Crossword Book Award in 2000. Through her novels, short stories and media articles, she critiques caste domination and social discrimination. Her works have been translated into English, French, Telugu, Kannada, Malayalam and Gujarati. She has been at the forefront of Dalit literary activism, and through the act of writing, she not only transgresses caste boundaries but also demolishes the conventional exclusions of language and genre.

Education is touted as a game changer and a springboard for the younger generation to break free from inherited occupations. In reality, do opportunities meet aspirations?

Let me tell you as a teacher and a Dalit woman—children from suppressed, oppressed and marginalised backgrounds study in spite of many odds stacked against them. When I was young, very few families educated their children. Now, everybody does. Girls and boys study. People are also aware of Dr Ambedkar's teachings. They realise that they have been oppressed and they have to fight back, demand their rights as equal human beings. This feeling is stronger in rural areas. But lack of economical backing and political will prevent them from actually achieving their goals. There are also psychological barriers placed in their way. This is not something other students will face. Now, I'm not saying they don't face any issues, they have other struggles, but these kids face great humiliation. Most of the faculty members are from higher castes. If all teachers can be sensitive, sympathetic, understanding and committed, massive changes can take place. But, unfortunately, that's not the case. Teachers are caste-oriented, they assume Dalits will not study. This is the image that's been created about the community. So teachers don't care about students from this background, they disregard them. They don't have an easy time at home either. There might be no electricity. The house may be small, with the whole family living out of one room, which is put to use as the living room, dining room, bedroom and kitchen.

Finally, when they get past all this and come to colleges and universities, caste becomes the mainstay there. Why did Rohith Vemula die? So many other students face the same thing. I feel terrible when I think about it. Why do they snuff out the life of a person who has faced so many hardships?

People can continue dreaming. What's hard is to make those dreams a reality. Currently, there are plenty of graduates. And not enough jobs. I go to speak in colleges around the state. They don't follow the UGC [University Grants Commission] pay scale, but have devised their own—they pay postgraduates four or five thousand to teach undergraduates. Naturally, the youngsters get vexed. So many go for coolie work. In my village, there's a boy with an MSc in Physics. He's a good, hardworking boy. But he's not managed to get a job. His family got him a cow. He now takes it out to graze.

How do we recognise and suitably reward women's work in the rural labour force? Is that even a possibility in a capitalistic economy?

The pay discrimination between genders is far less in white-collared jobs. But in rural areas, when women work in the fields and on road and building construction, they are made to work hard and paid poorly. In villages everywhere, agricultural work is on the decline. Women's experience and knowledge are not recognised; their skills are therefore dying. Since they have no other option, women opt for construction work. They either move to urban slums or commute long hours to get to their worksite and back. Unlike farming—which they knew well and did not have to travel for—they have to reskill themselves in the construction industry. In the course of their work, they are exposed to multiple levels of problems—chiefly, violence and insecurity.

The women are aware of how hard they work. They might not say 'I work like a man,' even though, in some areas, they work even harder than their male counterparts. And they know they are paid lesser than the men. But because they belong to the unorganised sector, they are not able to come together and fight for fair wages. Also, they're reluctant to fight, because they want that work. What will they do, if they lose whatever job they have?

Of course, I don't mean to say people are resigned to their lot. They participate in social justice movements. But for a country like India, the rural, agrarian society should be strengthened; only then, will there be real progress. It's not as if there was no exploitation in rural life. Landowners did exploit them. There was caste and gender discrimination. But what's happening now is far worse. There's a real struggle to find work, decent wages and fulfil basic needs.

Caste was a way of assigning value to someone's life. Physically demanding, dangerous and, sometimes, dehumanising occupations were reserved for the lower castes. Have we, as a society, done enough to break this?

Caste is very visible in rural areas. Unlike urban areas, it can be identified from the street you come from. As soon as it's known, communication and relationships break down. I live in a semi-rural area. When they find out your caste, you become a stranger. You are no longer a human being. It's very painful, a burden you live with your whole life.

Dalit women face discrimination not just from men, but also from the so-called high caste women. All women have problems. But Dalit women have additional problems because of their Dalitness. They are Dalits among Dalits. Only when their emancipation comes, can you call it complete freedom.

[In your book] you're talking about skilled people. Let me talk about sanitation workers and manual scavengers. They have been doing the same job generation after generation. Is this work reserved for their caste? Would a high caste person do this work if they were paid wages like in the software industry—say, forty lakhs—would they come forward to manually clean toilets?

Much of it is because, for hundreds of years, we've been oppressed, and now, without a trace of guilt, people talk as if we've grabbed all their jobs because of reservation. Even the so-called educated youngsters don't have any knowledge of social justice. They seem so casteist. It's such a sad state of affairs.

In a college I once visited, a girl asked me a question, which upset me greatly. She was a graduate, pursuing her higher studies. She asked me, 'Why are people still working as scavengers? We don't call them to our houses to clean our bathrooms or to clean our streets.' It was such a stupid question, about fellow human beings. She also argued that this has nothing to do with the Hindu religion. But it is what Manu said! *Manusmriti* pushes people to do the work that's assigned to their caste and legitimises the discrimination. In 1930s, Ambedkar had written about this in *Annihilation of Caste,* where he mentions the dos and don'ts listed by Manu. We've been trying to break free of all these stigmas and come up and yet people ask us if we get by because of reservation. Is that some kind of alms, a charity?

How does the social standing of women in rural Tamil Nadu compare with the state's own high performance on developmental and educational indices?

Let me tell you how Dalit women fare. I come from that background and I am aware of the issues. If you want to know their social status, the answer is, there is none.

Dalits, even today, try hard to prove their humanity, that we are human beings. The stigma and discrimination we face remains until we go to our grave.

Development only benefits one group of people. People who lived with and loved mann, chedi, maram, malai, mazhai [earth, plants, trees, hills, rain]—are now forced to prioritise money over everything else. But 'growth' and 'development' are destroying this. It destroys rural areas and people's lives. How can we call that growth and development?

As for education, it's fully commercialised. If you have money, you can get any degree and any job.

As a society, how can we value somebody's skill?

This is something I've been thinking about for a long time. As a teacher, I get a monthly salary. I earn at least ₹1,000 a day. Why don't we give the same to others? If we do that, it means we're recognising and rewarding their skills adequately. Now, I also get this salary whether I teach or not. In other white-collar jobs too, at the end of the month, the salary is credited. Similarly, why can a salary not be paid to agricultural workers? To women who do the transplanting work? They work under the sun and rain, standing on wet, squelchy earth, bending and stretching with aching backs. In fact, they should be paid more than me. The same should be given to women who make floor mats and those in all other unorganised sectors. Don't base the wage on their caste, but only on the skill. Isn't unorganised work also work?

Even if folk artists and craftspersons make some little money, their social status does not seem to improve correspondingly. Can this be changed?

In folk arts, it is not enough to appreciate the performance. You have to respect the performer as a human being. That's where the change has to come, in treating people with humanness, looking beyond their religion, caste, gender and even blood relationships. If you do it, you'll see the person and also find yourself appreciating the skill. Today, bharatanatyam is learnt mostly by Brahmins. It has a very high standing. The same is denied to kuttu and other folk arts and music.

Bharatanatyam artists are seen as important and respected and honoured wherever they go; why can't the same be the case for a kuttu artist? It is about respecting another human being. If I respect a person, everything about them will seem beautiful. If I think they are lesser beings, then whatever they do will appear mediocre. We don't value what they do because we don't recognise them as equal human beings. The same is true for gender. A woman is objectified and only seen as someone who gives pleasure and comfort. If they were treated as equals, with dignity, rights and freedom, there won't be any violence. This is what we are sorely lack in this country: seeing people as fellow humans.

The Man Who Drew Ten Thousand Designs

The birthplace of a Kancheepuram silk saree—where patterns and motifs are hand-drawn on old-fashioned graph paper with a 2B pencil—is the tidy living room of fifty-nine-year-old designer and fourth-generation weaver, B. Krishnamoorthy. As a designer, he creates new ones by borrowing from the old—'But only the idea, the outward shape'—and as a self-made archivist and educationist, he weaves up many reference catalogues. The design notebooks of this National Award winner are filled with drawings, over ten thousand of them, of parrots and peacocks, an army of elephants and horses; stunning variations of coins, lines, leaves and flowers; and the mythical yali—part lion, part elephant, part horse.

Unlike Krishnamoorthy, seventy-nine-year-old K. Veeraraghavan did not grow up around handlooms—his father was a contractor for the Public Works Department—and he picked up weaving in school. In the 1970s, Veeraraghavan bought rough cotton sarees locally and sold them in Karnataka and Andhra. The margins were poor—a rupee or two per piece. When that fell to fifty paise, he had to do something else. Around 1980, he began reproducing designs from the silk sarees on to cotton. He experimented with the yarns too, replacing the heavy sarees that didn't find takers, with lightweight ones. It was these sarees—rich in look and feel with designs similar to those on the famous Kancheepuram silk—that fetched Veeraraghavan the National Award in 1992.

Krishnamoorthy and Veeraraghavan are two of Tamil Nadu's 319,552 handloom weavers.[1] They not only belong to a well-known lineage—the famous Kancheepuram—but are also innovators and designers who build on the old. The turn of the twentieth century might have done well in romanticising the genius of the metropolitan artist. But those like Krishnamoorthy—in a little bustling town away from the limelight, their lives changed by an Industrial Revolution that happened two centuries ago in a far-away land—will never be valorised and rewarded in the same way.

The Kancheepuram weave has been part of this region's tapestry for centuries. Among the most famous weaves of India, Kanjeevaram or Kanjeepattu, as the silk is locally called, is fairly easy to identify—bright-coloured with contrasting borders and pallus. The pallu is linked to the body by a sturdy interlinking weave called the petni. 'Even if the saree tears, the petni won't,' asserted Krishnamoorthy. A handloom with three shuttles is used to weave the border. This method, called korvai, has one artisan weaving the body of the saree, and another, mostly an assistant, handling the threads of the border.

The motifs used are mostly traditional, handed down through generations of weavers; the sarees are woven using murukkupattu, the twisted three-ply silk thread from Karnataka; and the zari is 'pure', with 40 per cent silver and 0.5 per cent gold, sourced from both within the state and Gujarat. 'Though the newer colour palette tends to be pastel, borrowing from other cultures and regions in India, the sarees are traditionally ink blue, methi, bottle green, parrot green, black, mango yellow and maanthulir [the red of mango leaves],' said Krishnamoorthy, adding that the list was in no way exhaustive. 'All this put together makes Kanjeepattu unique.' Recognising this very uniqueness, a geographical indication was awarded to Kancheepuram silk in 2005–06. [2]

It takes 219 people to create a Kancheepuram saree, from the silk farmer to the buyer. Krishnamoorthy listed them out. 'It starts with mulberry leaves—the landowners, labourers, farmers, then the designers, dyers, warp twisters, zari makers, jala makers, weavers, salespersons. I've counted even the electricity guys; you need power to twist the yarn, don't you?'

The town that weaves this exquisite silk, just two hours from Chennai, is synonymous with its temples and has lent its name to both a spiced-up version of the humble idli and a sophisticated silk weaving tradition.

Handloom weaving is an ancient occupation in the region now called India. It finds mention even in the Atharva Veda, in which a passage 'personifies day and night as two sisters weaving, with the warp symbolising darkness, and the woof the light of day.'[3] In the seventh century, Kancheepuram was already thriving and finds glowing mention in the travelogue *The Great Tang Dynasty Record of the Western Regions* by Chinese traveller Tripiṭaka Master Xuanzang. Of 'Kancipura', the capital city of the Dravida country, he wrote:[4]

> The soil is fertile and crops are plentiful. It abounds in flowers and fruit and yields precious substances. The climate is hot. The people are courageous and fierce by custom and are entirely trustworthy. They are noble-minded and have broad learning.

The Kancheepuram region, likewise, has long been home to the finest weavers. Historian Pradeep Chakravarthy writes of thirteenth-century inscriptions in the town's Ulagalandhaperumal temple in

The Hindu.[5] The temple, 'is probably of Pallava vintage but inscriptions are from the Chola period,' from the time of Rajakesarivarman alias Tribhuvanachakravarthin Kulothunga Chola, who ruled the region between 1178 CE and 1218 CE.

> [One inscription] records a weaver who reclaimed some temple lands, built an irrigation tank and had the proceeds donated to the deity. There is a reference to Rajakesarivarman re-possessing the land given earlier to the weavers in the area since they did not cultivate it and returned it to the temple. ... [This] proves that the weavers were a prosperous group in ancient Kancheepuram.

In 1891, according to the census, there were 77,000 silk weavers in the then Madras Province, who had long ago migrated from Gujarat and spoke 'Patnlili or Saurashtri dialect'.[6] Krishnamoorthy and his family, descendants of those who came from Saurashtra, still speak this at home. Kancheepuram's weavers also migrated here from Andhra and Karnataka; now there are Chettiars who speak Telugu and Kannada and Tamil Mudaliars.

Twenty-five years ago, the town was thriving with over 70,000 weavers, and the villages around were full of looms, said E. Muthukumar, general secretary of Tamil Nadu Handloom Workers Federation. Today, according to official data, there are 36,521 weaving families in Kancheepuram.[7] The actual numbers might be even lower, he predicted. 'From what we know and see, many weavers have left the job. They've gone on to work in saree showrooms. Almost half the salesmen in the big silk saree showrooms in Kancheepuram are former weavers. Many have joined the catering business. And once they leave, they seldom come back.'

Krishnamoorthy unfolded a twenty-five-metre-long fabric, woven with 5,015 of his 10,000 exclusive designs. He had made two such pieces, but they were neither for a waist nor for a showroom wall. He did not hawk it for a big profit either. It is his dream to showcase his skill and produce a museum of designs for weavers and students. 'Titan Industries bought one at cost price—₹2.35 lakh, they keep it as a library of handwoven patterns. Just the wages to make this came up to ₹50,000,' he said, carefully folding the red cloth—the second sample he had kept for himself. 'It took me one year to draw all the motifs and punch them out on to 43,000 jacquard cards.' These cards are then used to repeat the pattern throughout a saree during the weaving process. 'Then it took another 2 years to set up a special 60-inch loom and weave it.' Did he send this to Guinness or any other world record? 'No,' he said, a little puzzled. 'But I don't think anything like this exists anywhere else. Maybe I should.'

Apart from his own work, he is keen to document the heritage designs too—'nothing fancy, those created by the weavers themselves'—and find new ways of keeping them alive. He handed me a three-fold brochure, a treasure with 114 drawings. 'The original designs compiled here are the true spirit, essence and the very breath of Kancheepuram sarees without which we can never imagine them. I want to publish a book with all these designs, for the purpose of education.'

He has carefully preserved the graphs drawn by his grandfather as well, about twenty of them, alongside many by his father and his siblings, all weavers. 'My grandmother's sarees, old samples, bits of cloth, all have beautiful designs that I improvise and build on.' His favourite patterns include: pattanikattam and muthukattam, in which tiny squares of thread are woven into the fabric; Ganga-

Jamuna, with two borders of the saree in different colours; and motifs inspired by temple architecture.

'The granite pillars of Kancheepuram's ancient temples, built by the Pallavas, are beautifully carved.' Krishnamoorthy showed me close-ups of sculptures that he and his wife Jayanthi have used in their creations: stylised elephants and horses and the beautiful annam or swan, with elaborately arranged tail feathers. 'But,' he was careful to add, 'we only borrow the idea, the overall shape; all the detailing inside is our own.'

Jayanthi is also from a weaving family in Bhuvanagiri near another temple town, Chidambaram. She started young, doing odd jobs and fetching and carrying thread and yarn when she was about eight, and learnt to weave long before her wedding. Now, she weaves, draws graphs by hand and helps Krishnamoorthy shade his designs.

For their wedding, Krishnamoorthy wove Jayanthi a saree: 'It was tomato-red with a navy blue border. We call it evening-morning border: one side is six inches, the other, three. The saree was covered with tiny, zari checks. It was a grand saree. She still has it!'

'He has to draw until eleven every night. Only then can he sleep,' said Jayanthi fondly, pointing to the tower of drawing books. Krishnamoorthy blushed as she turned the laminated pages, each quarter, half or full sheet containing a different design—half a fish, a handsome bird, a very large stylised mango—all his creations.

Krishnamoorthy's training too started early, not unlike many of his peers in Kancheepuram. What set him apart was very quickly recognising the need to specialise in design, and working with a single-minded focus towards it.

He began as a helper in his weaving household when he was a school-going twelve-year-old. After class ten, he trained in the actual weaving and designing from his father and grandfather as well as from two other weavers in town. He also learnt jala work—an old, complex technique of weaving motifs on silk sarees. He was then an apprentice for two years, weaving paavadais, or long skirts worn by girls, worked in a store in Kancheepuram as a weavers' coordinator. When he was twenty-one, he joined Co-optex—the Tamil Nadu Handloom Weavers' Society—as a weaver and later moved on to designing and drawing graphs. That is when his education in handlooms truly began and he honed his drawing skills. 'When in school, I had trained under art master Ramasamy sir. I knew how to draw graphs. It wasn't very difficult. Graph is the basic unit of designing, whether it's handlooms, powerlooms or bedsheets.'

In Co-optex, he visited and observed designs at other handloom weaving centres in the state. He developed two lines for them—the popular Puthinam sarees and traditional Kalakshetra patterns. In 2004, after twenty-four years of service, he missed the challenge of something new and opted for voluntary retirement. But it was his stint in Co-optex, designing as well as working with patents, that laid the foundation for a lifetime of innovating.

He set up a demand-based business model: weaving customised, one-off sarees, the designs based on the requirements of the customer, be it an individual or a retail store. This is different from the supply-based model of society weavers, who make pavus—a set of three similar sarees usually with traditional designs—which might be sold to different customers.

A saree with an inch of zari costs Krishnamoorthy a mimimum of ₹13,000–₹14,000 to make. This does not include the designing fee, about ₹2,000, and the cost of other materials like card and graphs, which are charged as used. He engages ten freelance weavers on ten looms of his own and produces around two hundred sarees a year.

His popularity brings students from Chennai's Stella Maris College and the National Institute of Fashion Technology, Haryana and Delhi, who spend a day talking to him and going over his designs, as part of their college training. Inspired by different batches of students often asking him, doubtfully, if the 114 designs on the brochure could actually be woven, he made them into a saree. 'They shouldn't think it's not possible,' he said, unfurling an inky black silk saree, with alternating gold and silver zari panels, each containing a new motif. Lines that were mere millimetres or half a centimetre in the design card, shimmered and shimmied up in thick bands. Mangoes, parrots, peacocks; animals wild and fantastical; buds, flowers and geometrical designs neatly lined the black base.

The patterns are stunning, the variations increasingly complex. There is, for instance, the traditional poun, gold coin design, in which a row of coins is separated by thin vertical lines. Then there is oval poun and vanki poun and an unusual sadhura or square poun, all geometrical variations of the original; there is mayil kann and kuyil kann, the eye of the peacock and koel. It is as much an exercise in documentation as creativity. How long did it take to weave this saree? 'Oh, this was nothing, just three months,' he said, folding the saree back carefully, mindful of the creases, until the whole thing became a black, gold and silvery rectangle of wisdom.

Despite the overwhelming enthusiasm of fine arts students from the city, only a few young people are interested in weaving as an occupation. Krishnamoorthy's two children work as software professionals in Chennai. 'They're not interested in weaving, it's a disappointment for him,' Jayanthi said, looking at Krishnamoorthy.

'Who will we pass on all our knowledge to?' he asked.

Despite Krishnamoorthy's angst, there are others outside of the traditional weaving families, if only a few, who are interested in taking up weaving. Veeraraghavan's son, forty-four-year-old

Sathiamurthy, has a diploma in textile marketing management and has worked with his father for almost twenty years.

Their family lives in the house Veeraraghavan's grandfather had built with local artisans and architects—quiet unlike the houses built today by contract labourers hired by mass market engineers. It is sumptuous, with a stout front door, the wooden frame carved with a thousand sharp details; the door is dressed in brass knockers and decorated with turmeric lines and vermillion dots. The living room with a double ceiling leads to other rooms opening into each other.

Much like architecture, mass production has changed the saree market as well. 'When I began fifty years ago, all sarees were handlooms,' said Veeraraghavan. 'Who heard of synthetic sarees and Surat sarees? There were low-cost cottons, which went to the villages. Even an agricultural labourer wore a cotton saree.' It was only when cotton sarees were replaced with synthetics and voiles that all the weavers in Kancheepuram, including the ones who produced lungis, flocked to producing silk sarees, too expensive for most people, even in the town of its production.

'Since 2000, powerlooms have mushroomed everywhere,' said Sathiamurthy. When a similar saree is available at a lower price, the customer cannot be blamed. 'It's not easy to tell the difference between handloom and powerloom sarees. The chief difference is the labour cost.' The wages paid to produce a powerloom saree are usually half that of what a handloom weaver makes, meagre as it is. Handlooms also have a hidden advantage—the employee is, often, also the boss. While the cheaper powerloom fabric gives an illusion of plenty and affordability, market capitalism has essentially messed with sustainability, be it in livelihoods or the environment.

Handloom sarees have a longer life, argued Sathiamurthy. 'The more you wash and wear, the softer it gets,' and they are usually a third heavier than powerloom ones. The life of the saree not only depends on the yarn and colours used but also on the skill of the weaver. 'If the recent awareness about handlooms had come ten or twenty years ago, the industry would not have collapsed, so many weavers would not have quit.'

In the 1970s, for a saree that sold for ₹24, the weaver was paid ₹3 or ₹4. 'It took about two days to weave simple cotton sarees,' said Veeraraghavan. 'So they earned about ₹60 a month. Now, cotton sarees are sold for ₹1500, and the weaver earns ₹300. But it's not enough!'

But this price and wage increase are still unsustainable because of a seemingly unrelated sector: agriculture. Many weavers also used to be farmers. The agrarian crisis has made it hard for weavers to live off just their wages. Cheaper powerlooms have further depressed an already distressed market. 'Only people who love and want handlooms buy it,' said Veeraraghavan. There aren't too many of them.

With poor sales and poorer cash flow, weavers struggle to get financial help from both banks and moneylenders. This is compounded by other events from time to time, like the implementation of the Goods and Services Tax (GST)—which pushed up the prices of the previously untaxed handlooms—and demonetisation.

In this unfavourable market, only designers and master weavers—who own more than one loom and engage other weavers to work on them—like Veeraraghavan, Sathiamurthy and Krishnamoorthy, manage to make a decent living.

'My father learnt dyeing and designing because he was interested in it,' said Sathiamurthy. 'He innovated by using the traditional silk saree's korvai designs on cotton sarees. It's a complicated weaving process and requires two people and three shuttles. There are only a few craftsmen willing to do it today.' For instance, only three of Krishnamoorthy's ten weavers work on korvai sarees.

Master weavers can afford to add a 20 per cent margin on the sarees. 'We need the margin to pay advances, to source new jacquard cards, among other things,' explained Sathiamurthy. 'For a silk saree that costs about ₹60,000, the silk yarn could cost around ₹4,000 and the zari around ₹15,000 to ₹20,000. Then there is dyeing the thread, getting the yarn ready to mount on the loom, making the jacquard design card, the wastage—usually about 20 per cent for thread and 10 per cent for zari—and, most importantly, labour charges. Finally, the stores add their own profit to cover overheads. But if it's an exclusive saree, then the price can be pretty high.'

For an ornate saree that costs a lakh, the labour charge could go up to ₹10,000. Depending on the design and the work involved, it could take a highly skilled and experienced craftsperson ten days at ten hours per day. Kancheepuram weavers use a throw shuttle, which is passed by hand between the warp threads mounted on the loom—unlike the faster fly shuttle commonly found everywhere in the country, except Banaras.

But a weaver who makes a simple silk saree in four days would earn only ₹1,000, or ₹250 a day. 'These are usually older weavers who are over fifty years and their spouses assist them. They're the only ones who stick on. Anybody younger is only interested in creating elaborate designs that fetch more money,' said Sathiamurthy. New entrants are only hired to assist. 'Would a twenty-five-year-old man want to labour ten hours a day, along with his wife, for just ₹250?' That is why, weaving is not aspirational.

Unlike sectors where State intervention hasn't always been beneficial, some of its policies have had a positive impact on handlooms. Besides, Tamil Nadu is considered a progressive state for weaving because of the number of weavers in the co-operative fold.

Co-optex, established in 1935, functions as the apex marketing body in Tamil Nadu, with 1.5 lakh weavers supplying to them. At the Chennai office, the managing director T.N. Venkatesh explained its operations. 'Whatever is produced by the 1,085 weaving societies across the state is marketed by Co-optex. Our interaction is more with the society and through the society's designer, to the weaver.' The organisation pays 40 per cent of a saree's retail price as weaver wages. 'In a few states like Odisha and West Bengal, they are comparatively lesser than Tamil Nadu, but in Varanasi, it could be very high, going up to a lakh for a saree. But remember, it would have taken the Banarasi weaver two and a half months to make it.' Societies hand out work for a set number of days, which vary with production targets and sales. An average silk weaver, said Muthukumar, makes twelve to fifteen sarees and earns around a lakh annually, for nine-and-a-half months of work, counting the breaks for monsoon, other holidays and to prepare the loom for the next round. Hardworking, independent weavers may even produce double that number, said Krishnamoorthy, and their earnings would correspondingly be higher at ₹1.5–₹2 lakh a year.

All weavers between the ages of eighteen and fifty-nine, both male and female, are covered by health insurance. They can avail scholarships for their children's education, old-age pension and free electricity up to two hundred units every two months. This is supplemented by national schemes like Jan Dhan—part of the National Mission for Financial Inclusion—and they are eligible for capital loans under the Pradhan Mantri MUDRA Yojana, which provides 'loans upto 10 lakh to the non-corporate, non-farm small/micro enterprises'.

Arignar Anna Silk Co-operative Society, formed in 1971, is among the six big and profitable societies in Kancheepuram, with 1,227 active members and an annual turnover of ₹44 crore. Over 200 houses were built for Anna's members as part of Co-optex's housing scheme.

Despite these initiatives, weaving societies have been dwindling. For instance, in Kancheepuram, their numbers went down from twenty-four in 2004 to thirteen in 2017. 'If a weaver works in a factory putting caps on pens,' said Krishnamoorthy, 'they get the same money as they would weaving, plus lunch. If he takes a bucket and serves food at marriages, he gets ₹500 a day.' Until 1995, weavers also got an annual bonus, said Muthukumar, of about 40 per cent of their annual wages. But when cooperatives were no longer profitable and could not compete with powerlooms, the bonuses were stopped and private players followed suit. A decade later, annual wage increases too stopped.

Even the weavers who have made money in handlooms encourage their children to get a degree and an office job. 'Where are the brides for weavers?' asked Sathiamurthy.

Inside the brightly lit, newly built showroom of the Anna society, half a dozen men assured me that nobody wants a weaver as a son-in-law. There was a time when weaver-grooms were sought out and bride's parents were willing to pay high dowries for them. Now, parents of girls prefer men with government jobs or 'company work'. The word 'company' encompasses all kinds of jobs—from industrial parks to security jobs to catering. 'Do you know why?' the men asked. 'Look at that screen.' A television was playing a video of the silk saree–making process on loop. 'Look at the heat; they have to stand in it the whole day.' If a woman is married into a weaver's household, the job of dyeing the yarn becomes hers. 'Why will anybody wish it on their daughter?'

Even the members of the flourishing Anna society, acknowledge that the Kancheepuram weaving industry is declining. Many weavers even work night shifts elsewhere to supplement their income. There are thousands of 'companies' around Kancheepuram, which send buses home to pick up the employees.

Weavers are selling their looms, while some hold on to them merely for sentiment. In fact, sentiment is everything, the men said, laughing. 'Do you know why we have time to talk to you today? Because it's an inauspicious day! Getting a wedding saree is not the same as a pant and shirt.' They showed me a monthly calendar with subhamuhurthanaatkal, or auspicious days, fit for weddings, and karinaatkal, or inauspicious days, printed below the dates.

Children of weavers have gone on to become doctors and engineers. 'I was told that third standard was a good education and was told to get into weaving,' said M. Varadarajan, who is on the board of Anna. 'Can I tell my children that? They're now studying in college.' The other weavers I met were also sure that nobody from the next generation is willing to take up this work. They estimated all weavers in Kancheepuram to be over thirty-five years of age.

Like many traditional livelihoods, weaving too cannot be learnt later in life, not even at eighteen, said Krishnamoorthy. 'It has to be taught when young. Why can't it become part of the curriculum? We cannot train young boys and girls, you see, that is banned under the Child Labour Act. So it has to be done institutionally. That is the only way to save weaving.'

Irai Anbu, an IAS officer well known across the state for his initiatives, clamped down on child labour when he was the

Kancheepuram district collector between 1997 and 1999. This was a game changer. Weavers still talk about it as if this happened in the recent past, about how since then no child has learnt the craft, essentially weeding out the next generation of weavers. But human rights watchers, then and now, applaud the decision because children were treated as bonded labour and were often overworked and abused.

Venkatesh however sees a 'positive shift' in the number of weaver children who are becoming weaver entrepreneurs. 'Weavers have so much inherent knowledge and skills that all they need is a little handholding. Then they'll do fabulously for themselves. They need to be informed by the retailers and organisations like Co-optex on what sells. That sync is very important,' he pointed out. 'I've had weavers come to me and say how they have grown old, but their children, with a college degree and digitally savvy, are now interested in running a few looms. The weaver sees a greater opportunity for the children; he is very proud that the next gen is on Facebook and Instagram. And they can successfully market the handlooms digitally. And, they come with the domain knowledge of a complex trade. The family will also still keep a loom at home, do some weaving, but the main income will be in sourcing and selling.'

But who are these young entrepreneurs selling to? All the women I met, weavers themselves or wives of weavers, wore synthetic sarees, which, no doubt are cheaper and don't wear out easily. Handloom cottons have moved to the cupboards of the wealthy, hanging beside scented sachets and modelled for social media.

Handlooms are now a niche market across the country. 'It's not going to be what it was in the 1970s or 1980s,' said Venkatesh. 'We have to live with this reality—a small set of highly skilled persons producing exquisite products in limited quantities. We are not going to deal in large numbers; be it supply or producers.'

Yet, there are more and more shops in Chennai's famous Pondy Bazaar, most of them selling Kancheepuram silks. They are crowded, always thronging with people, walking in eagerly, walking out with bags and bags of clothes. 'But they pack even a ₹350 saree in a cardboard box,' said Krishnamoorthy. It gives customers an illusion of a grand product, whereas only one in fifty that sells is an actual Kanjeepattu. 'The rest are low-end and synthetic sarees.'

The weavers' society stores have beautiful sarees that have so much zari that, sometimes, one can barely tell the colour of the saree. Weavers who are not part of the societies claim that these are not 'original' Kancheepuram silk. It is extraordinary skill that makes a Kanjeepattu, they assert, not the amount of gold in the saree.

Forty years ago, when Krishnamoorthy started as a weaver, the shelves were filled with traditional designs and local techniques. 'And there were very few fakes.' Now, sarees woven in other regions are passed off as Kanjeevarams, defeating the purpose of the GI. People are ready to buy these fakes—they are cheaper—and the layperson would be unable to tell the difference. Lookalikes of Dharmavaram and Banaras sarees too are woven in Kancheepuram, rather than the town's famous korvai saree.

Against market rationality, some customers also go for the most expensive saree, said Sathiamurthy. The prestige is in wearing a rich saree rather than in wearing something woven with great skill. This disregard for skills and crafts developed over centuries presents itself in the craze for engineering. 'Especially in Tamil Nadu and Andhra, if your child is not studying to be an engineer, God forbid ... where is the respect for the arts?'

But, Venkatesh believes that there will always be a demand for handlooms, even if only in a niche market. 'What is required of the people working in the sector is to guide people to make a discerning choice. Why do I invest so much in an organic cotton saree? Because the chemical-free dyes make it skin friendly. You're making a trade-off. I try to impress on people: don't keep saying handlooms are costly. Look at the chain of activity behind it.' This trend is of course visible in upmarket boutiques in cities, where customers throng to buy expensive handloom products. But not many of these upmarket stores transfer the returns back to the weaver. Customers also throng a Co-optex exhibition, and the sarees—linens in pastel shades and old revival designs in Kanjee cottons in affordable prices—are snapped up quickly.

Venkatesh is credited with the idea of attaching a photograph of each weaver to the saree. The initiative was widely praised and it lent dignity to the profession, recognising each weaver as an artist rather than just an unknown worker labouring over the looms. 'I must be very honest,' he said, 'the exercise of first tagging a weaver identity card was started by my predecessor and I sort of gave momentum to it. My thought was: a painter signs his painting, the author's name is mentioned in the book. When the focus of the arts is on the person who has done it, why should it be invisible for weaving?'

The very fabric of the weaving industry is changing, no doubt. Would the industry and the market grow to recognise designers like Krishnamoorthy? At the moment, it's not easy even for artisans like him.

'A customer might ask for five designs and I might spend three full days drawing them. But when they see it, they might reject four and take just one. What will I earn from it? A thousand rupees.' Showing me a beautiful saree in MS Blue, named after the celebrated Carnatic musician M.S. Subbulakshmi who wore that shade often, he said, 'Even today, I have an order for ten of these. A classic will never go out of fashion and will always be in demand.'

Nonetheless, customers do say they are bored of the same old peacock motif and ask for something different. 'So they tell me to draw it in flight or to design it with its nest.' Where do peacocks make a nest, I asked him. He laughed: 'They just want something different.'

Though drawing designs using CAD (Computer-aided design) software is easier and faster than drawing them by hand, it also makes copying them easier. 'There are around fifty designers in Kancheepuram. But only a couple apart from me draw by hand. The rest cut and paste. Cooperative societies have such big sales, but no skilled artist. They lift the designs and modify them. I don't have internet connection in the office. Every single design is my own!'

The trouble is, new designs—like Krishna eating butter or a dancing girl—tend to get duplicated quickly. 'It's become so easy to copy after computers came; whoever wants to, can take the handmade graph, which takes so long, and get it copied.' It is even easier to photograph it illegally. 'If I send a sample to a weaver, his neighbour can easily take a picture with a cell phone!' And quickly make and sell replicas of what was, until then, a one-of-a-kind design.

'You won't find these designs anywhere else. I draw them; my wife shades them inside by hand. It's team work.' Because there is no copyright—and no way to enforce one, in any case—Krishnamoorthy protects his work the old-fashioned way: by locking them up in a cupboard. 'This is the first time someone has seen these,' he said laughing, but with his eyes fixed on Sathiamurthy who had come along with me. He was showing us a huge scroll of graph paper with a drawing of deer roaming in a forest. 'We're working on a new wall hanging of six metres—a panel of Indian animals. It's been over six months, and we're nearly done. This is also for an award,' he said and rolled the sheet back up swiftly, the paper protesting the speed with a tup-tup-tup-tup.

Do awards make a difference? Sathiamurthy was quick to agree. 'Firstly, appa's award is encouraging for me. I too want to stay in handlooms. Secondly, they call award winners for exhibitions. And we reach out to new customers because of that.' Like in any business of selling, meeting with and talking to customers is vital. 'They give us suggestions, for instance, to make a saree into a dupatta. We got lots of orders for temple-border dupattas!'

Krishnamoorthy showed me his award-winning creation—a deep maroon saree, with a dark green pallu, a woman's hip-chain recreated in the border and miniature dancing girls on the pallu's edge. 'It took one month to weave this.' With fingertips pressing the gold buttas, he explained that it was the old jala technique that won him the National Award for silk saree weaving in 2010. His wife too won the same award in 2012 for a temple design saree. Hers is grander, the coin patterns stunning on the purple silk, the borders—one mustard, the other red—long and elegantly rimmed with gold. 'When we sent it for the award, we presented it with photographs of the sculptures in the temple pillars in Kancheepuram, which inspired our designs,' said Krishnamoorthy, showing me a laminated picture of Jayanthi receiving the award from Prime Minister Modi.

Though Krishnamoorthy insisted that the government has to encourage more designers and artists in cooperative societies, he is not sure if there are many other designers like him. The high cost of experimenting with designs is a detriment. 'You sink in lakhs to make the sarees. And time, to make these graphs by hand. It's all I have done every evening in these last few years,' he said.

Sathiamurthy, on the other hand, is sure there are not even a handful of innovators. 'Krishanmoorthy will be number one in the state. Even if there are skilled people, will they have so much interest and passion? He doesn't go out anywhere, people come here in search of him and his designs.' At office, Krishnamoorthy works on the computer. At home, on paper.

'All I know is design, design, design,' said Krishnamoorthy. 'This,' he pointed to the book of graphs, 'is what I love.' He flipped through the pages, where flowers bloomed, horses reared and parrots sat side by side.

But outside his house, in Kancheepuram and in other weaving centres in the state, weavers become servers in canteens and helpers on buses. They aspire to be drivers, watchmen and salesmen in saree showrooms. In the process, a craft that was learned and honed over generations is cast aside. There is no beautiful product to show for a day's hard labour, but there's food in the pot and a little cash in the pocket. This is how the weavers are rewarded—with jobs that pay them double what they once earned, but which require none of their extraordinary skills.

Making Wood Sing

On 15 August 1947, when India became an independent country, another quiet revolution took place. T.N. Rajarathinam Pillai, a legendary nadaswaram vidwan, played the Shanmugapriya ragam in front of Jawaharlal Nehru and other leaders. The centuries-old classical instrument he played on was modified only two years ago, by nadaswaram maker Ranganathan Achari, in a village over two thousand kilometres south of Delhi. A complex, handcrafted wind instrument, the nadaswaram, or nagaswaram, is played widely in weddings, temples and festivals and is central and important to the cultures of many societies in South India.

Ranganathan's son, N.R. Selvaraj, continues to make nadaswarams and also teaches the craft to his oldest son, Satish. His village Narasingampettai is on the road from Thanjavur to Mayiladuthurai in southeastern Tamil Nadu and is home to the four families who have handcrafted the finest nadaswarams for several generations. The village's fields are thick with paddy and plantains, its dusty streets are lined with coconut and drumstick trees.

It takes five days and exceptionally skilled craftsmen to get a block of wood to sing. The four families in Narasingampettai today, including Selvaraj's, who sculpt the nadaswaram by hand, make it look almost simple. The raw material is stacked like lumber in their backyards. In the workshops next to their houses, the wood is cut, shaped, filed and drilled, with a precision that comes with generations of practise. Nadaswaram players—many of them legendary musicians—have waited in these workshops for days for an instrument. Many have gone on to win awards and earn big money. But the makers of the instrument earn a profit of a thousand rupees a piece, or an additional five hundred if they get lucky.

Yet, every morning at ten, fifty-six-year-old Selvaraj, a fourth-generation nadaswaram maker, comes to his small workshop on Thachar Street—named after the occupation of the people, tachar meaning carpenter. Thin and wiry like his two assistants, he fetches iron files—some over two feet long—from the poojai room to start the day. On the wall beside the framed gods, hang the portraits of his late father and grandfather, and below sits Selvaraj in a checked lungi and banian, making a nadaswaram.

Deftly mounting a cylindrical block of wood on the pattarai, or a wooden lathe, Selvaraj told me about his village's long association with the wind instrument. 'The nadaswaram is a mangalavaadhiyam,' an auspicious instrument. 'It originated in this area, in a village near Mayavaram. My great-grandfather, Govindasamy Achari, went there to learn the craft.' Today, it is Narasingampettai that is synonymous with nadaswaram.

Filmmaker and music enthusiast Rajiv Menon spoke of that important day seventy-two years ago: 'You hear this announcement on All India Radio by the celebrated Indian radio broadcaster Melville De Mello: "Let us listen to auspicious music by Mr Thiruvadudhurai Rajarathinam Pillai." Delhi's choice of going with with TNR, as he was popularly called, was a source of great irritation in Mylapore, the bastion of Carnatic music. But the nadaswaram was chosen as it was 'auspicious', 'positive' and 'bright'.

In its earlier version, the nadaswaram used to be shorter and its pitch, higher. The players struggled to play popular ragams like Shankarabaranam. TNR asked Ranganathan to modify the instrument for a clear madhyamam—one of the swaras of Carnatic music, with two pitch positions of shuddha and prati.[1] The musician also wanted the nadaswaram to become a concert instrument. Carnatic musician and author T.M. Krishna writes about this transformation in *A Southern Music*:[2]

> In the early twentieth century, the nagaswara changed from being a short high-pitched instrument (timirinagaswara) to a longer and lower-pitched instrument (barinagaswara). Many attribute this change to Vidvan T.N. Rajaratnam Pillai and to his assertion that he would render kutcheris like vocalists, seated, using the longer length to rest the instrument on the floor.

'To make this modification, my father went to Thiruvanaikaval near Srirangam and learnt more techniques. Then he made six nadaswarams in its new avatar. TNR tried it out and loved it. He told my father not to give them to anybody else,' said Selvaraj.

TNR wanted to play with singers and, in the older format, the nadaswaram and human voice could never mix, pointed out Menon. 'You know that iconic song, *Nalandana* in *Thillana Mohanambal* where the lyrics are followed by the instrument playing as if it were repeating the words? That would not have been possible without Rajarathinam Pillai.'

And, by extension, Ranganathan.

Speaking above the whine of the hand-turned lathe, his body juddering as he drilled, Selvaraj explained that although it was his great-grandfather who introduced a new vocation to the village, it was his father who gave the world a new instrument. The innovation was well received and nadaswaram vidwans who played on it won titles and awards. The nadaswaram makers, though, continue to toil in their workshops.

Lathes lay strewn around the floor and unfinished nadaswarams leaned against short walls. The adjoining poojai room was lined with iron files, some of which belonged to Selvaraj's father. Selvaraj calls them 'ayudham', a word that can mean either weapon or tool in Tamil.

The instrument is traditionally made of two parts. The hollow wooden tube is made from aachamaram or Indian blackwood, which does not absorb the saliva that tends to collect in the nadaswaram's interior and hence does not swell, retaining its tonal quality over many years. The anusu, or flared bell, is made from vaagaimaram or rain tree wood.

'But you can't use fresh blackwood,' Selvaraj warned. 'It has to be at least seventy-five to a hundred years old. Young wood will bend and bow, like a palanquin.' They use the wood from lintels and pillars of old houses. 'But we face a lot of trouble transporting it. We're stopped at checkposts and asked for a bill. Which seller, tell me, will give me a bill for old wood?' To further insult the injured trade, they are accused of smuggling sandalwood. The popular refrain in these parts 'Aachamaram aacha pocha?'—is the wood all right or a goner?—is drawn from the difficulty of procuring the right wood. It might look smooth and shiny on the outside, 'like the skin of snake gourd', but it might turn out to be knotted and cracked on the inside. It is difficult to gauge how many instruments a log can make until it is cut.

The geography—not of where the tree comes from, but of where the used wood is sourced from—too influences the quality of the instrument. 'Wood from Pondicherry seasons well because of the moisture levels and soil from the region. It's a pleasure to work on it. The pillars and beams look thorny on the outside, but are very good on the inside.' Selvaraj is also fond of wood from Karaikudi. 'But Cuddalore and Panruti wood is harder to work on as it is tougher and denser.'

In August 2013 when I first met him, Selvaraj explained the complex process of turning a pillar into a musical instrument. 'First, you cut a block of aachamaram that's 2.5 feet long, with the top end at 1.75 inches and the bottom at 2.25–2.5 inches. This is then mounted on the lathe, chiselled, drilled, hollowed out and shaped.' These few short sentences play out over many hours, with three men—Selvaraj and his two assistants—two leather ropes, one lathe and a roomful of wooden files.

'It's important that the bore is aligned right. If the alignment is even slightly off, the instrument will be flawed,' said Selvaraj, dousing the bore with water to prevent the wood from heating up due to the drilling. 'The next stage, bramastaram, is the most important—it's what makes the nadaswarm speak; that is, gives it the tonal quality.' He pierced the wooden tube with a flat file and it turned on the lathe, slowly, as his assistants pulled it with leather ropes, straining every muscle to 'churn' the wood impaled on the file. As it rotated, the file smoothened the bore and when he was satisfied, Selvaraj removed it to check. Then, he drew a chalk line on the wood and marked out twelve spots using a thin strip of coconut frond for measurement, over which one of the assistants drilled holes. It looked deceptively easy, but one turn too many and the instrument would have been destroyed. One part of the instrument was ready.

To make the anusu, he cut a block of vaagaimaram into a 7.5-inch square, and shaped it carefully using chisels and files. He then screwed the anusu on to the body.

Satisfied, Selvaraj placed the nadaswaram to one side, and began work on the next cylindrical block of wood, which too would be ready, in four or five days, to await its vidwan.

S. Muruganandam, a player from Karaikal, was already in the shop. 'Even someone who's about to begin learning will bring a player along to check it. Sometimes, you want some corrections done on it and the craftsmen do it right here,' he said.

In the Tamil month of Aadi that falls between July and August—when weddings and auspicious events are not held, and the players are not busy—music fills Thachar street as prospective buyers test new instruments. Selvaraj only sells directly to his customers, and sometimes, he personally delivers the instrument, especially to those who might be coming from far, even from outside the country. 'But we'll never send it through someone else. What if they keep ours and palm off an inferior one to the buyer?'

Muruganandam blew into the seevali—the handmade reed mouthpiece at the head of the nadaswaram—a couple of times. The sound was sharp and short. He turned on his shruti box to fix the pitch and then played a song, his cheeks puffing, his head moving gently and his fingers covering and uncovering the holes on the body of the nadaswaram, coaxing complex tunes from the initially reluctant instrument.

Selvaraj listened carefully, as he applied slaked lime on a betel leaf. He tucked it into his mouth and asked the player, 'What do you want corrected?' Though makers don't play the instrument, they can tell when the shruti is off. Muruganandam confirmed what Selvaraj had suspected: 'The notes are difficult.' Selvaraj unscrewed the anusu, chose a file, dabbed a little water on it and inserted the file. It fit snugly into the wood. After a few rounds of smoothening, he checked it against the light.

'For some swaras to be heard better, the inside of the nadaswaram is smoothened with an iron file after mounting it on the lathe; for some, it's enough if it's done by hand. He knows what to do,' said Muruganandam, acknowledging the skill and genius of the maker.

Fitting the anusu back, Selvaraj stood up, let his folded lungi down and handed back the instrument. When the musician tried the nadaswaram again, both player and maker knew it was perfect.

Narasingampettai's nadaswaram is yet to receive a geographical indication tag.

Without it, middlemen routinely pass off other mediocre and cheaper nadaswarams as ones made in this village. 'Players will know only when they play it,' said Selvaraj, 'but even if you place ten similar-looking instruments in a row, we can tell the difference.'

Nadaswarams are made in other places as well. 'Outwardly, it looks just like ours. It is relatively easy to get the shape. Working on the wood on the inside is what requires great skill. I know how to do it as I watched my father. The others don't, and their instruments don't speak.'

Selvaraj wondered if the Narasingampettai nadaswarams can command a premium if they get a GI—'Maybe, I could ask for ₹10,000, and maybe players would then pay ₹8,000'—but he is unsure if premium pricing will work without adequate awareness about the tag.

Not far from Narasingampettai, the Thanjuvur veenai—India's national instrument and one of its most ancient ones—was the first musical instrument to receive the GI in 2013,[3] but it hasn't done much to improve the lives of the fifteen families in the region who make the instrument and continue to remain in debt.

Half-a-dozen men were hard at work in a workshop when I visited two years after the GI was introduced. Sunlight slanted in and picked out the hand-carved details on a veenai, making the brass frets on the stringed instrument shimmer. They were making an ottu veenai—put together by attaching different parts that are crafted individually, as the name implies. The other kind, ekantha veenai, is carved out entirely from a single jackfruit tree.

In another workshop across the road, N. Govindarajan, a third-generation veenai tuner, was checking the pitch of a new instrument. His father Narayanan Achari was a popular craftsman known to all the older vidwans. Govindarajan had always had an ear for shruti, which he has put to use for over half a century. But his skills will, very likely, fade with him. Upstairs, his daughter was in the middle of a class, teaching veenai to young girls. Her instrument, over forty years old, was tuned by her grandfather—the nadam, or tone, gets betters as the veenai ages. Her notes were clean and clear. The students sat in front of a Saraswati idol, the goddess with a veenai on her lap.

Veenai making is not a skill that can be mastered quickly. 'It's very difficult,' said M. Narayanan, the then president of the Thanjavur Musical Instruments Workers Co-operative Cottage Industrial Society Limited. 'There's not a single stage that you can call easy.' The sizing has to be precise and the only measuring instruments they use are 'eye precision and experience.' The instrument—a work of art—is sold as a 'product', whose price is determined by the cost of raw materials and labour.

Jackfruit wood, from which veenais are made, lends the instrument its soothing tonal quality. It ages well too. The wood was easily available during Narayanan's father's time. There used to be many orchards in the area but the trees were chopped down and the land sold as real estate. Now, the makers have to travel to Panruti, over three hours by road, to source wood that is thirty to forty years old.

Though the number of people learning the veenai seems to be going up, the makers have not benefitted from this. Their products are made on pre-order from retail showrooms. In principle, it seems like an arrangement that should work well: the makers don't end up with old or unsold pieces. However, for an instrument that retails between ₹12,000–₹25,000, the craftsperson earns around ₹300–₹500 a day, making four or five instruments a month; it barely covers their living expenses. Like nadaswarams, the prices of veenais too have not gone up by much. In fact, fifth-generation craftsman Senthil Kumar feels that the margins are down to 10 per cent of what his grandfather earned. Family members help out to cut down labour costs. But Narayanan's sons opted for better-paying jobs—one is an engineering graduate settled in Singapore and another is an MBA graduate working in Chennai.

Narayanan has pinned his hopes on the GI, for which he credits advocate Sanjai Gandhi, who is responsible for obtaining the tag for many products in the state. 'We were told more people will come here directly to buy the veenai and that the name will be globally known.' But the law and the tag alone might not bring about miraculous changes, without support from the government for sourcing the wood and marketing their goods. 'There's no sales tax now; that's helpful.' Pensions for elderly craftspersons and training centres to teach the craft are also the need of the hour. 'Then, you're preserving the craft, the tradition.'

In his house, Narayanan proudly showed me an exquisite veenai: the resonator was carved with Ashtalakshmis, the front panel with Saraswati and the neck with creepers. 'This will fetch ₹35,000–₹40,000. Maybe a foreign tourist will buy it.' Though many foreigners visit their workshops and admire their handiwork, praise alone does not lift families above the poverty line or keep a craft alive.

The annual turnover of Narasingampettai's nadaswaram industry, Selvaraj estimated, is around ₹19.2 lakh. 'There are six master craftsmen in four workshops. In each workshop, about eighty instruments are made annually and sold for an average of ₹6,000.' The monthly turnover, at each workshop, averages at about ₹40,000. This is used to pay for the wood—now selling at ₹35,000–₹40,000 a ton, the wages for the assistants at ₹500 a day, and, of course, the family's expenses. Three generations ago, a nadaswaram sold for ₹3 and when Selvaraj's father just started out it went for ₹12. Between 2003 and 2018, the price of the instrument went up 1.66 times; the cost inflation index for the same period went up by about 2.5 times.[4]

The asking price for a nadaswaram in 2019 is ₹8,000, but not everybody settles for it. 'Younger musicians test the instrument and they're usually so happy, they give me what I ask. They want my blessing to grow in their careers.' But the established artists begrudge the price, claimed Selvaraj. 'They don't get concerts and programmes like before. In most weddings, they have a "radio set", or a band or light music.' Even if there is a nadaswaram in weddings, musicians play film music rather than Carnatic music, rued Selvaraj. 'Only when the thali is tied, they play a keerthanai.' The days when a nadaswaram vidwan used to play a single ragam all night are gone. The players plead with Selvaraj to reduce ₹1,000 here, ₹1,500 there. 'When people cite economic reasons and refuse to pay me my full price, I just take it as God's will. This is how much grain he's willing to give me. Andavan padiallakaran.' God measures out the grains.

Music colleges seem to be mushrooming and this should ideally push up the prices of nadaswarams. But with fresh-out-of-college musicians willing to do concerts at half the price of what a senior player would charge—₹10,000—the senior players further shy away from investing in new instruments. They instead ask Selvaraj to smoothen the inside of their old nadaswaram.

The player's spittle can accumulate and form a coating in the hollow instrument. Nadaswaram makers like Selvaraj oblige when old ones are brought to be smoothened. 'They say they might only play for a few more years, and with nobody in their family learning, a new instrument is pointless. They also tell me their instrument was made by my father. For the sake of my business, I can't ask them to buy one they don't want, can I? And when they do buy a new one, they offer to pay the old rate, when they last bought an instrument.' The wood and wages in the meanwhile, would have of course, shot up.

Selvaraj added that their lives have indeed improved a bit. 'But if we have to do better, it cannot happen without the co-operation of the nadaswaram players. Their lives and lifestyles have dramatically changed. But we languish, with no access to wood and no help from the government.'

Years of drought, frequent since 2012, have also hurt the supplementary occupation of Narasingampettai's nadaswaram makers: farming. People in this region, who used to farm with water from the river Cauvery and its tributaries, are now dependent on groundwater and deep bores, which too are drying up, and sometimes on water from the Mettur dam. Selvaraj sold two acres of his land when his daughter got married in 2017 and he has been solely dependent on the nadaswaram since then.

Like his father, Selvaraj is an inspired craftsman. He is now trying to make three-piece nadaswarams, and eventually five, to make it easier for the players to carry it around and re-assemble when needed, 'like a clarinet'. The three-piece instrument is already ready and was even tested by a player, who found it to be pitch perfect. But Selvaraj would like to sell it only when the five-piece version is ready. Selvaraj's new instrument could add to his father's legacy.

To recognise the contribution of Ranganthan, TNR wrote him a letter on 14 September 1955—now a yellowing paper, mounted on old calendar sheet, laminated and carefully folded. The letterhead mentioned all of TNR's titles in Tamil and his address:

> Akila India Nadaswara Eka Chakrathipathi
> Nadaswara Chakravarthi
> Isai Ulaga Jyothi
> Isai Mannan
> Mannan Sangeetha Ratnakaram Nadaswara Everest
> Isai Sigaram
> Thiruvaduthurai Adeenam Mahavidwan
> T. N. Rajaratnam Pillai
> Sivaji Mahal
> Thiruvaduthurai P.O, Narasingampettai, Thanjavur Zilla

Holding the letter delicately, Selvaraj summarised its contents. 'TNR tried getting his nadaswarams made in several places. But nowhere did the shruti "speak". Then, he came to Narasingampettai and here, Ranganathan, son of Narayanan Achari, made him an instrument. TNR was pleased with the tone and clarity of sound. He believed that even players who weren't highly skilled could play this nadaswaram well. He recommended that the government give awards to the craftsmen. He asked the nadaswaram players from the

Isai Vellalar community and the state and central governments to reward the families that make the instrument.'

Folding up the letter, Selvaraj said, 'But nothing has happened till now.' It has been sixty-three years. TNR remains the Nadaswara Chakravarthi. Even in his lifetime, he positioned himself as a star, said Menon. 'He acted in a film. He went about in a car. When he travelled to his village by train, he'd pull the chain and get down and would happily pay the fine for the privilege! He had so much money. When he got down in Thanjavur, his fans would throng the station. He would walk away from the station playing the nadaswaram. He was instrumental in getting his village a railway station.'

'As well as electricity', said Selvaraj when I recounted this to him. 'When Nehru asked him what he wanted, as a token of gratitude, TNR asked for electricity. And he got it!'

But Ranganathan Achari, the wizard who made the instrument, is not known outside the world of nadaswaram players. His grandson, tired of the toil and little recognition, wanted to drive a tourist van.

Selvaraj's house has a red-tiled sloping roof, an elongated living room painted green, a thinnai with slender pillars and a narrow ramp at the entrance to roll up mopeds. The workshop next door stands in contrast—plain, flat-roofed and contemporary.

As the eldest son—nadaswaram making was and remains an inherently male profession—Satish is expected to learn and practise the art. But initially he had other plans. Over lunch—cooked by Vijayalakshmi, Selvaraj's wife, on a mud stove fired by wood chips and scraps from the workshop—Satish talked about his love for automobiles. 'People have pictures of gods or their parents on their cell phone screen. I have a van!' Everybody smiled as he showed me his phone, except the parrot from a neighbour's house, which was busy eating rice and red pumpkin sambhar from a small steel plate.

In 2013, then in his early twenties, Satish was doing what he loved: driving. From a family car, he progressed to a seventeen-seater tourist van. When I visited them again two years later, Satish—sitting cross-legged on the floor, with a tonsured head and a t-shirt labelled 'Pepe Jeans, London' worn over a pair of ankle-length trousers—asked, in a complete turnaround, 'Who will even know what a nadaswaram is, if we don't take it up? The customers who come here might be so much older than me, but they treat me with respect and don't dismiss me as a young boy. Even you have come here because of my grandfather's name, because of my father's fame.' He recalled customers who visited his grandfather to tell him their lives had improved after playing his nadaswaram.

Selvaraj's uncle, Sakthivel, as the elder of the family, was the first to coerce Satish. But others played a role too. His sister Durga would say: 'When we go to a temple and tell them we are from Narasingampettai, we're treated like VIPs. We get to go near the god and have a closer darshan.' Satish's friends reminded him, 'You don't have to fold your hands in front of an employer for a day's leave to attend a family function, you can work in your own time.'

And of course, there was his father: 'If Satish and Sabari [Sakthivel's grandson] don't take it up, Narasingampettai will lose respect.' The art of making nadaswarams is seen as prestigious by the makers themselves and hence there is an enormous pressure on the younger generation to carry the legacy forward. 'My sons have to, who else is there?' said Selvaraj. What about his daughter? 'Women don't make this; my grandmother assisted my grandfather. But my wife has never come to the workshop and my daughter wasn't interested.' But he is certainly not against it. 'Women drive planes, buses, autos ... they can do this too. It's only a handicraft, isn't it? In fact, there's a woman ghatam maker.' He was alluding to the late Meenakshi Kesavan who received a Sangeet Natak Akademi award. Selvaraj then wondered aloud. 'Maybe, an instrument made by a woman might fetch a better price?'

With the enthusiasm of a new convert, Satish is now convinced that his younger brother too will take this up. 'See, after his engineering, if he takes up a job and that company closes, he'll have to find another one. But here? There's always going to be work. And you never have to retire. You can work as long as you live, as long as you're healthy. Ninety, even hundred.'

While Satish has come around to the idea of taking up the family's occupation, he also wants to continue with his tourist business. He probably will need to do that. His younger brother Prakash, who has a bachelor's degree in engineering, too might have to pitch in. The income from making an instrument alone can no longer sustain a family. The prestige, of carrying forward the family name, won't pay the bills. And it will definitely not pay for a load of wood.

The succession dilemma also plays out in Sakthivel's family, who live down the road. His grandson Sabari is keen on academics but his father Senthil Kumar, who has made nadaswarams since he was fifteen, is certain that his son, when he takes up the family occupation after his education, will improve it. 'He'll modernise it,' said Senthil, showing me a lathe that is turned by a motor. 'Nobody—including my father—thought this was possible. But it works beautifully.' The motor is handy given how hard it is to find labourers. 'Now we wait for them to arrive with folded hands!' Sakthivel quipped, his words laced with sarcasm and his mouth stained with betel juice.

Selvaraj doesn't plan on getting a motorised lathe, not until his boys have mastered the process of making nadaswarams. 'We cannot start by working on a machine,' agreed Satish. 'Besides, that will work only with electricity. Whereas, you can make it by hand anytime, so it's important to learn this first.'

Despite their obvious pride, the men yearn, as any artist would, to be recognised by society.

Selvaraj has won honours from musicians and he is thrilled about them. But a government recognition is something else. The last honour the makers received from the government was in 1955, during the then chief minister K. Kamaraj's regime. 'T.N. Rajarathinam Pillai made it happen for my father. Nothing has come after that. We make the nadaswaram with so much precision. I have requested the government to honour my uncle, who is older than me. If he gets it, maybe something will come my way as well.' Why, demanded Sakthivel, are all awards and recognitions reserved for the players, while craftsmen from the village where the parinadaswaram was first made languish unrecognised?

'The younger generation will be motivated, that's why,' was Selvaraj's explanation for why they want it so badly. Selvaraj, who picked up this craft inspired by his father, to do an occupation that would bring him respect and dignity, believes that he deserves a national award.

'Who will know Narasingampettai if not for the nadaswarams?' asked Durga. 'Tirunelveli is known for halwa, Thirupachetti for aruvals, Palani for panchamrutham. Our village has nadaswarams. How can we let it go?'

The Kuchaali and the Korai

The grey, rectangular workshed is in the greenest part of Tirunelveli district. The road leading to it in Pathamadai village twists and turns through paddy fields, ponds pink with lotuses and a horizon blue with hills. But the route is forgotten once you are inside the shed, with its high windows and hot sunlight. Everywhere, there is colour: in the mats that grow on the looms one thread at a time, in the bundles of brightly dyed korai, and in the special wedding mat with the names of the groom and bride—'Girish weds Sneha'—in deep purple, jade green and rani pink.

Sitting by the looms placed on the floor, their pallus drawn over their heads, are the weavers of the famous Pathamadai pai, or mat. They stretch their legs, cross their feet and press their big toes against the tripod that anchors the loom, as they chat, mind the children and calculate wages. There are about a hundred weavers in the village, mostly women from the Muslim community. Of the twenty in this group, five are state and district award winners. They earn, on an average, nine rupees an hour. Yet they queue up daily for a chance to weave the mat that has both an interesting past—it was once gifted to Queen Elizabeth—and future—it received the geographical indication tag in 2012–13.

At least five generations have made floor mats in Pathamadai, said S. Zeenath Beevi, who heads the women's self-help group cooped up in this workshop. She spent her whole life in the village, like her grandmother, mother, sisters and daughters. They have woven mats since they were ten, but have only this workshop on rented land to show for their craftsmanship, even as their rich mats adorn grand homes in towns and cities. Often, customers complain about the high prices of the mats—ranging from ₹1,500 to ₹5,500, depending on the size, material, complexity and count—about why they are charged so much for something to sleep on. They don't factor in the experience and knowledge of several generations and the backbreaking labour of women who spend the entire day bent over floor looms in a small cemented room.

Mat making in Pathamadai has a long and fascinating history. In 1917, civil service administrator H.R. Pate published an account of the weavers in *Madras District Gazetteers: Tinnevelly*. He praised the mats for their 'superior composition' and 'considerable reputation', and admired the fine texture of the best ones, which remain undamaged even when 'crumbled in the hand like a pocket handkerchief'. Of the process and the people, he writes: [1]

> Its manufacture, which is now the monopoly of four or five Muhammadan families, appears to be of purely indigenous origin and to have evolved itself from long experience in the production of the coarser varieties. The excellence of these mats has been acknowledged by the award of medals to their makers at several public exhibitions, amongst them the Delhi exhibition of 1902.

Mindful of their time—each hour lost is nine rupees lost—the women explained the process of making the mats, as they sat at their looms, weaving with the kuchaali—a four-foot long wooden needle—and coloured threads, their hands keeping time with their eyes, swift and graceful at once, the movements repetitive, almost meditative. They chatted, yelled to each other across the room and instructed little boys in lungis, shirts and caps who drifted in and out. Young ones cried until a mother or an aunt scooped them up and on to a hip. Through all this, the sound of the kuchaali and achu, a piece of wood that compresses the korai, remained steady, without missing a beat, as the mats grew from the looms.

Pathamadai's famous mats come in two varieties. Fine mats are typically made from commercially cultivated korai—a tall, grass-like plant—belonging to the Cyperus family. The superfine variety, also called pattu pai or silk mat, is made from wild korai that grows along the river Thamirabarani in the region. 'Wild korai becomes shiny and beautiful when soaked in water for over a week. Any other variety will rot if left to sit in water for that long,' said Zeenath. The gold studs on her nose and ears and the prints on her synthetic saree caught the afternoon sun and glowed, like her silk mats. The height of the korai limits the width of the mats to three feet. The length can vary, from the usual six feet to nine feet.

Sourcing the korai is not easy. The women get it from deep inside Karambai village on the way to Kallidaikurichi, with the help of farmers. Zeenath's grandparents used to bring the grass back home by bullock cart. Now, the women carry it back in auto rickshaws.

It takes the women an hour to weave five to eight inches of a fine mat, the length and speed increasing with experience. There are about 50 korai threads per 9 inches for a fine mat, whereas there are 100–140 for a superfine mat. Though it does not look dense on the loom, after the mat is woven, the korai fibres are pushed closer and twisted, compressing a band of colours a few inches apart to two fingers' width.

During Zeenath's parents' time, the workday started as early as half past five in the morning. 'Growing up, life wasn't easy. When it rained, the thatched roof leaked. How could mats be made then? There was work and some money for about six months. The rest of the time, our families lived off loans. When we sold mats, we repaid them.'

Zeenath could not educate all her children—only her son and the oldest of her three daughters, Rahmath Meeral Beevi, are graduates. Zeenath requested the local bank manager to employ Rahmath, but they offered a meagre salary of only ₹1,200 in 2013 to work in the accounting and computers section. Eventually, Rahmath got married, and she now weaves mats. And so it goes on, the women working in their own homes or next door in the workshop, resting in the afternoon when it is hot. Late in the evening, after the housework is done, they listen to the radio, chat with each other and weave.

Nearly all the women in the group are related, by birth or, more often, by marriage. 'We don't give our daughters in marriage outside,' said Zeenath as a cooker whistled from her house next door. Lunch was getting ready and the chatter in the room got louder. Women came and went, delivery dates were discussed, one waited for her wages, another measured the portion she had completed the previous day with an inch tape. A long and complex calculation later, she was paid ₹105.

'Marrying within the community helps keep the skills alive,' said historian, writer and award-winning filmmaker Kombai S. Anwar. 'I've seen this in Kadayanallur village near Tenkasi as well, where the women marry someone from within the village. That way, the daughter-in-law, who knows the weaving tradition, is an asset.'

Some of the women did not wish to be photographed and explained that theirs was a close-knit, conservative society. A few younger women, including Zeenath's youngest daughter, have opted to wear the burqa, while their mothers continue to dress as they always have, in sarees, with the pallu drawn over their head and tucked behind the ears.

Thirty to forty years ago, it was the men who made the mats. Zeenath's father K. Rahamathullah is an award-winning mat weaver. She held out his visiting card, which had a stern photograph of him, with 'National Award 2003' and 'Shilpa Guru Award 2011' printed above his name. He also used to be a medicine man and the muezzin, calling his village men to pray at the palli vaasal.

The men gradually drifted away from mat weaving because of the low wages, whereas the women find working from home to be an advantage. 'We are women,' said S. Kyrunnihsa, Zeenath's eldest daughter, emphasising the gender. 'In our society, we cannot go out and work. We can do this from our homes. That's why we take this up.'

The men mainly used to weave the expensive superfine mats. Back then, there was no workshop or a cooperative society, like now. Each house had its own loom and made one superfine mat a week. 'That was their only income,' said Zeenath. The men mostly soaked the mats in the canals and river, while the women did the actual weaving. But now, the men want an education and a day job. 'Even if they earn only ₹5,000 doing other jobs, they prefer those to this,' said Zeenath's sister-in-law, Kavva Beevi.

Zeenath's twenty-one-year-old, with a degree in mechanical engineering that cost her ₹1.5 lakh, only recently landed a job in a textile store. 'How can it help when everybody has an engineering degree, when there are colleges everywhere, and all the children are following each other like a herd to the gate?' she asked. 'Why, I pay ₹1,500 for my son who is in class one in the nearby English medium school,' jumped in Kyrunnihsa.

The roomful of women excitedly shared their opinions on how to get more men involved in the occupation. If men come in, they argued, the daily wage would automatically increase, ways to decrease the drudgery would be explored, and the products might sell better since the men would be able to travel far and wide with the mats.

But they eventually conclude that even if the economic situation were to improve, their sons would not work on the looms. 'They won't be patient,' said Zeenath's sister, Mohamed Regina. 'They are interested in other things.' Many of the men have also migrated to the Gulf countries, with salaries ranging from ten thousand to a lakh rupees.

Zeenath's husband, her aunt's son, too worked in Saudi Arabia for fifteen years in a vegetable shop and returned home in February 2018. They stayed in a series of rented houses till 2013 when they finally built their own. It was also the same year in which the women rented a piece of land, on which their workshop now stands.

Zeenath and Kavva got twenty women together, many of them single and contributing to their family income, to form a self-help group. It cost ₹1.2 lakh to build the shed. One of their clients, a Chennai-based upscale saree store, lent half the amount, while the owner of the land lent the remaining. 'We have repaid the store in mats,' said Zeenath. They also secured a bank loan of ₹6 lakh to get them started. Divided among them, each has to contribute ₹800 a month towards paying back the interest of 4 per cent.

Zeenath and Kavva work tirelessly to not only keep the unit running but also to think up new strategies for expanding. 'But it's very hard,' said Zeenath. 'The rent for the land on which the workshop stands is going up. It started at ₹1,200 a month. It might go up to ₹1,800 soon. The electricity bill last month was ₹1,300, because we pay commercial metre rates.' Since the majority live in rented houses, they cannot install looms at home. The National Bank for Agriculture and Rural Development took on the cost of the one-member staff and the rent. But Kavva and Zeenath still had to take a loan of ₹20,000 to purchase stock and put up the signboard. 'The money disappeared quickly,' they said.

Though superfine mats sell for ₹5,500, they don't sell often enough to cover the many costs. Moreover, weaving them is nearly as painstaking as weaving a silk saree.

The wild grass has to be first soaked in a tank, like the cement one outside Zeenath's house, for about ten days till it rots and the pith comes apart, to enable the outer sheath to be split into thin strips. 'In my father's time, they would soak the bundles of korai in the river water. But since the river is two–three kilometres away, we don't take it that far unless we go there to wash clothes.' Teasing the threads out—a week's work to pull out enough strips for one mat—is hard, delicate labour that takes a toll on their eyes.

The women in the group are each paid a wage of ₹800 for this work, about ₹114 a day—for a job that calls for a bent back, a keen eye and nimble hands to carefully tear a blade of korai into four or six pieces of the same length and width. For a superfine mat requiring more work, they are paid ₹1,000 for the weaving that takes seven to ten days and another ₹1,000 for finishing it.

The only easy part of the work is the dyeing. Since the threads are fine, they soak up the colours quickly, but only if they are chemical dyes. Natural dyes—they procure Japanese ones—would require the threads to be soaked in them for a day. The dye also has to be pounded first.

The teak wood loom is hard to make, especially with just one or two carpenters left in the village. Each loom, which comprises of twelve pieces of wood, costs ₹4,000. 'All these are old,' said Zeenath, waving her hand around the room. 'It's especially hard to find spares for repairs. The carpenters are not interested in replacing just a part. They have to run around to source it. What profit will they make?'

Every month, the group forks out ₹50,000 to source commercially grown korai—difficult to find and expensive—from Karur and Veeranam among other places, sold by the handful at ₹400. 'The set up that we have now—with eight looms—barely provides work for all twenty members,' said Kavva. 'It's so tight that when one woman gets up, another is waiting to take her place to weave.'

'We have been doing this work for decades and generations. Look at my mother-in-law, her back is bent with age,' said Zeenath. 'But even today, she can only eat if she weaves mats.' She did not push for nor receive the government pension for senior citizens because those with children are not eligible for it. But the children have their own families and little money to begin with.

'We are not criticising the government, we're only asking for a few things.'

Zeenath was particular that I see two things in Pathamadai: their retail store and the big machine installed in the courtyard of her house, custom-built for them by the Rural Technology Action Group (RUTAG), IIT Madras. Two team members visited their workshop and measured the height, width and breath of the korai, before making the machine. Once the machine was installed in 2017, four women from the group went to Chennimalai in Erode district to learn how to use it.

An unfinished orange-and-straw-coloured mat sat on the machine's loom. Zeenath was visibly proud of it, which she believes can possibly make their lives easier and more productive.

RUTAG was funded by the Tamil Nadu Handicrafts Development Corporation Limited (TNHDC) to establish a common facility centre in Pathamadai. The then chairman and managing director of TNHDC, Santosh Babu, told me that the government had sanctioned fifty lakhs to revive Pathamadai mats by providing machines, trainers, a marketing platform and a salary for a designer, and that they were partnering with RUTAG for three years.

The RUTAG website mentions that four electronic jacquard handlooms will be installed in Pathamadai and predicts an increase of 200 per cent to 300 per cent in productivity. It might just be the intervention that will entice youngsters, perhaps, even young men, to take up the work.

Though the women acknowledged the good work done by the design institute, this only solves a part of their problems. 'Even people in Tirunelveli don't know we make these mats,' added Kavva.

'What they also need to do better is marketing.' Zeenath used the word 'marketing' in exasperation and in longing, about ten times in five minutes. The women are willing to produce any product, yoga mats for instance, as long as there is a demand for it. They already go beyond mats and make purses, penholders and coasters.

Though Poompuhar, a government retail store, takes mats from them, they only transfer the payment after a sale. 'Superfine silk mats have a limited market—mostly, people from Tirunelveli and, often, Brahmins who insist on silk mats for their weddings,' said Zeenath. Weddings in their community of Labbai Muslims must also necessarily have silk mats.

Gita Ram, chairperson of Crafts Council of India, has a Pathamadai mat that is seventy years old. 'It was made in the 1950s,' she said, showing me old samples of Pathamadai weaves in the showroom in Chennai. 'An average mat easily lasts for decades.' Ram has a long association with the Pathamadai weavers. When she asked schoolgoing girls, the last time she was in the village, what they would like to do later in life, all six said they wanted to join the civil services. 'It's perceived as safe for girls.'

Does the GI tag give the Pathamadai mats an edge? 'GI is something to be proud of,' conceded Ram. 'Except, customers only look at the price and colour of the mats. They don't care whether it has a GI or not.'

Despite the hardships and the low income, mat weaving is still popular in Pathamadai because of three simple reasons: social constraints placed on the women, lack of other acceptable opportunities and the awards given to the weavers, which add prestige to the livelihood.

Textile showrooms in nearby Tirunelveli prefer to hire younger, educated girls. But the disinterest is mutual. 'The trouble with that kind of work is that you end up neglecting your house. Here, you can manage all of it,' the women said. Working away from home also involves spending money. 'A bus ticket is twenty rupees one way. If you have tea and a vada, you'll spend a hundred on the journey. Plus, it will be mentally exhausting. Considering all that, mat weaving seems like a good alternative,' argued Rahmath. She was also certain that education alone does not guarantee a good job or salary. 'For a lot of government jobs, you need to write exams. You need to spend time and money to prepare for it. If you go to work in some local company, you can't really expect much. Maybe four thousand or five thousand rupees.'

'There really is nothing else for us to do in this region,' the women chorused. None of them own any land. 'We live in rented houses, where do we go for farm land?' they scoffed. Sometimes, there is agricultural labour and there used to be beedi rolling work. 'You can roll beedi if there's space enough to sit, whereas, to weave a mat you need a space of 6 feet by 12 feet to install a loom,' said Zeenath. But they voluntarily stopped doing the latter even though it was a popular cottage industry. 'Tell me, do you get any disease weaving? That's why more women are coming here now. Mat weaving wasn't doing well sometime back. But now? It's thriving.'

Kavva added another reason for it: 'We're proud of the hundred rupees we earn every day. And we want to provide employment for more women.'

Despite their entrepreneurship and ambitions, the women frequently refer to themselves as 'kinnathu thavalai', a frog in the well. 'What can we do? We're just women who are stuck inside a room,' is another refrain. Their sense of self is hardly close to the truth.

Much of the progress—including formal financial inclusion—happened after they started their own kuzhu, or group. Until then, they were part of the village cooperative, which they found to be restrictive, as everything they produced had to be sold exclusively to them. 'That's how coops function, so it wasn't unfair,' said Zeenath. But selling directly to the customer brings in better prices, a profit of a hundred to two hundred rupees. 'So Kavva, who is sharper and ten years younger, and I decided that we should have looms of our own. And we started the group.'

Zeenath constantly thinks of the innovations they could bring in to market the product better. The palette she uses on the mats has expanded. 'Previously, we used just five colours—red, green, violet, orange and rose—along with the natural ones.' I pointed to the plain, straw-coloured mats on the floor and asked if those were the natural-coloured ones. 'No, these we buy from the bazaar for rough use. They are machine-made.' Another voice in the room called out, 'But they're also craftspersons like us,' referring to those who make them. 'They need to make a living too, don't they?'

Mat weaving is an art as much as it is a craft. It involves not only keeping the cotton threads taut or fixing new threads on the loom or even weaving but also the complex calculation that goes on in the maker's mind as she chooses a coloured korai thread. The eight looms in the workshop that day were testimony: each unfinished mat had a different pattern and colour scheme, each a mark of individuality of the weaver. Design weaving calls for good eyesight and skill. The cotton warp threads are lifted up and down so that the korai weft threads make the design. 'It's very difficult,' said the women, and acknowledged Zeenath as their leader and trainer. Now, Zeenath pointed out, the people who weave names on mats are literate. 'My mother, who died five years ago, wasn't schooled. But she was gifted and blessed by Allah. Her deep interest in the art enabled her to recognise designs and patterns and weave names.'

'The Tamil Muslim community is very entrepreneurial,' said Anwar. 'They aren't confined to one geography. It spans from Pulicat in the north to Kanyakumari in the south. Many are into trading. Some have become big corporates, but the majority are content with their small and medium enterprises. It's also a very cohesive group, very supportive. If you're willing to put in the hard work, people will help you.'

Running their own show helped Zeenath and her team build a customer base. They took their work to a few fairs and exhibitions in Chennai, which gave them the confidence to approach javuli stores, or clothing stores. Soon they started supplying to boutique stores in the city.

Pathamadai weavers are invited by other weaving communities to train other mat makers. The women once stayed in Chidambaram, a temple town, for twenty days to teach weavers, for which they were paid ₹100 a day each.

'My grandmother also used to train people,' added Kyrunnihsa. She shouted across to the eighty-year-old, whose name is also Kyrunnihsa, and asked her to list the places she had been to. 'Manamadurai, Erwadi, Madurai. And four or five villages,' came the reply in a voice hoarse with age.

In 2018, I met Kavva and Regina when they came to Mumbai for an exhibition. The women stood in a stall with posters about Pathamadai mats, korai samples and a few handmade purses. 'One lady came and bought eighteen money purses as give-aways for a sumangali poojai,' said Kavva, referring to a Hindu religious custom. An eager client bought all their mats too. 'They'd start at half the price,' she said, sighing, not pleased with their enthusiastic bargaining. With three days to go for the exhibition to end, they had only one unsold superfine mat. It was rolled up and encased in a beautiful drawstring bag. Customers asked to see it, admired it, and walked away, their eyebrows in their hairline, when they heard the price—₹5,000. 'This is the problem,' said Kavva. 'We don't know how to tell people what's special about the mat.'

Even a hundred years ago, the Pathamadi mat was a niche product:

> In spite of their artistic merits, however, it is difficult to see that the mats are of much practical value; they form a delightful spread to sleep on, especially in the hot weather, but for all the uses to which mats are generally put they are by their very fineness and

> delicacy less suitable than the ordinary coarser articles. Their production is expensive, and for a mat about 6 feet by 3 feet a price varying according to the texture of the article from ten to thirty-five rupees is asked. There is unfortunately no real demand for them and consequently no market; the few sales that are made are usually the result of hawking on the part of the makers themselves.[2]

But this is precisely why the women harp on getting some support on marketing. 'The wild korai is medicinal. It's cooling when you sleep on it,' said Zeenath. The mats also have a long life. 'I know of women who still have their mother's wedding mats.'

Her daughter held up one for me to photograph. It went a couple of feet over her head. When I complimented Zeenath on the cheerful design, she said it was a faded one. But four years of frequent use later, the words 'R. MOHAMED MUSTHAFA WEDS K. MOHAMED FATHIMA' and the date '25-05-2014' are still clear, bright and beautiful.

These hardworking artisans, with a keen desire to improve their lives, need more than just help with marketing or a small parcel of land—their ask is about two thousand square feet—to build their own workshop. A holistic approach that understands the community and all its needs will take it far. Without that, they will continue to struggle in a market that favours and rewards all that is cheap, fast and plenty. 'Write about us,' the women said as I was leaving. They want people to know how hard it is to do this work, apart from running their homes, and how they pay for saapadu and sowriyam, or food and comfort, with their earnings: nine rupees an hour.

'Does the Thanjavur Veenai Inspire the Same National Passion as the Stradivarius Violin?'

Prabha Sridevan served as a judge of the Madras High Court from 2000 to 2010 and was the chairperson of the Intellectual Property Appellate Board from 2011 to 2013. She was named one of the fifty most important persons in intellectual property in 2012, 2013 and 2015 by the magazine *Managing Intellectual Property*. In 2014, she was tasked with heading an intellectual property rights (IPR) think tank by the central government to formulate India's IPR policy. She is a prolific writer and has published articles and books in English and Tamil, besides translations of Tamil fiction into English.

Can intellectual property rights be a tool of social justice? Have there been instances when IP has helped empower a community, gender or people?

Yes, certainly. Geographical Indications of Goods [Registration and Protection] Act (GI Act), the Protection of Plant Varieties and Farmers' Rights Act (PPV) and the Biological Diversity Act are legislations which deal with intellectual property rights that are designed to include and share, in contrast to the Patents Act, which is designed to exclude and appropriate. The latter is monopolistic while the former three are not. The introduction to the GI Act speaks of increasing the prosperity of the producers of goods registered under the Act. The PPV Act speaks of recognition and protection of the rights of farmers and the acceleration of agricultural development. The Biodiversity Act mentions conservation of biological diversity, sustainable utilisation of resources and equitable sharing of benefits. If these acts work well, they can surely be tools of social justice. I am not going into detail here, but just giving you an idea of what is available.

Let's take the case of Assam's famous Muga silk which has a GI. Promoting GIs has benefits that go beyond just IP protection. In the northeastern states, which are rich in tradition, culture and biodiversity, much of the art and craft forms have local origins, in terms of material and the making. This forms the basis for the GIs. The golden yellow Muga silk of Assam was registered in 2007. But only two people had applied to be its authorised users till 2014. In 2015, two GI camps—one in Guwahati and another in Lakhimpur, Assam—created awareness among stakeholders from thirty-three villages. The organisers learnt that producers were simply unaware of the benefits of GI, and could not fight against fake products that were passed off as real Muga silk. This is, by no means, unique to Muga silk, but a problem with GI products across the country. Dr Prabuddha Ganguli, the Ministry of Human Resource Development Intellectual Property Rights Chair of Tezpur University, who was associated with the GI camps, said that the response from Muga makers [to the camps] was staggering. More than ninety people applied to be registered as authorised users.

State governments must take note of this initiative and replicate this success across the country. With some imagination and effort, they can make the legislation work in favour of the producers, so as to maintain quality and prevent GI products from going extinct.

Many crafts and products from Tamil Nadu have received a GI. Two of them feature in this book—Pathamadai mats and Kancheepuram silk. While the GI is encouraging, it hasn't helped them financially. Why is it hard to replicate the GI success stories from elsewhere, in India and world over?

Other countries have been far more successful with marketing and branding. Look at the premium a bottle of sparkling wine from France commands over another manufactured in a similar manner in the US, only because of the name champagne, which is a GI. That's the advantage champagne has. Indians travelling abroad will pay extra for that GI. But what's in our backyard is not given its due.

The Thanjavur veenai, which has a GI, may not be made for long because of paucity of wood. The number of makers is already dwindling; soon they might all turn to other occupations. What does this tell us? Granting a GI alone is not enough. The government has to nurture the product and support the practitioner. But what does it do instead? When a severe cyclonic storm in 2013 felled jackfruit trees, among others, the wood was sold as timber. Why couldn't they have given them to the veenai makers? The nadaswaram makers, similarly, are always on the lookout for aachamaram. They also want a GI for their product. But, is the tag alone going to solve their problems? The Thanjavur veenai probably has a more hoary history than the Stradivarius violin. But, does it inspire the same national passion as the violin?

Of course, GI owners also have a role to play in promoting their product. But unfortunately, they are not as vocal or powerful as trademark and patent owners. Take the weavers of Kancheepuram silk, which has a GI. They are abandoning their great craft and going to work in colleges and companies nearby. Long ago, their profession was well respected. In the early twentieth century, a weaver and designer from Kancheepuram called Muthu Chettiar came to Madras. He had thirteen annas in his pocket. His sarees were exquisite and the elite in the city queued up to buy them. His most famous creation was the MS Blue saree. I remember wearing his sarees. It made people envious. Can you imagine weavers like him today?

Of the options available—trademarks, patents, copyrights, GI, PPV, biodiversity—what would, in your opinion, work best for India?

Geographical indication is one of India's strengths. Everything we grow or make is specific to a region. There are so many examples we use in everyday conversation, which I had written about in an article in *The Hindu*: 'Leave your Kolhapuri chappals over there,' or 'Come in and wash your hands with Mysore sandal soap,' or 'Have those idlis made with the Coimbatore wet grinder,' or 'The Darjeeling tea in the Jaipur pottery cup,' or 'Where did you buy that Sanganeri print?' All of them are GIs. And these rights need to be strengthened and protected.

PPV, biodiversity and traditional knowledge can all be used to our advantage. However, there are uncertainties in these legislations—the near mindless interpretations of some provisions, lack of understanding by the officers in charge of implementing the Act about the hows and whys of the Acts. These defects should be addressed. We are prolific creators of works that are governed by the Copyright Act. Given the right impetus, we can be leaders in any area. Our people do not lack an innovative spirit. You may have read of the spurt in patent registration by IITs. So, I will not restrict our capacity to create intellectual property.

How can IPR work hand in hand with the call now to bring skills and knowledge out in the open, and make it shareable.

We already have Acts that speak of benefit sharing, so the owners of the rights are recognised. The Copyright Act speaks of fair use, and so do the other acts, which shall not constitute infringement. We have compulsory licensing provisions in the Patent Act.

In fact, a question like this is difficult to answer because each IP has its own defined space and dynamics and as I have often repeated in the case of IP, one size or one hat does not fit all.

Draupadi Plays a Final Game of Dice

In two hours, the girl became a gypsy. Slender and sharp-featured, she peered into a hand mirror and applied a pasty foundation. Her face and fingertips turned blue, her 'look' for the lead role. She dusted her face with talc. With steady hands, she lined her eyes with kohl, drew a neat black circle on her forehead and filled it with kumkum. She stained her lips a deep red, tied her hair into a bun, and pinned false hair beneath it. S. Tamilarasi was ready for the lead role in *Draupadi Kuravanchi* to be performed in Chennai's prestigious Narada Gana Sabha.

Kings, queens and clowns rushed in and out of the green room, and the sound of their ankle bells flared and faded. A little boy made faces at his moustachioed reflection while another adjusted his red skirt and glittering crown. Many of the actors were children, and all of them were students of the Kattaikkuttu Gurukulam, a Kancheepuram-based school that teaches kattaikkuttu. This is a form of therukuttu, a rural theatre performance hugely popular in Tamil Nadu.

The younger ones sat around their teacher, Tamilarasi, fascinated by her. Traditionally, men dressed and performed as women. She is only the second woman to become a professional kattaikkuttu artist, barely a year after P. Thilagavathi became the first.

Their guru, P. Rajagopal, was the one who made this possible. Born in a family of traditional performers, Rajagopal acts, writes and directs plays and teaches the Perungattur bani of kattaikkuttu—the name derived from his village in Tiruvannamalai district. This elaborate theatre form includes song, dance, make-up, drama and dialogue and is typically performed through the night at village festivals in north and central Tamil Nadu. It takes extraordinary stamina and skill to last the eight hours.

In Tamil villages, kuttu begins at ten in the night. There are no mikes and chairs, or a raised stage—just a well-lit open ground, often near a temple. The orchestra plays four instruments: mridangam and dholak for percussion, harmonium for chords and the wind instrument mukaveenai. The kattiyakaran, or narrator and clown, is the first to appear. He entertains the audience and initiates the story. The lead performers are ushered in around midnight. There is an air of mystery as they come dancing behind a cloth screen and a collective gasp goes up among the audience when the richly dressed performers emerge. Until the sun rises, the crowd is held captive as they sing, dance and bring alive stories from the great epics—stories of kings and queens, gods and gypsies, warriors and clowns.

The art gets its name—kattai meaning wood and kuttu meaning theatre—from the heavily decorated wooden gear that the lead actors wear on their head, shoulders and chest. This art form is also unusual in that the performer combines singing and prose dialogue with acting and movement or dance, in contrast to other South Indian theatre forms, such as kathakali or yakshagana, 'where the singing has been delegated to a separate person, thus opening up the possibility, for example, for more facial expression and for a form of "classicisation,"' said Hanne M. de Bruin, a Dutch national who did her PhD research on the dance form. She is also married to Rajagopal.

Kattaikkuttu, in its current form and style, can be traced back to about four generations. There have been mentions of kuttu in ancient Tamil literature, including the *Silapadigaram*, but 'we don't know what type of theatre that was,' said Hanne. 'Its history has not been written, like the histories of many other popular forms. What we have is oral history that goes as far back as people can remember. It's very clear, though, that such a complex form doesn't come out of nothingness. They must have evolved, sometimes quite fast, to what we now call kattaikkuttu.'

The form typically changes with the geography. What is performed in Kancheepuram might be different from its rendition in Salem or Dharmapuri. 'But we don't exactly know how widespread this form is, how many people perform it, or even how many people watch kuttu.' Given the swelling crowds at the performances, the number of viewers probably exceeds those who watch live theatre in Chennai, 'but we have no figures.'

The core of kattaikkuttu performers were traditionally confined to two caste groups in northern Tamil Nadu—the Pandarams and the Vannars, who fall under the most backward castes. However, nowadays, the majority of performers are Vanniyars, who come under the backward caste. The art has always been open to other communities as well, said Hanne. Rajagopal too began teaching anybody who wished to learn, including women and girls.

During my first visit to the Kattaikkuttu Gurukulam in December 2014, the group was rehearsing under Rajagopal's supervision. The children call him thatha, grandpa, while Hanne is paati, grandma.

Training for kuttu starts early in life. Rajagopal recalled performing when he was barely five. 'One of my first memories was acting as Krishna. I was very small. They made me sit on top of the pandal and drop a sari down to Draupadi.' He quit formal education when he was ten to join his father, C. Ponnusami, in his theatre company as a professional child actor. In 1990, he established the Kattaikkuttu Sangam in Punjarasantangal village of Kancheepuram with sixteen artists from different companies. Along with Hanne, he founded the Kattaikkuttu Gurukulam, a Tamil medium residential school, in 2002. Run by the Sangam and in the same village, it offers students the opportunity to learn the art form without having to drop out of school.

The Gurukulam is path-breaking, as it offers a dual curriculum, free of cost—in addition to the regular subjects taught at schools, students also learn singing, acting, dance, music and other arts. A fee of ₹8,000 is charged annually for the hostel, and includes food, uniforms, medical insurance and counselling. When I reported on the school in 2016 for *Open* magazine, a third of the fifty-four students were girls. The teachers are hired from nearby villages, while international volunteers teach English through drama and storytelling.

Until Rajagopal's intervention, in these all-night performances that are physically demanding, men played women's roles. Families, for their part, worried that their daughter's marriage prospects would be ruined by their presence on a public stage, performing alongside men and exposed to the male gaze. Keen to address these concerns, Hanne and Rajagopal started an all-girls programme at the Gurukulam to encourage more female participation in this male-dominated theatre. They believe kuttu can, and should be, a dignified full-time profession for both men and women. Hanne pointed out that while their girl students are open to portraying both male and female roles, adolescent boys often hesitate to play the opposite gender at the Gurukulam.

Most of the young male graduates of the school are reluctant to take up kuttu as a full-time profession. They, as well as their parents, prefer higher education in order to get white-collar jobs to taking up the physically demanding kattaikkuttu, which also continues to carry the stigma of caste labour. The money does not look good either. Professional theatre companies divide the earnings, between ₹20,000 to ₹30,000 for a performance, among the thirteen to fifteen members, usually twelve performers and three musicians, after paying for the expenses. During the kuttu season—mid-January to mid-October—top troupes do 150 performances, while others average between 50 and 100.

The trouble is in tiding over the lean months. A full-time performer may be out of a job during the monsoon, but their individual earnings of ₹800–₹1,000 per performance must also pay for the upkeep of costumes and musical instruments, apart from regular household expenses. A performer and teacher at the Gurukulam, Kailasam, said, 'Some of us, like me, teach or make the wooden gear and costumes to supplement our income.' Others work temporarily as farmers and coolie workers, but many are in debt.

'The indebtedness has to be seen in a certain context,' said Hanne. Artists take loans, called an 'advance', for high rates of interest. Before, advances were provided by company owners to bridge the lean season. Now, these advances 'have taken on very different proportions, are often provided by persons outside the acting profession, carry a high rate of interest and are seen as representing the "worth" of an actor.' Both the lender and borrower are aware that the loan might not be repaid at the end of the season. Performers still borrow, for they have no other option.

But this has not stopped some of Gurukulam's students from taking to the art form full-time and desiring the recognition and fame it brings. Parents too give in when the children are passionate and adamant. 'How can they say "no"?' asked Rajagopal. He should know: his father did not wish to foist the art on his son. Except, Rajagopal was keen. 'There were reservations,' explained Hanne, 'because the word therukkuttu was used derisively, and actors were not accepted socially.'

Twenty-two-year-old Doraisamy, an actor and teacher at the Gurukulam, loves kuttu because of the adulation. People laugh and clap when he plays the kattiyakkaran. He finds the crowd's appreciation and acceptance to be addictive. And so do Thilagavathi and Tamilarasi, who fought many battles to be able to do what they love.

The Gurukulam started classes a year after the then eleven-year-old Thilagavathi was introduced to the art by her uncle, also a kuttu artist. She enrolled in its first year with two of her male cousins.

Back then, Thilagavathi did not know too much about the art form. She was charmed by the Gurukulam though. All she had seen until then were thatched-roof huts and simple meals in her village, Mettu Mulluvadi in Vellore district. 'Back home, we were five girls and there was little money. Only my father, a kuttu performer, earned something. My mother ran the house and looked after all of us. We didn't even have a proper roof like this,' she said, pointing to the terraced house we were in, of her classical dance mentor, Sangeetha Iswaran, in Chennai. Thilagavathi recalled being overjoyed by the many uniforms for different activities, thrilled to see the ceramic tiles in the building, and fascinated by the pencils and notebooks.

'It was all so fancy; I really enjoyed it.' She drew out the word 'fancy' for effect. 'At the school, everything was new and surprising. The white-skinned foreigners especially so!'

Academics did not interest the young Thilagavathi. 'But kuttu? That was great. You learn it by listening, and I could do that very well. However long the dialogue, I picked it up in two minutes.' By the time she was fifteen, she started getting lead roles. 'I was doing well. When I started menstruating, my mother visited me and that was all. Life went on pleasantly, until one of my friends back home in the village got married when I was sixteen.' That put enormous pressure on her, with relatives pointing out that it was time for her, the oldest girl in the family, to get married as well.

'It was a tough time. I was to have married my maama, my mother's younger brother. They said that if I went up on the kuttu stage, I would no longer be a "good girl".' She was alluding to how her community views girls who perform on stage, especially with men—as sex workers.

Now in her late twenties, Thilagavathi still looked only about sixteen. Her face was animated, and her hands and eyes matched up. 'There was such a big uproar. I told my parents, don't listen to what the others say. If you trust me, let me act.'

Around that time, she got a chance to go to the UK for two weeks to perform *Pagadai Thugil*—Dice and Disrobing—an adaptation of the *Mahabharata* by Rajagopal. She was with three other girls, accompanied by Rajagopal and Hanne. That trip helped silence the critics.

Though the social pressures never quite went away, Thilagavathi did not let it break her desire to perform either. She dropped out of school after class ten and became a full-time kuttu performer, encouraged by Hanne. 'Paati used to say that no girls performed, and that it was time someone broke that barrier. I decided to do this at any cost.'

Besides, she added, she did not really know what to do outside the world of kuttu. She might have gotten married and had two kids. How can it compare with what she loved to do? She refused to get married at eighteen when her parents compelled her to. 'Not that they have stopped asking. They don't order me to get married any more. They request me now!'

Thilagavathi got more of a 'voice' in her family when she started supporting them financially, and she continues to take care of her sisters' education, from the ₹15,000 she makes during the season. 'It is possible to make a good living from the art. It only requires initiative.' She also supplements her income by taking hour-long lessons, which she charges ₹1,000 for. 'But my father does not see the possibilities. That's why he thought getting me married was the best option. I would then become somebody else's problem!' But problems only begin after marriage, she argued. 'And, my lifestyle is such that I travel so much. Unless I find someone supportive ...'

During the kuttu season, she goes back to the village to perform. She is the only woman among the sixteen artists in a senior troupe called Mandaveli Amman Nadaga Mandram in Tiruvanamalai. 'I am like a rani in that troupe. The men take care of everything, and they are particular about my privacy.'

While she finds her colleagues to be respectful and understanding, it is the audience that brings her back to the stage, every time. 'Every kuttu experience is special. Sometimes, fans don't even wait for the show to get over. They come up to me during the performance and give me money. It's a sign of appreciation.' Her fans have given her sarees along with matching nail polish, hair clips and sticker bindis. Once, when she acted as the gypsy—her trademark role—she received a five hundred rupee note, a novelty.

Tamilarasi's journey has been no less difficult. Though it was her father who admitted her to the Gurukulam when she was nine, he began insisting that she quit during her early teens when some of her classmates were pulled out of the school by their parents. 'That was the first time I stood up to my father. I told him I did not ask to learn this: "You put me here, and now I want to continue."' Though her mother was, and continues to be, supportive, her father was swayed by popular opinion. 'My father said he was only trying to forewarn me, to prevent my name from being ruined. But I stood firm.' At fifteen, her determination to make a career out of kuttu solidified.

Although Tamilarasi has three older siblings, who are all married, it is her income that helps her mother run the household. 'She is careful with money, unlike my father.'

Tamilarasi still has to constantly fob off snide remarks, the most common being: 'You are a kuttu dancer, who will marry you?' She always replies that somebody will, and that she will not let marriage end her career.

In her early twenties now, Tamilarasi teaches at the Gurukulam as well as performs in their productions. 'Kuttu is far more complicated than most other performing arts,' she said. As it combines many forms on one stage, one needs 'a good voice, great foot skills and incredible breath control.' Given how slight her frame is, she is often asked where she gets her energy from. 'When I am singing and dancing on stage, I just become the character.'

Her voice is rough, but her diction is excellent and her throw astonishing, which is perhaps why she plays the lead in many of the Gurukulam's productions. But she didn't take to kuttu at once. Her singing was off-key and she struggled to memorise the lyrics. Only the dance came effortlessly. Noticing this, her guru and teachers encouraged her to try lead roles, even the heroic male ones. She did, and was soon a big hit on stage. When she was younger, she was just excited to wear the elaborate male costumes. Then, she grew to enjoy the characters' complexities, like those of Arjuna and Abhimanyu, her favourite male roles. Her aptitude for the epics comes in handy for her sister, a schoolteacher who makes it a point to consult the performer in the family before her mythology lessons. 'She has no idea who is whose mother, father, brother,' Tamilarasi mocked her sister.

It is when she plays Draupadi that she is truly transformed. 'Draupadi is my role model. She's so powerful, so strong.' Her enactment of this compelling character in *Karnatic Meets Kattaikkuttu*—a collaboration between Carnatic musicians T.M. Krishna and Sangeetha Sivakumar and kattaikkuttu artists led by P. Rajagopal on a Mumbai stage in 2017—was gripping. Ordered to come to Duryodhana's court, her pride hurt, she became fierce, angry, and stood taller and straighter. When she was dragged by her hair, she spun dizzyingly eight or nine times, round and round the stage, a chilling tableau of a young girl in a white saree, running away from the clutches of a power-drunk man. Every eye in the audience followed her, stunned when she was dragged to the court. They cursed and flinched when she was thrown at the merciless king's feet. Despite the familiar story, Tamilarasi had the audience in her clutches, making them fear with her, pray with her and root for her.

She was pleased to perform for an urban audience but prefers a boisterous rural one, whose enthusiasm adds energy to her performance. 'In city auditoriums, they use mikes. It distorts the voice, and I am conscious of how I deliver my lines. The audience is in the dark and they are all so quiet. Of course, they clap for comedy scenes, during entries and exits. But how do I know if they like what

I'm doing?' She would, on a village stage—with the passionate crowd on its feet, the air energised by their hooting and clapping, their appreciation demonstrated with blessings and requests to perform in their village again.

Both the women are determined to share their training and take kuttu to more people.

During the off-season, Thilagavathi works in Katradi, an NGO founded by Iswaran, where she teaches disabled children using kuttu as a tool. She also aims to visit schools and introduce kuttu to a thousand kids a year. 'I went to see thatha and paati last week. I got an award—Sahitya Akademi's Yuva Puruskar—and went to show it to him. I had to thank my guru. Who would know me but for him?'

Meanwhile, Tamilarasi has put together a fun half-hour programme, called Masala. It is an amalgamation of storytelling in English and Tamil with acrobatics, clowning, fighting and, of course, strong kuttu elements. Her idea is to make the art form exciting to even the uninitiated. She learnt acrobatics and clowning for three months at the Dimitri school in Verscio, Switzerland. Though she had earlier visited England for workshops with Rajagopal, Hanne and other students, it was her first trip abroad on her own. While there, she conducted two kuttu workshops, taught step classes and received training in rhythm, clowning, acrobatics and classical dance. Her biggest takeaway from her trip to Switzerland, though, was that art was venerated and the teaching of it respected, and that it paid well.

Hanne too agreed that the challenges today are biased pay scales for classical and folk arts, stepmotherly treatment of folk arts and the dismissive attitude to them in the cities. 'Why are our shows covered only when we perform in Chennai? The Sangam's annual festival has seen some grand versions, and even that got very little coverage.' The village shows are bigger, longer and draw thousands of spectators. 'Why are we not invited to theatre festivals in the city? To Chennai's December music season? Why are we paid a pittance, compared to a classical musician, who might earn ten times more than what we do? They are just five people in that troupe, we are fifteen.'

Her whys are unsettling and hang without answers. Rajagopal, through his art, has addressed some of them—patriarchy, for example, through his twist to Draupadi's story in *Pagadai Thugil*. In his version, she challenges Duryodhana to a final game of dice, pledging her chastity, and wins. 'When this is performed, audiences are ecstatic,' said Tamilarasi. Won't the last scene take place only at six in the morning, I ask. 'Of course, but people wait, 2,000 of them, some standing all night.'

How do we decide where an art form is headed, if it is thriving or fading? How does one measure its shifting boundaries? It is difficult to debate this as we don't have actual figures, said Hanne. 'Who knows how many performances there were in the 1930s? In the 1950s? We cannot make unsubstantiated, emotional statements that we cannot prove.'

What we can do, she argued, is look at the potential of the form. 'Kattaikkuttu is not dying. How can it be, when there are over 2,000 people watching the Mahabharata performances? The question we must be asking is, where would we like to see it ten years from now?' If a performance in a small village gets fifty viewers, a staging during a big festival attracts a few thousands. 'Big companies and women in the cast attract a specific audience too. The "dying argument" seems to serve only one purpose: the dance has to die in order to be rescued, and be "purified", etc.' To underline the irony in her statement, she threw in a heartful laugh.

The art form, Hanne predicted, will face its biggest challenge—and crisis—when agriculture crumbles. 'Then kuttu will also disappear,' not unlike other rural livelihoods that are all intrinsically related to agriculture. 'For me, that connection is so crucial. Because the most important occasions for kattaikkuttu performances are related to the agrarian season. When agriculture goes down fully or becomes totally commercialised, then I see a lot of problems for kuttu as it is performed today in villages.' It is exactly what sickle makers fear, and what nadaswaram players and makers worry about. Just like farmers who encourage their children to take up other jobs and move away from agriculture, kuttu performers too want an easier life for their children. 'Kuttu is a form of physical labour,' said Hanne. 'They don't always take pride in performing it and are ashamed of it, for whatever reasons. This prevents them from opting for kattaikkuttu as a full-time profession. They do not use their artistic talent.'

The school's website too talks of how society perceives the art:[1]

> Kattaikkuttu enjoys little social standing and respect although it is complex and profoundly meaningful. The urban, educated middle classes tend to think of kattaikkuttu as a theatre that lacks sophistication and taste and they question its ability to be "contemporary". Therefore, parents in rural and urban areas hardly ever envisage kattaikkuttu as a sustainable and dignified career for their children.

Wouldn't something like the Gurukulam encourage more people to take it up? Doesn't the admiration performers like Tamilarasi and

Thilagavathi receive inspire others? 'We have tried everything,' said Hanne. 'Rajagopal has built a new generation of performers who are professionally trained and who, when they leave the Gurukulam, are not burdened by debts. But the reality is that today we are not able to put up our own company, perhaps because many of our talented alumni students are not interested in the professional rigour Rajagopal demands, or have opted—often giving in to parental pressure—out of the performing arts. This year, because of lack of funding and no support from the state government, we are down to half our strength. Those who leave us, go and do other things, including setting up their own companies and drawing on students trained at the Gurukulam, which is fine, but ...'

The school's mandate itself, in many ways, is fulfilled. Rajagopal wanted to train the next generation of performers; he did. He wanted to open it up to women; he did this too. He wanted professional performers to enjoy good education and not, like himself, have to forsake school in order to become an actor; he accomplished that as well. He still performs, his steps perfect, his expressions sublime. In a performance I watched in an open-air theatre in Chennai, he became Krishna, his face painted blue, his eyes smiling and sharp at once; he walked the stage singing, acting, with a golden flute in one hand, his kohl-rimmed eyes taking in the audience, instructing the orchestra, smiling like the calendar prints of gods. And then he was Duryodhana, in an auditorium in Mumbai. His body bristled with the arrogance of a king who refuses to accept defeat, his face—framed with a tall crown and wooden ornaments—was haughty, humble, angry and sad, in turns. As his power and stature fell, so did his physical form—he was reduced from his great height to a man who kneeled and crawled and begged black ants to not tell Bheema that he was hiding in the Kurukshetra bhoomi. That minute, everybody—his students playing the orchestra and performing with him, the audience, other artists in the wings—was in awe of the man with a grand vision for a great art form.

On Art as Labour

’t is labour, hard labour
Tying my crown really tight
to perform fast spins.

With a silver plate and a band of pearls
on my forehead, (kattai) ear and shoulder,
ornaments and a shining breast pendant,
bells tied around my feet, I perform tirelessly.
(’t Is labour)

What’s the art in Kuttu they ask?
It’s easy to speak of its shortcomings.
When you do not immerse yourself in it
you will never be able to recognise and enjoy its finesse
(’t Is labour)
Kuttu starts at ten at night.
It finishes when it gets light
and even then we should look fresh and focused.
Bigwigs, I tell you that it’s labour, hard labour.

—P. Rajagopal [Translated by Hanne M. de Bruin]
From: *Karnatic Meets Kattaikkuttu: A Musical Conversation between T.M. Krishna and P. Rajagopal*

The Dance of the False-Legged Horse

She has been dancing since she was eleven, through the eighth month of her pregnancy, and when she was nursing her young children. When they cried, she fed them and went back to the performance. Fifty-six years later, when she wears the ornate papier-mâché horse on her waist, over her royal costume, and attaches the tall wooden stilts to her legs, she is just as agile, not missing a single beat of the Maratha drums, for N. Kamachi is the queen of poikkal kuthirai.

Literally meaning false-legged horse, the dance came to Tamil Nadu when Thanjavur was ruled by the Marathas.[1] An art form that demands great stamina and skill, it was once favoured in courts of kings and now precedes the deity in temple processions. It used to be quite popular at weddings and festivals, till it was replaced by other forms of entertainment. Now, more than half the artists have quit. Others, like Kamachi, her husband T.A.R. Nadi Rao and their family, are carrying forward—with difficulty—a tradition that came south with Rao's predecessors, the Marathas.

'My husband's ancestors came to Tamil Nadu as drummers and dancers, and stayed on,' said Kamachi, narrating the story she had heard from her husband's grand-aunt. Along with the dance, they also brought Maratha culture with them. Kamachi picked it up when she got married, a very young eleven-year-old bride, who learnt to wear her pallu over her head and speak fluent Marathi. She also learnt their dance.

As we sat around the dining table in their house in Vadakku Vassal, Thanjavur, Kamachi's oldest son Sivaji Rao showed me his parents' old wedding invitation. The shelves and walls were filled with medals, shields and certificates. There were photographs of Kamachi and Rao, standing proud, just like the king and queen they become in their dance.

Kamachi was born and raised in Pattukottai, where Rao and his parents came to perform. As Kamachi stood admiring their poikkal kuthirai act, Rao's mother noticed the pretty girl. 'Why don't my son and her get married?' she asked Kamachi's mother, who readily agreed. But there was opposition from the relatives. 'They are a family of kuttu dancers,' they scoffed. Rao's family was persistent, and the wedding happened in 1960, when the eleven-year-old girl child married a man nine years her senior.

Soon after her marriage, Kamachi's father-in-law, who was the first to introduce women dancers in poikkal kuthirai, was keen that she learn dancing.

'In his father's time—they were five brothers who were all performers—one of the men dressed up as a woman. My mother-in-law and her sister were perhaps the first women poikkal kuthirai dancers.' Sivaji, who has done some research on the art form, dated this to about seventy years ago.

Rao's father was frank about his intentions—the dance would support her and the family. The young girl was confused. She prayed to her favourite local goddess, Mahamayi, to guide her.

Even all these years later, she got emotional as she recalled the moment she said yes—a decision that shaped the rest of her life.

In the beginning, she could not grasp the dance of the poikkal kuthirai, which made her husband, who was teaching her, angry. The family appointed another teacher to train her in karagattam, or karagam, which involves dancing with a pot balanced on the head. Kamachi spoke of her first performance on stage the way a mother would describe her child's first walk—'*Thathaka, bhuthaka*'—imbalanced, wavering and unconfident. But the organisers thought otherwise; they showered her with coins. 'Not ordinary coins, silver ones.' She gathered them up and came home a dancer.

Her dancing progressed. She learnt a new form—kuravan-kurathi aatam or gypsy dance, vigorous yet joyous and playful—and began performing with her husband. 'But I was famous for karagam. I performed all sorts of tricks. They were ready to change the dates of the festivals if I was busy.'

Karagam dancers usually deploy tricks to entertain the audience as well as to showcase their balancing skills. Kamachi had a few up her pot, like the soda bottle trick. 'I opened it with my teeth and drank the fizzy liquid without touching the bottle.' The cost: her teeth. 'All these are false.' She opened her mouth for me to examine. The ten bottles she drank a day also left their mark on her stomach and made her oesophagus sore. 'I cannot eat spicy food or drink anything fizzy anymore.'

If she had any regrets, she did not show them. Instead, she continued with the story of her dancing career—she finally had her first poikkal kuthirai recital in Tiruchendur when she was thirty. 'It was torturous; I practised walking on stilts on this very road, outside the house, for two days.' She managed to retain her balance on the third day. The poikkal kuthirai dancer was born.

Kamachi flipped the pages of an old album she had ordered Sivaji to fetch from another room. Together, we admired the young dancer in beautiful flared skirts and gossamer half-sarees. No one could have guessed that in some of them she was expecting or already a mother of several children. The dummy horse too concealed her pregnancy. 'I nursed my children until they were two. Once, when we went to that town with a lot of coal ...' As she paused to remember the name, her son helped out. 'Yes, Neyveli. My younger son started crying. The organisers asked me to feed him and come back on stage.'

Kamachi's career was liberally peppered with applause and opportunities, more than she could manage. There was no bias then, unlike now, of seeking out only young women dancers for performing. 'I was a mother of two sons and two daughters. That did not matter. It was the dance that mattered, nothing else.' Back then, the dance was well respected too. 'Unlike today, when the moves are lewd and the costumes revealing, I wore a full dress—a long skirt, blouse and a half-saree.'

These days, organisers want the dancers to look glamorous. Kamachi used the harsh Tamil word—'kavarchi'—a reference to seductive roles and costumes in films. 'What's worse,' added Sivaji, 'is how many troupes agree to do that sort of thing.' With the attention shifting to their looks and costumes rather than their talent, many women performers are hesitant to continue dancing. 'If I go and announce regulations to all the artists, they will tell me to shut up and sit at home!' But Sivaji also acknowledged that the government seemed keen to ban obscene performances that are passed off as folk art. 'It might be our only chance.'

She reeled out the names of the district collectors who presided over the functions in which she had danced, guzzled soda and spit fire with a mouthful of kerosene. All for a few coins that would augment the family's income. 'I had children to educate, a family to feed. So, I danced three styles each evening.'

She berated me for not bringing up her salary. 'Ask me what I got!' she commanded, but went on to tell me without missing a beat. 'Back then, I got five rupees for a programme.' She paused dramatically. 'My husband? Three rupees!' Nearly a third less. The ten or twelve rupees the family made together just about covered household expenses. 'If I took a silver coin, I could buy a big measure of rice, vegetables, meat and also save a few annas for movie tickets.'

'It wasn't like there was a choice. We had to eat you know.' That is why women began dancing. 'There was an abundance of arrack then and the men were quite fond of it. If they earned ten rupees, they'd drink away seven. The next day, there'd be no money for rice.' The women did their men and families a favour by becoming professional dancers.

Kamachi calls the dummy horse Ayyanar, after the enormous clay horses that guard the village deities in Tamil Nadu. 'I see it as vehicle of the gods. I see my art form as divine.' Maybe that is why, she wondered aloud, her reputation has never been maligned. 'Nobody ever calls me a street performer. Of course, the officials and organisers know me as a dancer. But when I go out in society, I look different. Without make-up, I am a different person.'

It takes her over an hour to transform herself. She carries her wares in modest plastic containers. Inside, there is everything a dancer will need. As I watched her get ready for a performance—for a documentary we were shooting for PARI—she applied the make-up deftly; all the powders were natural, the white, yellow and vermillion bought from a naatu marundhu kadai, or country medical store, that sells local herb mixes. She swept up her hair into a bun, pinned flowers on them, lined her lips with black, and just as I wondered about the startling, dark outline, she filled it with red—'not lipstick, that's a weak colour, this paint won't come off'—and the effect was stunning.

She changed from her cotton saree into dancer's velvets. She wore her blouse and pyjamas, wrapped a towel over her bosom and sat on a chair. Her younger son Jeeva Rao helped her get her stilts on. He first tied the horizontal stick to her feet and then fixed the vertical ones on it. The wood and flesh were held together with white canvas straps. These were old-fashioned wooden stilts: tall and tapering. Kamachi scoffed at the newer stilts available today—stockier and shorter—just like she scoffed at those who dance for 'dappan kuttu', as the beat of a non-classical drum is commonly called. Only those who dance to sangeetham—according to her, traditional music with devotional lyrics—are real performers.

The stilts are made from the roots of the banyan tree, a lightweight wood that does not wear down easily. 'Now they use any and every wood,' said Sivaji in exasperation. Neither do they adjust the length of the stilts according to the person wearing them. 'A taller person will need a shorter one, otherwise he'll not look like a horse. He'll be a giraffe, won't he?'

As Kamachi and her husband slipped on their ankle bells, I picked up one of them and my hands sagged; a pair weighs over seven kilos. The bells were large and loud, like the ones used on cattle. 'The smaller ones won't be heard over the sound of stilts,' explained Sivaji. Kamachi lifted her hands and the dummy horse was lowered over her head till it came up to her waist.

When it was time to perform, she leaned on an assistant and climbed the few steps down from the dressing room to the performance space—the neighbour's yard. The papier-mâché horse, painstakingly handmade by Sivaji over six months and which cost ₹50,000, was rich and elegant, studded with mirrors and decorated with gold strips.

Though Kamachi described poikkal kuthirai as 'deiviga kalai', or godly art, her husband called it deadly. 'One wrong step when you're wearing all the gear, you'll fall heavily.' The stilts, ankle bells, the horse and costume together weigh about twenty to twenty-five kilos.

The whole ensemble looked bulky and awkward when they walked. But once the drumming began, the elderly couple danced gracefully and vigorously, making their drummers, one of whom was Jeeva, sweat. 'These drums, the kondalam, are the preferred instruments of the Marathi goddess Tulja Bhavani. Both the drums and the dance are central to Maratha culture and were played at the Maratha king's court in Thanjavur. They were also played in all functions, not just as an accompaniment for the dance,' said Sivaji, continuing his commentary.

'As part of the dance routine, we break coconuts placed on an assistant's head, slice raw bananas with a sword and perform stunts with live torches. All this is meant to reflect the valour of a yesteryear king—that he could similarly chop the enemies' heads and protect his people.' Sivaji is as good a dancer as he is a storyteller, and is especially adept at the kavadi style, but he was not performing that day.

The slicing and breaking looked impressively dangerous; the sword was long and the stick heavy, but Rao made it look effortless. When the couple held their horses together and took short, swift, circular steps, their outfits dazzled; the glass and sequins caught the sun and glinted. I closed my eyes and imagined how grand it might look in the dark of the night, lit only by handheld torches.

As poikkal kuthirai's popularity grew, so did the couple's stature. Official functions gave them opportunities, income and a name. 'But it was in 1982 that we really made it big,' said Kamachi. 'Five artists from Thanjavur were selected to go to Delhi for three months during the Asian Games. We were paid twelve rupees each a day,' for an event that was estimated to have cost the government ₹700–₹1000 crore.[2]

The family needed the money. They also had to pull Jeeva out of school, who was to write his class ten exams that year, and took him along. 'My husband said that if he came, there would be another ten rupees a day. Jeeva agreed, and my husband made him wear a peacock costume and perform with us.'

They were to lead Appu, the elephant mascot. 'It was bitterly cold in Delhi. But we had to be up at four, bathe and go for the rehearsal. Two days before the event, we were taken to the venue and had to stay there.' At the stadium, they had a feeling of being locked up—'*adachitaanga*'. 'There were many enemies and saboteurs out to disrupt the programme; so it was understandable.'

Their participation in the international event created a market for them back in Thanjavur. 'Many people asked me to perform here and there. There were times when, for ten days, I couldn't shut my eyes. I danced night and day.'

But lately, she has had to cut back on her programmes. 'I cannot dance for hours like I used to.'

The third time I met her in 2015, Kamachi paused our conversation around three in the afternoon. 'It's time for you to eat,' she said, and served rice, sambhar and vegetables on a plantain leaf. When I complimented the food, she protested, 'But this is hardly good food!' Kamachi has fond memories of her mother-in-law's cooking, which had a Marathi flavour. They loved their fish and liked meat. She mouthwateringly described a smoked brinjal recipe, its flesh mashed and cooked with onion, chilli and tamarind. 'They ate a lot of dried fish.' She burst out laughing as she said the Tamil word for it—karuvaadu; it is revered and ridiculed for its legendary smell, depending on whether one is a fan or not.

Having fed her guest, Kamachi spoke about her past and the art form's future prospects. The past dazzled in her words. As for the future, she was not sure if hopes and prayers would fix what policy and apathy had strangled.

The current rate for a troupe performing poikkal kuthirai is around ₹40,000, and the troupe includes dancers of karagam, kavadi, mayil or peacock and maadu or bull, along with the dummy horses, drummers and assistants. The luggage usually fills a 'kutti yanai', or small elephant, as mini lorries are called. It takes an hour and a half to put on the make-up and another hour to pack up, and this time too is factored into their costs. The stilts they use need the support of assistants, who need to be paid as well. So, organisers would rather have karagam dancers, who work out cheaper, than poikkal kuthirai artists.

B. Kolappan, a senior journalist with *The Hindu* who has followed and written extensively about performing arts in Tamil Nadu, said that there is a huge demand for folk performers during the season. 'Almost every community, except Brahmins, have their folk deity temples now, modelled after Vedic temples. Non-Brahmins are asserting their link with religion. Their economic upliftment is reflected in the temples they construct for their folk deities. Today,

Mutharamman and Sudalaimadan temples are concrete buildings with fine decorations. Poojais happen there regularly, and so do folk festivals. When I was in class five, I remember folk art forms were gradually waning. In the last thirty years, there's a terrific revival, and there's a large number of troupes.'

Panagudi M. Siva, who plays the nadaswaram in naiyandi melam—a folk ensemble that sometimes accompanies a poikkal kuthirai performance—substantiated this.

'During the season, in Tirunelveli, Tuticorin, Kanyakumari, and Virudhunagar, folk artists are very busy. Sometimes, advance is given for a season five years ahead!'

With eight members, leading naiyandi melam troupes charge about ₹45,000–₹50,000 to perform on all three days of a village festival, and this amount includes the transportation cost. After the performance, the money is split seven ways—one part each for two nadaswaram players, two tavil players, two pambai players, and a half part each to the one who keeps the pitch and another, the beat.

Kolappan further asserted that the demand is so high that it is sometimes difficult to book folk artists. 'Unless you block their dates well in advance, you might not get the person you want. For my village's kodai thiruvizha in 2018, I had to put together a team of musicians from different areas. The players for magudam and mandam—percussion instruments of kuttu—came from different places, and so did the annavi, the main singer. The busiest months tend to be Panguni, Chithirai and Vaigasi months of the Tamil calendar—corresponding to the time between mid-March to mid-June—when outdoor performances take place. This is street art, not something performed in an auditorium.'

But these opportunities are limited to the summer months, when village festivals take place. 'At the end of the season, performers without vices—who don't splurge on drink—can earn about a lakh,' said Siva. 'After July, until the following March, the going is very hard.' And the money, hard to come by.

Sivaji calculated that a folk artist might get eighty to a hundred programmes a year, although some years it might be half of that. The earnings from this have to last them the whole year. The Raos only manage to make ends meet because they are also farmers. Their dwindling opportunities were recently hit by another unexpected problem: a whole new set of rules regarding the length of the events and how late they can go on into the night. 'When we go as a troupe of fifteen and charge ₹40,000 for a performance, organisers are reluctant to hire us when the event itself is barely two hours,' said Sivaji. 'It's impossible to be a full-time artist and run a household.'

'These days, performances are half-hearted because people completely unrelated to the art are getting in. There were other dancers in Thanjavur. But they have abandoned their horses, and given up the art because they got no opportunities.' Sivaji summed up the situation with a Tamil saying: '*Kazhudai thenju katterumba aachu*'—the donkey grew smaller and smaller, until it became an ant.

Poikkal kuthirai is doubly devastated, economically and culturally. 'You cannot live off the income of the dance. Look at the abysmal payments for folk performances,' said Kamachi. 'Sometimes you get awards, but can you eat them?' asked Rao.

The community fought for a raise. Sivaji estimated there to be about one lakh folk artists in Tamil Nadu, hailing from various communities, and about three hundred artists' associations, with four in Thanjavur. Associations, or sangams, are vital because, as Sivaji put it, 'If everybody claps, it is heard better.' After the demand from folk performers, state-run cultural organisations doled out ₹800 per person per performance post 2013. Before, it was only half that. 'Bharatanatyam dancers, for a troupe of five, get ₹25,000–₹30,000. It clearly shows they respect those art forms more, doesn't it?' asked Sivaji. Let alone Chennai, even in their own town, and other smaller towns, classical artists are picked over folk artists.

The art form's future is a touchy subject with Kamachi. On the one hand, she is devoted to it, both her sons dance and drum, and her grandson is enthusiastic about learning. But the future looks uncertain as the art form grows more unviable as a full-time livelihood. Mother, father and son reeled out the various discriminations and deep prejudices they often face.

'My sons ask why I keep pushing them to take this up when we have suffered so greatly from lack of patronage. It was hard to find brides for them. A relative, whose daughter I sought in marriage for my older boy, refused. He said that I would make his daughter dance like me on the road.' The hurt in Kamachi's voice was evident. This played out again when she looked for grooms for her daughters. 'A vegetable vendor, a gardener, a fish seller—they are also professionals. So are we!' Yet, she recognised the prejudice that folk forms and artists face. 'It would have been entirely different had we danced bharatanatyam, wouldn't it have?'

Folk arts were not looked down upon always. '"Folk artist" has come to mean all sorts of things. It wasn't so bad earlier. My in-laws have travelled for four days by bullock-carts to perform in Chettinad. They were treated well and rewarded with gold coins. Now, people openly say, "These arts are meant for people from lower castes and classes." Why is it perceived that way?' asked Kamachi.

'Schools and colleges have folk performances too. But do any of the children continue performing outside of school? No,' said Sivaji.

Again, the reservations are the same—performing folk arts would tarnish the person's name, especially a woman's.

Rao is also deeply upset about the art form's place in Tamil society. 'In Dubai, Istanbul and London, they celebrate this art and press us to stay longer. But in Tamil Nadu, poikkal kuthirai is not regarded highly anymore; other forms of entertainment have displaced this.'

'Given a choice, people would prefer our dance. That's why they present classical forms first at events. If not, the crowds will watch us and leave,' said Kamachi. 'All organisations that promote the arts in India are guilty of some kind of discrimination. We are asked to sleep and stay in schools and verandas, while classical performers are given good hotel facilities.'

Kolappan brought this up too. 'Folk artists sleep in a corner of the temple they perform in. It is a difficult life. The work is tedious, and sometimes, inhuman. And while people encourage them—by coming in big numbers to watch them perform—they are yet to perceive them as artists. Are appreciation and pay alone enough without respect?'

Continuing to draw parallels with classical music, he said, 'Classical performers don't need to do it full-time. Look at the leading Carnatic vocalists—they didn't start their careers as full-time musicians. They let go off other jobs only when their music picks up.' But that is not a luxury available to folk artists, who have little means to survive outside of their art.

Kamachi and Rao threw up another challenge, as artists: 'I can dance to bharatanatyam beats, can that dancer handle mine? Will a vocal concert or bharatanatyam recital go along with the procession of the deity?'

After leading lives of indignation, they are taunted at death too. 'To get compensation due to us in case of accidental death, we have to shuttle between departments for days,' complained Sivaji. 'And who comes to the funeral when a folk performer dies?'

Though money was never freely available in Kamachi's household, there was never a poverty of talent. If Kamachi has fame, Rao and his sons have awards. Their list is impressive: Rao received the Kalaimamani from the Tamil Nadu government, and so did Sivaji, recently. In 2013, Rao and Jeeva received the Sangeet Natak Akademi award from the President, for their drumming.

When I asked Kamachi if she was unhappy about not winning awards, she held Rao's framed, gilded certificate and said, without a trace of jealousy, 'My only wish is that my husband wins more.'

Kamachi never went to school, but she listed the names of big and little countries—a long roster—that she has visited. Her grandson, who accompanied the family to Delhi for the Sangeet Natak Akademi award ceremony told her, 'It was the dummy horse that took all of us on a flight. I too will dance.' Kamachi is delighted that he is eager to learn the form.

Yet, she asked, 'Where is the future in this? If the next generation become carpenters, or sell fruits on a push-cart, they can make a living. But dancing?'

Then again, the dancer in her wants, more than anything, for her sons and grandson to take the art forward. 'Even today, when I wear the ankle bells, I'm energised. When I remove them, I feel drained.' When she is not a dancer, her responsibilities crowd her: she needs to feed the chicken, pick up a titchy one that might have fallen into the gutter, fetch water, cook dinner ...

Late one evening in her Thanjavur house, Kamachi and Rao were showing me pictures from their Germany and Turkey trips. A sudden rain drummed and lashed on the roof.

Kamachi was the first to run upstairs to save the paddy harvested from the two acres of land they own. Her family joined her a few minutes later. When she came back, though she seemed happy to have saved the sacks of grains in the nick of time, she also looked tired. But she was not going to get much rest. Early next morning, the family was going to Sivagangai for a programme. That meant packing all the gear, travelling for three hours, make-up for two, and then the dancing. She would return home late that evening. It sounded extraordinary. For Kamachi, it was just another day.

'Physical Labour Is a Trigger for Art'

T.M. Krishna is a vocalist in the Carnatic tradition. He writes and speaks about issues that affect the human condition and culture. Krishna has authored books on art, including the pathbreaking *A Southern Music: The Karnatik Story* and *Reshaping Art*. He is the driving force behind the Chennai Kalai Theru Vizha, which opens arts and artists to new audiences and environments, and Svanubhava, which aims to cultivate a sensitivity to the arts among future generations. He has been part of inspiring collaborations, such as performances with the Jogappas—transgender musicians—and co-conceptualising and performing Karnatic Kattaikuttu, an unusual aesthetic conversation between art forms and communities that belong to two ends of the social spectrum. He received the Ramon Magsaysay Award in 2016 in recognition of 'his forceful commitment as artist and advocate to art's power to heal India's deep social divisions'.

How and when did performing arts become a livelihood? Were they ever seen as a sustainable livelihood option?

We need to think about whether arts need to be sustainable in the traditional sense of a market; the buying-selling transaction. It's similar to wondering whether education or healthcare need to be private. I believe that both should not be privately owned. They are products, yet they are not. But, with art, things get complicated, because while people understand the absolute need for education and healthcare for every member of society, they are not convinced that art is essential.

The other aspect is patronage. We may have replaced the feudal king, zamindar and chieftain with the corporate honcho and bureaucrat, but our relationship with these characters has not changed. Within this structure, gender and caste inequality continue to live. The corporate says, 'I'll give you shows,' and the government bureaucrat says, 'I'll give you recognition, awards, tours and money for projects.' Except for some Dalit art forms, this is today's ugly model.

No art form is sustainable only through the sale of tickets. Even with 15,000 people paying ₹5,000 per head, a film music show cannot happen if the corporate does not put in crores. This is true of any performance, whether in a village or a city. It needs buffering and cushioning, which can only come from the corporate or the government.

Support cannot be removed from the performing arts anywhere in the world. The Kennedy Center gets huge grants from the American government. In Europe, the mayor of each city provides grants for museums and performances. As much as I am suspicious of corporate intentions, I can't run away from the fact that they are an important part of the ecosystem today and I will not dismiss them as unnecessary. Crowdfunding will work up to a point but beyond that you need the state government or corporate. So, it's always going to be a combination of these resources that can make art sustainable.

But—this is a catch-22 situation—we have not yet got to the point where we can assert that art is a necessity. We still talk about art being a luxury, just pleasure, and that's deeply problematic. Hence, all those in a position of power who control opportunity or the purse strings believe they are doing art and artists a favour. This needs to change. As a society, we need to truly realise the intangible, irreplaceable, ethical and social necessity of art.

It gets even more complicated if you go down the hierarchy. The classical forms sit on the cushy part. Beyond that, the patronage system has collapsed. You won't get a corporate to sponsor oyilattam performers, who depend much more on state support and government grants.

But there are some art forms that sustain themselves in villages. For example, there are four to five hundred performances of kuttu in the villages every year. I don't think they get paid great amounts of money. But performances are happening and there is a cultural demand for this form locally.

But there are art forms that have been unable to compete with mass culture such as cinema; they have now become curio pieces, which the state then wants to display occasionally as 'our culture'. The state will provide a stipend of ₹3,000 a month but will not engage with the art form or discuss how to revive its cultural gravitas. For example, how do we make oyilattam important to various cultural spheres? Rather than saying I'll protect it, you must think, how will I enrich it?

This is where India has failed completely. Except for spurts, there is no sustained cultural engagement from the government. The problem is that they think of cultural engagement as giving grants to four musicians, conducting four festivals and giving some money for archival purposes. I applaud it, but this is very limited. It does not address the larger picture of why these artists are suffering and the very essentiality of the art form itself. What does it represent and what are its cultural, social and political contributions? These are the questions the government must be asking.

In Tamil Nadu, are we protecting the culture we are so proud of?

No. We do nothing. Forget mainstream Brahminical Carnatic music. What has the state done to sustain Tamil art forms? Nothing. Various art traditions of the state sustain themselves through local support and patronage. The moment this is reduced, especially if they do not belong to the cultural elite, it becomes a desperate struggle. The state has done very little to truly celebrate, what we like to call, Tamil culture. Support has been small, reactionary, sans any serious engagement and completely lacking in a cultural vision. This is primarily because we do not recognise the arts as socio-cultural enablers. They are viewed merely as culture-specific entertainment mechanisms.

As a counter to the Brahminical Carnatic world, the Tamil Nadu state government has built music colleges that teach Tamil isai and other art forms; students from across the state learn music in these institutions. But where do they go after passing out? Take nadaswaram for example. Artists from Tamil Nadu survive because they perform in kutcheris in Kerala, which has done far more for the nadaswaram than we have. Money and respect also comes from Malaysia, Singapore, the UK, Canada and Australia; wherever Sri Lankan Tamils reside. They are the true patrons of the nadaswaram and tavil. The other occupational option for them is teaching in government music colleges.

There is a great deal of talent but we do not know what to do with it. We believe that if we build performance halls and colleges of art or conduct festivals, art will come alive. It just does not. The truth is that governments in Tamil Nadu proclaiming [they care for] Tamil culture are just making a political statement. If they cared, they would create cultural hubs that work in education, socio-cultural intersections, and theorise and organise the learning and practice of Tamil art forms. Let us also not forget all the interconnected occupations, such as instrument makers. We have done absolutely nothing for them.

Communities kept art forms alive, sometimes forcing it on the next generation. For the same reason, lots of artists have been stigmatised because their art 'outs' their community or caste group. To avoid caste oppression, the practitioners,—particularly their children—move away from the art. What can be done to keep those art forms alive outside of the casteist silos? Are there any successful examples?

This usually happens with caste groups that fall in the lower rung of the hierarchy. Most art forms in India are largely caste-specific with minimum expandable bandwidth. Across the country, caste is our marker, like ethnicity might be a marker in, say, Poland or other parts of Europe.

The answer probably does not lie with the art but with caste. Unless you engage robustly with the caste issue, you're going to have this problem. You can have artistic engagements and conversations within each artist community, which essentially means within a caste group. But we also need artistic conversations to transcend these limits. And they are not easy or simple. One has to be very careful that there is no question of appropriation or condescension.

The other question is: How do we create an environment where you empower the community to feel proud of their art and culture? In my book *Reshaping Art*, I talk about the idea of identity and its inversion. That is, when you talk about the upper spectrum of the caste group and culture, identity needs to be collapsed. When you look at the lower spectrum of society, caste identity needs to be enabled and invigorated. An Arundhatiyar must own their identity and say, 'This is my beautiful music.' Then, the musician within the Arundhatiyar community will be respected. In turn, the community will also realise their cultural expanse.

The issue with art forms that fall in the subaltern—and I don't have clarity on this since it's so complicated—is that, at one level, we need the art form to permeate and grow, but, on another level, you also wonder what happens to the community that held the art form. It's what happened to the Devadasis—their art was appropriated.

That's why I think empowering the community that already holds the art form is a starting point. No Dalit community is told that their cuisine is great, their dance is great, their music is great; that they are central to Indian culture. Can we get there?

The changing political and social climate is disrupting a lot of art forms. Kaniyan kuttu is badly affected by Sanskritisation of worship; bharatanatyam, after it moved into the hands of the upper caste, became a pay-to-dance-in-the-sabha thing; folk dances like poikkal kuthirai are marginalised by the advent of cinema sub-culture, among other things. Again, what's the fix for this?

Everything is going to be appropriated by mass culture. If you belong to the top caste spectrum, you'll proudly say, 'Look, they took this from me. Carnatic music comes in the movies.' The stand-up comic Alexander Babu said something very relevant in this context. He talks about a boy asking a maama in a sabha, 'Isn't this what Rahman put in his song?' The maama says, 'Yes da, you think they'll give him Oscar for nothing?' That's a fascinating sociological statement. What they are saying is: Look, Rahman needs Naatakurinji raagam.

But, as you go down the hierarchy, it becomes more difficult because you don't have the power to contest appropriation. And before we realise it, mass culture twists and morphs the actual practice. Gaana is subaltern fusion music that evolved in the city of Chennai; it's a new culture, about a hundred years old. This art form has Urdu, English, Telugu, Tamil, and was originally part of funeral music. It is the voice of Dalits, manual scavengers and daily wage labourers. The lyrics traversed everything—politics, social moorings, ethics, morality, sexuality, conflict, oppression, protest and hope. Then, gaana moved from being sung at funerals to becoming an entertainment by itself. In cinema now, the item number is a gaana song. It has vulgarised the form as just a song for gyrating dance. Now, what songs do people want to hear? The gaana that is in cinema.

We need to accept that we cannot compete with mass culture, but we can make sure other narratives are powerful, alive, vibrant and engaged. How do you do this? One way is by giving local panchayats grants to sustain art and culture, particularly art that belongs to their localities. Here, you must have some cultural body in every panchayat. It shouldn't just be about music; it could be about painting, dance, craft, etc. Then, creation of local art spaces takes place.

Even if you want to look at it from the tourism perspective, the possibilities are phenomenal. Every panchayat becomes a place for people to see art, culture, music and dance. It'll take you ten years to put this in place and will need more than just money and space. We need to instill pride in the local, distinct and unique subcultures. Heterogeneousness must be normalised, and sharing should be the basis of this new cultural initiative.

Folk artists often say that their art forms receive stepmotherly treatment. They are not given the space—culturally and socially—to perform, in the way that classical artists do. And

monetarily, there is no comparison. Can this gap ever be bridged? And why is it important to do so?

Can the gap ever be bridged? I would like to say yes, but I really don't know. The problem comes from what we value and want to project as valuable art and culture. Unfortunately, the culturally and economically privileged do not see folk artists as sophisticated or evolved. This unquestioned, discriminatory aesthetic practice is rampant, even among the so-called progressives. And those from oppressed communities who want acceptance among the cultural elite slowly give up or hide their own cultural markers in order to fit into the upper-cultural aesthetic space. Unless we address these anomalies, I am not sure how we can reach any sort of economic or social parity. The words folk and classical need to be entirely demolished.

A private sector bank will be happy to sponsor a Carnatic concert in Chennai. You know why? One, the bank knows that it caters to the middle and upper middle class who have money and many of whom are its customers. They'll take a hundred tickets for privileged customers, and they'll sell the rest. Two, they see being associated with Carnatic music as high culture. Suppose we say, instead, let's have kuttu, they are not going to support it. Even the treatment, hospitality and honorarium given to a classical musician and a folk musician are disparate. It's a complex battle.

In *Reshaping Art*, you speak of art as a necessity or luxury. How does one explain the need for art—as we know it and consume it—to someone who walks seven kilometres for water? How do they respond and react to art? Is art for them also a leisurely pursuit?

Are we presuming that the person who walks seven kilometres for water does not sing? Or does not know dance? Painting on the walls of homes, the red and yellow lines in the door corners, and kolams, all that is art. So, every individual knows art, it is natural. They may not intellectualise it or even call it art, but they just "do". The question of it being a necessity or not is irrelevant; it is life. It is people like you and me who decide that art is not needed for the poor; that sanitation, education and healthcare are priority. But how can any of this be offered if we do not enter the cultural spaces of their homes? Because within that home resides art.

I meant art as a leisurely pursuit, in the sense that we take time off from our daily life to consume art.

This argument is similar to how we have explained intellectual evolution. We moved from being hunter-gatherers to becoming agriculturalists. Once we did not have to travel so much to get food, our physical efforts reduced and we had time to do other things. This is the standard accepted model of how the mind developed. Many arguments on intellectuality come from this very unfortunate hierarchy. Like the often-stated point that only those who have leisure have time for philosophical or artistic pursuits. But others too, spend time on art. They go to village festivals, listen to kuttu songs and watch movies. So, everybody is engaging with some form of art in their lives.

Don't forget that people paint a mud pot before they use it. Why? Won't rice cook otherwise? They do it because there's an eye for the idea of aesthetic. And it naturally exists in every culture across the globe. The idea of aesthetics and beauty, however culture-specific it may be, has always been part of every livelihood engagement and it's not linked to wealth. We link it to wealth only because we want to be highbrow about thought and culture. We are propagating a fraud. Therefore, we ask, why do the poor need art when they don't even have time for food? But you can't deny anybody access to art and culture in the name of poverty. One is to deny someone access. Another is to ignore the culture that exists within them. We do both. And then when their art and culture is dying, we say, 'Oh no, let's archive it.'

I think leisure itself is an interesting idea. Leisure cannot be associated only with extra available time. It's a state of mind. You could have six free hours, and still not have leisure. When the person working eight hours a day breaks into song, how does that happen? The whole idea of physical work is quite fascinating. We—the upper castes and classes—have no clue about it. For generations, we got other people to do our work. What happens in the mind when you're engaging with physical labour is the question we should be asking.

I think physical labour is actually a trigger for art. Why did the fisherfolk sing? It was a way of changing physical hardship into a song. But they didn't sing about physical hardship. They sang about the sky and the water, converting what could be painful into a celebration. Though they were at sea for seven hours to catch fish, they were smelling the air, celebrating the water, looking at the birds. They know everything about the shift of the wind, not just occupationally, but as people that are connected to the environment.

I think the problem here is intellectual elitism, of the idea of the intellect itself. The intellectual endeavour of art has been linked to its articulation. Intellectual endeavour of the art is about being within it. That is why subaltern cultures paint, sculpt, sing and dance. This is their pain and their celebration, and is what keeps them connected to all that surrounds them. And only leisure can produce it. This is true leisure, and this is found within, in the emotions and the experience, not in spare time.

How does the caste hierarchy influence the purpose of art—as knowledge and as labour? You had written about it in the book and also in your conversation with P. Rajagopal of Kattaikkuttu Gurukulam

Rajagopal mentioned it casually to me, that's why it found place in the book. He kept talking about his art form as 'ozhaipu' or labour. I'd never thought about Carnatic music as ozhaipu in my life. I've never been trained to think that way. The idea of knowledge creation then becomes murky. I've been handed down something that is accepted as knowledge, and I am told that I am creating knowledge. Why, I could even attain moksha. The trajectory is very clearly written down. Art forms within oppressed castes become a caste obligation at some point, and they're told, this is physical labour. Never in their mind, in their training, do they realise they are creating knowledge.

This is disturbing, that an artist does not realise their own wisdom and intellectual and social contribution through their artistic practice. Even all of us who have had interactions with 'folk art forms' have never dealt with this fundamental idea. We say, 'Yeah, yeah, this is a beautiful art form, you should bring it to the city,' but then, there are fundamental structural issues that we do not address.

Firstly, I have to ask myself the difficult question. Am I creating knowledge? But what does it mean to create knowledge? Why are aesthetic practices that exist beyond the Brahminical not embraced as knowledge?

Like I have said in my book, those who practise art forms that exist beyond this exclusive circle have to use tools that the classical practitioners used to get where we [classical artists] are. I understand that this idea has many pitfalls but I think we should deal with them and move ahead. If we do not, it's difficult to challenge knowledge.

Why has the classical become knowledge? Because we have written and spoken about it. We [classical practitioners] have been discussed for hundreds of years and the white man too has looked at our texts. Beyond the temporal we also say, 'Ultimately, all this is just nada and a process of self-realisation.' This is also knowledge. An edifice is built. And I am sitting on that edifice. How can you ever question me? But the rest are just ritual, social, local art; the only thing we are willing to grant them is ethnicity.

How does society place a monetary value on performing arts? Has this changed with time?

There is an attitude in this country that artists should not make money. We use the Sanskrit term 'ananda' to denote what the reward should be. The person that's singing our music of ananda cannot say, at least publicly, that they will not sing unless they are paid a lakh. Because the moment they place a monetary value on the art, their art loses its elevated status and becomes commercial. We believe that musicians should somehow live in poverty or make just enough for a living. If this is the perception even at the top tier of art, we can only imagine how bad it gets as we go down the ladder. This is the cultural bane of this country.

Notes

Introduction

1. Office of the Registrar General and Census Commissioner, India, dataforall.org/dashboard/censusinfoindia_pca/.
2. 'Extreme Inequality in Numbers', Oxfam International, oxfam.org/en/even-it/india-extreme-inequality-numbers.
3. Jean Drèze and Amartya Sen, *An Uncertain Glory: India and Its Contradictions*, Allen Lane, 2013.
4. Amit Basole, 'The Skilled and The Schooled', *The Caravan*, 1 January 2018, caravanmagazine.in/reviews-essays/india-struggle-knowledge.
5. 'Sewer Death Cases', National Commission for Safai Karamcharis, ncsk.nic.in/about-us/sewer-death-cases.

Let Them Eat Rice

1. Abhishek Waghmare, 'NE Monsoon Worst In 140 Years, 144 Farmers Dead, Tamil Nadu Declares Drought', *IndiaSpend*, 10 January 2017, archive.indiaspend.com/cover-story/ne-monsoon-worst-in-140-years-144-farmers-dead-tamil-nadu-declares-drought-89699.
2. 'PR NO. 040', Director, Information and Public Relations, Chennai, 16 January 2017, cms.tn.gov.in/sites/default/files/press_release/pr16017_040.pdf.

3. Sharan Poovanna, Dharani Thangavelu, 'Centre Releases Drought Relief for Tamil Nadu, Karnataka', *Mint,* 1 April 2017, livemint.com/Politics/QROT9cz6QAiz9YIrb7iG0I/Centre-releases-drought-relief-for-Tamil-Nadu-Karnataka.html.
4. Dharani Thangavelu, 'Tamil Nadu Farmers Begin Strike for Loan Waiver, Drought Relief Package', *Mint,* 4 April 2017, livemint.com/Politics/9nO9H1Mmgxce1ucB4mqArN/Tamil-Nadu-farmers-begin-strike-for-loan-waiver-drought-rel.html.
5. 'State/UT-wise Number of Suicides Committed by Persons Engaged in Farming Sector During 2016: Answers Data of Rajya Sabha Questions for Session 246', Open Government Data (ODG) Platform, data.gov.in/resources/stateut-wise-number-suicides-committed-persons-engaged-farming-sector-during-2016-ministry.
6. Meena Menon, 'NCRB's Silence on Farmer Suicides: RTI Reply Reveals Why Organisation Has Not Released Data Since 2016', *Firstpost,* 21 March 2019, https://www.firstpost.com/india/ncrbs-silence-on-farmer-suicides-rti-reply-reveals-why-organisation-has-not-released-data-since-2016-6276811.html.
7. P. Sainath, 'In India, Farmers Face a Terrifying Crisis', *The New York Times,* 13 April 2018, nytimes.com/2018/04/13/opinion/india-farmers-crisis.html.
8. 'Policy Note 2018–19', Agriculture Department, Government of Tamil Nadu, p. 44 cms.tn.gov.in/sites/default/files/documents/agri_e_pn_2018_19.pdf.
9. 'Policy Note 2018–19', p. 35.
10. Vishwanath Kulkarni, 'From Green Revolution to Millet Revolution', *BusinessLine,* 26 March 2018, thehindubusinessline.com/specials/india-file/from-green-revolution-to-millet-revolution/article23356997.ece.
11. Chitrangada Choudhury Aga, 'Debal Deb: The Barefoot Conservator,' *Mint,* 9 August 2014, livemint.com/Leisure/

bmr5i8vBw06RDiNFms2swK/Debal-Deb--The-barefoot-conservator.html.

12. Aga, 'Debal Deb'.
13. Podhumani and Jeyabal peg their income at ₹61,000 per acre: ₹49,000 from the sale of thirty-five sacks of paddy at an average of ₹1,400, plus ₹12,000 they hope the straw will fetch. Their input costs come up to ₹25,750 per acre. The 'profit' of ₹35,250, divided by nine hundred hours of labour over ninety days—roughly five hours per person per day—puts the labour cost per hour at ₹39, or around ₹200 a day per person per acre of field cultivated. The extent of land under cultivation varies each season depending on the availability of water, which is only getting scarce by the day.
14. 'Women's Participation Is 75% in the Production of Major Crops in the Country: Radha Mohan Singh', Press Information Bureau, 15 October 2018, pib.nic.in/newsite/PrintRelease.aspx?relid=184202.
15. 'Gender and Land Rights Database', The Food and Agriculture Organization, fao.org/gender-landrights-database/data-map/statistics/en/.
16. 'Women in Agriculture', Global Agriculture, globalagriculture.org/report-topics/women-in-agriculture.html.
17. 'State-wise and All-India Average Daily Wage Rates by Occupation and Sex for the Month of December, 2018', Ministry of Labour and Employment Labour Bureau, Government of India, pp. 2–3, labourbureaunew.gov.in/WRRI_DEC_2018.pdf.

Singaravelan: Fighting for the Bulls

1. 'Value of Output from Livestock Sector', National Dairy Development Board, nddb.coop/information/stats/outputvalue.
2. '19th Livestock Census–2012: All India Report', Ministry of Agriculture, Department of Animal Husbandry, Dairying and Fisheries, Government of India, dahd.nic.in/sites/default/filess/Livestock%20%205_0.pdf.

3. 'Press Note on 20th Livestock Census', Ministry of Agriculture and Farmers Welfare, Department of Animal Husbandry, Dairying and Fisheries (Animal Husbandry Statistics Division), Government of India, 27 September 2018, http://dahd.nic.in/sites/default/filess/Press%20Note-20LC.pdf.
4. S. Panneerselvam and N. Kandasamy, 'The Kangayam Cattle, A Retrospective and Prospective Study', Tamil Nadu Veterinary and Animal Sciences University, 2008, p. 16, http://kangayambull.org/wp-content/uploads/2015/11/The-Kangeyam-Cattle-Retropectiveand-prospective-Study.pdf.
5. The breed survey, though conducted separately, was envisaged as part of the overall activities under the nineteenth livestock census in 2012 and the estimates are derived by disintegrating the figures of livestock census. Therefore, the breed survey results provide useful insight into the results of livestock census as well by maintaining the consistency in the reporting periods.
6. 'Estimated Livestock Population Breed Wise: Based on Breed Survey 2013', Ministry of Agriculture and Farmers Welfare, Government of India, dahd.nic.in/sites/default/filess/Breeding%20Survey%20Book%20-%20Corrected.pdf.
7. 'Milk Production Estimates from Exotic/Crossbred Cows in India during 2014–15', OGD PMU Team, Open Government Data (ODG) Platform, 30 August 2016, community.data.gov.in/milk-production-estimates-from-exoticcrossbred-cows-in-india-during-2014-15/.
8. 'Animal Husbandry Policy Note 2015–16', Animal Husbandry, Dairying and Fisheries Department, Government of Tamil Nadu, p. 52, cms.tn.gov.in/sites/default/files/documents/ah_e_pn_2015_16.pdf.
9. Karthikeya Sivasenapathy, 'Kangayam Cattle Pride of Tamil Nadu: Past and Future Strategies for Their Improvement—A Farmer's

View', *Compendium of Invited Lectures and Abstracts*, Tamil Nadu Veterinary and Animal Sciences University, 13–14 February 2015, p. 239, 14.139.252.116/compendium/Compendium_2015.pdf.

10. K. Venkataramanan, 'Tamil Nadu Ordinance to Permit Jallikattu: An Explainer', *The Hindu*, 23 January 2017, https://www.thehindu.com/news/national/tamil-nadu/Tamil-Nadu-ordinance-to-permit-jallikattu-an-explainer/article17082141.ece2.

Fifty Feet Above ...

1. Sarah Tucker, *South Indian Missionary Sketches: Part 2*, J. Nisbet and Co., London, 1842–43, p. 39.
2. Tucker, *Missionary Sketches*, p. 39.
3. Arun Janardhanan, 'Cyclone Gaja Damaged Nearly 1 Crore Coconut Trees, 70,000 Farmers Hit: Tamil Nadu', *The Indian Express*, 4 December 2018, https://indianexpress.com/article/india/cyclone-gaja-damaged-nearly-1-crore-coconut-trees-70000-farmers-hit-tamil-nadu-5477078/.
4. Jency Samuel, <Tamil Nadu's Palm Trees Withstood Cyclones and Climate Change, but Neglect Threatens Their Survival', *Scroll.in*, 16 Feb 2019, scroll.in/article/913260/tamil-nadus-palm-trees-withstood-cyclones-and-climate-change-but-neglect-threatens-their-survival.
5. R. Panchavarnam, *Panai Maram*, Panchavarnam Pathipagam, 2016.
6. 'Policy and Historical Background', Commissionerate of Prohibition and Excise, Government of Tamil Nadu, cpe.tn.gov.in/policy.html.
7. Prabhu Chawla, 'Tamil Nadu Chief Minister M.G. Ramachandran Reintroduced Prohibition', *India Today*, 31 January 1987, indiatoday.in/magazine/indiascope/story/19870131-tamil-nadu-chief-minister-m.g.-ramachandran-reintroduced-prohibition-798461-1987-01-31.
8. '34th Annual Report', Tamil Nadu State Marketing Corporation Limited, 27 December 2017, http://tasmac.co.in/forms/TASMAC_Annual_Report_2016-17_English.pdf.

9. B.V. Shiva Shankar, 'Telangana's Green Drive Promises More Toddy Down the Line', *The Times of India,* 12 July 2016, timesofindia.indiatimes.com/city/hyderabad/Telanganas-green-drive-promises-more-toddy-down-the-line/articleshow/53174041.cms.
10. Shankar, 'Telangana's Green Drive.'
11. George Monbiot, 'The 1% Are the Very Best Destroyers of Wealth the World Has Ever Seen', *The Guardian,* 7 Nov 2011, theguardian.com/commentisfree/2011/nov/07/one-per-cent-wealth-destroyers.

Welding Work and Worship

1. K. Rajan, 'Iron Age, Early Historic Transition in South India: An Appraisal', Padmashri Amalananda Ghosh Memorial Lecture, 25 August 2014, iks.iitgn.ac.in/wp-content/uploads/2017/01/Iron-Age%E2%80%93Early-Historical-transition-in-South-India-K-Rajan.pdf.
2. T.S. Subramanian, 'Kodumanal Reveals More Hidden Gems', *The Hindu,* 19 May 2013, thehindu.com/news/national/tamil-nadu/kodumanal-reveals-more-hidden-gems/article4728296.ece.

Thaka Thari Kita Thaka

1. S. Samanth, 'A Mecca of Music', *Livemint,* 4 October 2008, https://livemint.com/Leisure/BTQPlNEEtYBvTfBEOcPw0J/A-mecca-of-music.html.
2. T.M. Krishna, *A Southern Music: The Karnatik Story,* HarperCollins, 2013, p. 339.
3. The artistic community of 'Devadasi parenthood in the Tamil region began to formally call themselves the Isai Vellalars (literally, music cultivators, the Vellala being a cultivating community),' writes T.M Krishna in *A Southern Music: The Karnatik Story.*
4. Manu S. Pillai, 'The Reinvention of Bharatanatyam', *Mint,* 24 Feb 2018, livemint.com/Leisure/1y3EA1cpOU9eOW5TAMCtTJ/The-reinvention-of-Bharatanatyam.html.

5. Charulatha Mani, 'Of Love and Longing', 8 November 2013, thehindu.com/features/friday-review/music/of-love-and-longing/article5329771.ece.

The Man Who Drew Ten Thousand Designs

1. 'Handlooms and Textiles Policy Note 2018–19', Handlooms, Handicrafts, Textiles and Khadi Department, Government of Tamil Nadu, p. 8, cms.tn.gov.in/sites/default/files/documents/hhtk_e_pn_2018_19.pdf.
2. 'Registration Details of Geographical Indications', Office of Controller General of Patents, Designs and Trade Marks, Ministry of Commerce and Industry, Government of India, ipindia.nic.in/writereaddata/Portal/News/367_1_Registered_GI.pdf.
3. Sabita Radhakrishna, 'A Rich Textile Tapestry', *The Hindu*, 20 June 1999, thehindu.com/folio/fo9906/99060060.htm.
4. Li Rongxi (tr.), *The Great Tang Dynasty Record Of The Western Regions*, BDK America, Inc., 1996, p. 282, bdkamerica.org/system/files/pdf/dBET_T2087_GreatTangRecordofWesternRegions_1996_0.pdf.
5. Pradeep Chakravarthy, Chola Temple with a Pallava Surprise', *The Hindu*, 22 June 2007, thehindu.com/todays-paper/tp-features/tp-fridayreview/chola-temple-with-a-pallava-surprise/article2272787.ece.
6. *Census of India 1891*, Eyre and Spottiswoode, London, 1893, p. 141, ia600205.us.archive.org/22/items/cu31924023177268/cu31924023177268.pdf.
7. *District Statistical Hand Book 2016–2017*, Kancheepuram District, p. 73. cdn.s3waas.gov.in/s31543843a4723ed2ab08e18053ae6dc5b/uploads/2018/04/2018042565.pdf.

Making Wood Sing

1. T.M. Krishna, *A Southern Music: The Karnatik Story*, HarperCollins, 2013, p. 46–48.

2. Krishna, *A Southern Music*, p. 407.
3. TNN, 'GI for Thanjavur Veena Gives Makers More Leverage', *Times of India*, 26 May 2014, timesofindia.indiatimes.com/city/trichy/GI-for-Thanjavur-Veena-gives-makers-more-leverage/articleshow/35611999.cms.
4. 'Notified Cost Inflation Index Declared by Income Tax Department under Section 48 for FY 2018–19', incometaxindia.gov.in/charts%20%20tables/cost-inflation-index.htm.

The Kuchaali and the Korai

1. H.R.Pate, *Madras District Gazetteers: Tinnevelly, Volume 1*, Government Press, 1917, pp. 218–220, ia601003.us.archive.org/32/items/GazeetersTinnevellyVol11917/Madras%20District%20Gazeeters%20Tinnevelly%20%20Vol-1-1917.pdf.
2. Pate, *Tinnevelly*, pp. 218–220.

Draupadi Plays a Final Round of Dice

1. 'Traditional Tamil Theatre', Kattaikkuttu Sangam, kattaikkuttu.org/new-page-2.

The Dance of the False-Legged Horse

1. S. Gopalakrishnan, 'Tanjavur and the Performing Arts: Interview with Rama Kausalya', *Sahapedia*, 28 March 2017, sahapedia.org/tanjavur-and-the-performing-arts-interview-rama-kausalya
2. Bibek Debroy, 'Calculating the Cost of the Games', *Financial Express*, 5 August 2010, financialexpress.com/archive/column-calculating-the-cost-of-the-games/655554/.

Versions of some of the essays in the book have previously been published as:

Let Them Eat Rice—'Where Farming Means Two Full-time Jobs', People's Archive of Rural India, 29 February 2016; 'Small Farmer, Big Heart, Miracle Bike', People's Archive of Rural India, 7 March 2016.

Singaravelan: In the Shadow of the Bulls—'Bulls in Her Backyard', *The Hindu Sunday Magazine,* 8 March 2015; 'Slipping Hold', *The Caravan,* 1 October 2016; 'Livestock Landscapes: Jallikattu, Local Breeds and More', *Seminar,* July, 2017.

Thaka Thari Kita Thaka—'Let's Dance', *The Hindu Sunday Magazine,* 2 June 2013; 'Kali: The Dancer and His Dreams', People's Archive of Rural India, 20 December 2014; *Kali Wants to Dance,* Story Weaver: Pratham Books, Delhi, 21 March 2018.

Making Wood Sing—'Narasingapettai's Nadaswaram Makers', *The Hindu Sunday Magazine,* 12 April 2015; 'We Make The Music, They Play It', People's Archive of Rural India, 13 April, 2015.

Draupadi Plays a Final Round of Dice—'Tamilarasi Shanmugam: Drama Queen', *Open,* 31 July 2015.

The Dance of the False-Legged Horse—'The Queen of Poikaal Kudhirai', *The Hindu Sunday Magazine,* 3 May 2015; 'The Dance of the False-Legged Horse', People's Archive of Rural India, 13 October 2016.

Acknowledgements

It Takes a Village to Write a Book

My enormous gratitude to everybody who told me their story. Without your time and trust, this book would not have been possible. I am thankful to you and your families for your hospitality during my visits, and for your patience every time I called with questions. I would not be able to repay all of you for the love, laughter and looking after.

Thank you:

My mentor P. Sainath, for teaching me how to tell stories, and for your generosity and support.

Nirmala Lakshman, for the idea for the series on vanishing livelihoods that led to this book, and for your faith and encouragement.

R. Krithika, TP, and my daughter, Lasya, for reading every word, twice, and pushing me to finish it. I would never have completed this manuscript but for you. I owe you three crates of jam.

My editor G.S. Ajitha, for believing in me and this book back when it was just an idea.

My editor Janani Ganesan, for all the handholding and guidance and for making the process such fun. I couldn't have asked for more. I promise to send you a lifetime supply of thengapoli.

Priya Iyer, for your sharp eye and all the crucial last-minute catches.

Shri Gopalkrishna Gandhi, Justice Prabha Sridevan and T.M. Krishna, for your support with the proposal, stories and interviews.

Everyone who gave me long and short interviews, in person, over the telephone and by email. Your inputs were invaluable.

Arun Janardhanan and Kombai S. Anwar for helping me with contacts and crucial feedback.

Amit Basole, Jaideep Hardikar, Baradwaj Rangan, Chitrangada Choudhury, Lavanya Shanbhogue Arvind, Subha J. Rao, Poo.Ko. Saravanan, Padma Ramesh, Neeraja Arjun, Chitra Satish, Kalaivani Ramalingam, Sharmila Joshi, Aravindan Kannaiyan and Mohan Ramamoorthy, for being sounding boards, reading various stories and for your feedback.

Karthikeya Sivasenapathy (Soundaram Ramaswamy), Karunakara Menon (Kali Veerapathiran), Hanne M. de Bruin (Tamilarasi Shanmugam), S. Sathaiah (Anthony Rayappan) and Gita Ram (Zeenath Beevi), for introducing me to the protagonists.

The editors of the publications at PARI, Pratham Books, *The Hindu*, *Open*, *The Caravan* and *Seminar*, where shorter versions of some of these stories were published.

The National Foundation for India, for the fellowship to write the ten-part series on 'Vanishing Livelihoods of Rural Tamil Nadu'.

Cho Dharman, for the epigraph.

Perumal Murugan and P. Rajagopal, for lending me your verses.

Kavitha Muralidharan, A.R.Venkatachalapathy (Panaiyey) and Hanne M. de Bruin (Art as Labour), for the English translations.

Team PARI, for being there.

And my family and dogs Puchu and Shingmo, you are the best!

Muralidharan and Malathy (Appa and Amma), Karthik (my husband) and Arjun (my brother), for supporting me in every way.

My daughter said I could be anything I wanted to when I grow up—so I decided to be a storyteller. Thanks, my darling.

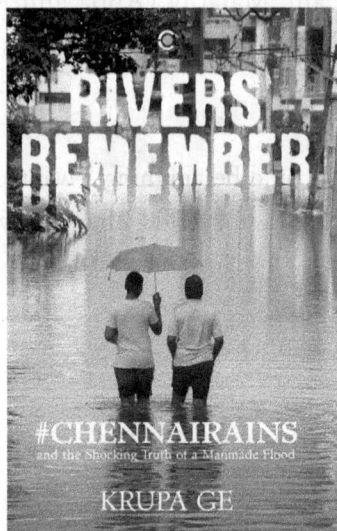

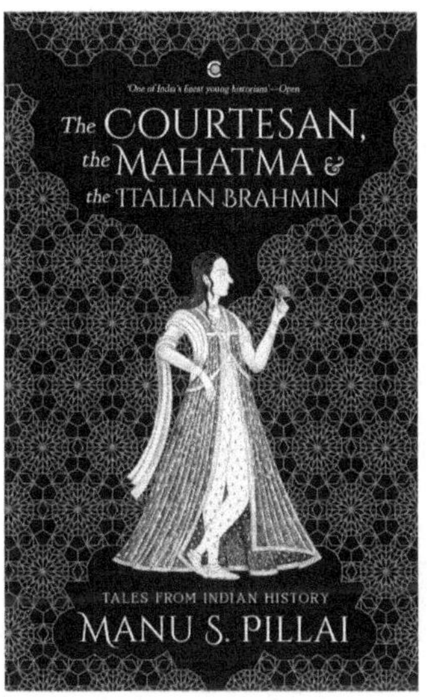

A collection of fascinating essays that dig out unheard of historic personalities and re-imagine episodes in Indian history, accompanied by beautiful illustrations.

'Published propitiously in times that have most certainly been wrenched out of joint, Manu Pillai's book is an important contribution.'
—*The Tribune*

'Mr Pillai's book—well-researched and accessible—does a yeoman's work in uncovering nuggets of history of which a general reader usually might have been unaware.'
—*Business Standard*

'This book is that old cliched thing: a must read.'
—*Deccan Herald*

'Pillai weaves magic with words and details of other time and place, transporting the readers to a not so distant past. ... Exquisite illustrations by Priya Kuriyan only added to the brillant pallete of historical nuance.'
—*The Kochi Post*

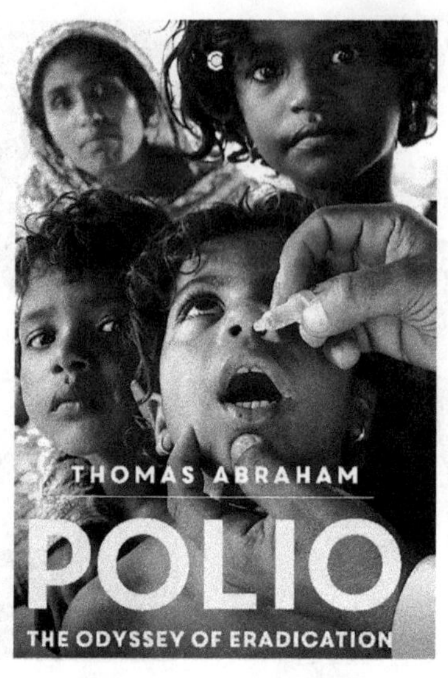

A riveting, thriller-like account of the world's most ambitious eradication drives.

'A must-read for anyone interested in global health, mysteries or how the unimaginable might become possible.'

—CHELSEA CLINTON, Vice Chair, Clinton Foundation

'Addresses the huge question of why polio eradication has become such a singular focus of the global health community.'

—DEVI SRIDHAR, Professor in Global Public Health, University of Edinburgh and Co-author of *Governing Global Health: Who Runs the World and Why?*

'Authoritative, insightful and occasionally jaw-dropping.'

—ALEX PERRY, Author of *The Rift: A New Africa Breaks Free*

www.ingramcontent.com/pod-product-compliance
Lightning Source LLC
Chambersburg PA
CBHW071547210326
41597CB00019B/3147

* 9 7 8 9 3 9 5 0 7 3 2 3 3 *